COMMERCIAL BUILDING DESIGN

COMMERCIAL BUILDING DESIGN:
INTEGRATING CLIMATE, COMFORT, AND COST

BURT HILL KOSAR RITTELMANN ASSOCIATES

MIN KANTROWITZ ASSOCIATES

VNR Van Nostrand Reinhold Company
_____ New York

Copyright © 1987 by Van Nostrand Reinhold Company Inc.
Library of Congress Catalog Card Number 86-28977
ISBN 0-442-21156-2

Printed in the United States of America

Van Nostrand Reinhold Company Inc.
115 Fifth Avenue
New York, New York 10003

Van Nostrand Reinhold Company Limited
Molly Millars Lane
Wokingham, Berkshire RG11 2PY, England

Van Nostrand Reinhold
480 La Trobe Street
Melbourne, Victoria 3000, Australia

Macmillan of Canada
Division of Canada Publishing Corporation
164 Commander Boulevard
Agincourt, Ontario M1S 3C7, Canada

16 15 14 13 12 11 10 9 8 7 6 5 4 3 2 1

Library of Congress Cataloging-in-Publication Data

Commercial building design.

  Includes index.
    1. Commercial buildings—Design and construction.
  2. Commercial buildings—Environmental engineering.
  3. Public buildings—Design and construction.   4. Public buildings
  —Environmental engineering.   I. Burt Hill Kosar Rittelmann Associates.   II. Min Kantrowitz & Associates.
  TH4311.C66   1987   725'.2   86-28977
  ISBN 0-442-21156-2

ACKNOWLEDGMENTS

MAJOR CONTRIBUTORS: This book was edited and major portions were written by:

Harry T. Gordon, AIA, Burt Hill Kosar Rittelmann
Associates
Justin Estoque, Burt Hill Kosar Rittelmann Associates
Min Kantrowitz, Min Kantrowitz Associates

Other authors were:

G. Kimball Hart (Hart, McMurphy & Parks)
Brandt Andersson (Lawrence Berkeley Laboratories)
Ron Kammerud (Lawrence Berkeley Laboratories)
William Babcock (Booz, Allen & Hamilton)
Kirk Renaud (Booz, Allen & Hamilton)
Eric Hjertberg (Booz, Allen & Hamilton)
William I. Whiddon (William I. Whiddon & Associates)
Michael Sizemore (Sizemore/Floyd)

In 1979, the U.S. Department of Energy issued Program Opportunity Notice DE-PNO2-79C30142, (Passive Solar Commercial Buildings Design Assistance and Demonstration). This was in support of the Solar Heating and Cooling Demonstration Act (P.L. 93-409). The information in this book is largely based on the results of this program and on the individual building projects which were included.

SUPPORT AND GUIDANCE: The continuous support and thoughtful guidance of Ted L. Kurkowski and Ron Lutha of the U.S. Department of Energy, and Ron Kammerud of Lawrence Berkeley Laboratories have made this project possible. Dr. Frederick H. Morse, Robert Shibley, Robert Holliday and Michael Maybaum of the U.S. Department of Energy were also instrumental in the administration of this program. Steven Ternoey and others at the Solar Energy Research Institute made significant contributions to the initiation and successful continuation of this program.

PROJECT TEAM MEMBERS: Team members for individual building projects are listed in the Appendix. Data monitoring services for individual projects were provided Faruq Ahmed (Burt Hill Kosar Rittelmann Associates), and Don Frey and Joel Swisher (Architectural Energy Corporation).

TECHNICAL EXPERTS (DESIGN REVIEWERS): Sarah Harkness, AIA, Lawrence Bickle, P.E., P. Richard Rittelmann, AIA, Bruce Hunn, William Lam, Michael Sizemore, AIA.

TECHNICAL MONITORS: William J. Fisher, Donald L. Anderson, Peter G. Rockwell, Robert Mizell, Tom Sayre, Robert Floyd, Robert Busch, Harry T. Gordon, William I. Whiddon.

PRODUCTION AND STAFF SUPPORT: Karen Ruckman, René L. Carter, Judith A. Klein, John Taschek, Lynn Perkins, Jan Wilson, Terri Humphrey.

CONTENTS

INTRODUCTION

Integrating climate, comfort, and cost concerns into a well-designed commercial building is a challenge for designers, consultants, and clients. While no solution is perfect, it is possible to reach an appropriate balance among these factors to solve each building problem. Climate-responsive buildings, designed with a careful understanding of the interrelationships among functional demands, cost constraints, and climate-related opportunities, often achieve this balance because of a unique and careful design process. This book describes that design process, presents a number of case-study buildings, and analyzes performance in terms of cost, occupant satisfaction, and energy use. By understanding the lessons learned through these buildings, this approach can be applied to new design problems.

How well do climate-responsive commercial buildings work? Concern about building operating cost has fluctuated dramatically within the past few years, along with changes in the price and supply of electricity and fuel. Yet organizations and institutions that use commercial buildings must plan for the long-term lives of buildings, lives in which operating costs will continue to affect profitability. Designing and constructing buildings that carefully use energy by being "climate responsive" makes sense over the long term of building life, whatever the current costs of auxiliary energy. But there are questions: How well do climate-responsive, nonresidential buildings actually work? Do they really save money? What design strategies work best? Do occupants' needs for comfort interfere with building function? This book answers those questions through in-depth examinations of a diverse group of buildings, from design and construction through evaluation of energy, cost, and occupancy performance. Analyses are based on field tests of actual buildings in use, and constitute the largest known data base for evaluating the design, cost, and performance of new and retrofit climate-responsive, nonresidential buildings.

While each building is unique, designs can be improved by analyzing experience. Every new building or retrofit is designed to resolve its own unique set of problems, opportunities, and constraints. No one building ever totally solves the problems presented by another, but lessons learned from approaches and concepts tried in one building can incrementally help improve the design of others. This is particularly true for climate-responsive, nonresidential buildings, where the interaction among climate, comfort, and cost increases the challenge of good design.

The purpose of this book is to help architects, engineers, and builders produce better climate-responsive, nonresidential buildings, by presenting new and useful information about a group of innovative energy-efficient buildings that have been thoroughly field-tested. This diverse group of passive solar nonresidential buildings, with their different climates, functional programs, organizational contexts, financing, designers and construction techniques, employs a wide range of experimental approaches. In analyzing building design and building performance, this book describes the most successful approaches as well as the less successful ones, in terms of design, construction costs, energy use, and occupant satisfaction.

By systematically examining how buildings are designed and operated under a real world set of conditions, the authors hope to inform the next "generation" of climate-responsive design. What worked well and what is worth repeating? What is a good idea, and does it need to be refined? What experimental approaches experienced consistent problems? How can these problems be solved in the future? The answers to these questions can guide designers, clients, and users toward energy-conserving buildings that are better in their energy performance and in their support of human activity.

The "Problem": Skepticism about nonresidential, climate-responsive design. Early attempts at climate-responsive design were almost entirely residential in scale, and directed at certain highly motivated pioneers, i.e., those who would tolerate large temperature swings and peculiar-looking buildings in return for direct financial savings and the satisfaction of publicly demonstrating their commitment to a resource-conservative philosophy and life style. Nonresidential buildings were assumed to be unlikely candidates for energy-efficient or passive solar technologies because of their high internal heat gains, large volume, and rigid environmental conditions. Furthermore, solar heating and daylighting were expected to increase cooling loads, which were already considerable. Thus, the design approaches for residential design were deemed inappropriate for larger, more complex buildings. One reason was the concern about technical building performance under the demanding and relatively inflexible programmatic requirements of the work environment (e.g., stringent requirements for a narrow comfort band, fixed working hours, and workstation locations). Another was uncertainty about how building users would respond to climate-responsive buildings in which they had no direct "stake" (e.g., no direct financial pay-off, no philosophical commitment, and no "pioneer" spirit). The questions became, "Can people who don't stand to benefit directly from financial or philosophical rewards be satisfied in energy-efficient, passive solar buildings and can these users successfully learn to operate these dynamic, flexible buildings to optimize energy savings?"

The "Solution": Examine the potential of energy-efficient nonresidential buildings through design and field testing. In 1979, the U.S. Department of Energy (DOE) instituted a large design development and field test program in response to these questions. The program, the Nonresidential Experimental Buildings Program, was intended to build a body of practical information on the design, construction, and performance of nonresidential, energy-efficient buildings and to investigate the potential of passive solar technologies to meet commercial building energy requirements. The program is the largest known attempt to guide design and simultaneously evaluate construction and operational costs, actual energy use, occupancy effects, and reactions in climate-responsive, nonresidential buildings. There were three phases in the DOE program: design, construction, and performance evaluation. Over 300 building owner/designer teams applied to participate in the program, but only the best 35 were selected. Of these, 22 buildings located across the country completed design; 19 completed construction.

PROJECT LOCATION MAP

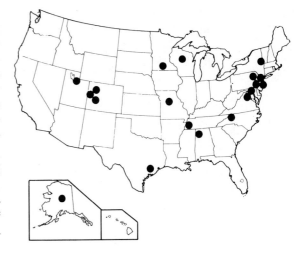

Design Process: In the design phase, each project team established a "base case" building, a nonsolar building which the owner would ordinarily build. Team members calculated heating, cooling, lighting, and other energy requirements, taking into consideration internal loads, building occupancy, schedule, climate, and construction practices. Teams then developed an alternative design, using passive solar approaches to heat, cool, and light the building, and calculated the design's performance using a variety of energy- and cost-prediction tools. The tools ranged from complex mainframe, energy-simulation programs like BLAST (Building Loads Analysis and System Thermodynamics) to simpler, hand-calculated procedures. A panel of technical experts reviewed these project designs in a series of meetings. The review was aimed at ensuring that designs effectively integrated strategies for passive cooling, lighting, and heating with each other, the building, and the auxiliary mechanical and lighting systems. The review provided valuable feedback from the earliest stages in design through final preparation of bid documents. Twenty-two building teams completed the design phase.

Building Construction: In the construction phase, incremental costs associated with the energy systems were identified. While a portion of those costs were reimbursed through DOE cost-sharing funds, actual building construction costs were obtained by the organizations and institutions for whom the buildings were being designed. As a result, only 19 buildings were actually completed. Photos and logs of the construction process for these 19 buildings identify issues, problems, and processes that are unique to the energy-efficient designs and that might be applicable to other buildings in the future.

Performance Evaluation: The final phase, performance monitoring, included one complete year of monitoring actual cost and energy performance in each building. The evaluation was intended to provide information about these basic hypotheses:

- Actions of the building's occupants can help reduce building energy requirements.
- Inclusion of passive solar features enhances the ability of the building's occupants to perform their job responsibilities.
- Operating costs for these buildings will be significantly lower than for comparison buildings.
- Use of passive solar features reduces auxiliary fuel requirements for heating, cooling, and lighting.

To test these hypotheses, information was gathered each week from each building about actual energy use (disaggregated by fuel type and end use), occupancy patterns and conditions, weather, and energy costs. By comparing monthly patterns to those predicted for both the base case and the innovative building, the project team and technical monitors could analyze the basic patterns of building energy use.

Monthly logs completed by building managers, and question- naires completed by both full-time and part-time building users also yielded qualitative information about how users re- sponded to and interacted with the building's passive solar components. Twelve building teams completed a full year of performance evaluation.

THE BUILDINGS

The 19 completed buildings constitute varied responses to a wide range of design constraints and opportunities. Each de- sign team faced a different climate, program, client, budget, and site. Yet each unique building design used passive solar and advanced energy conservation techniques to meet a significant portion of the heating, cooling, and lighting loads. Brief descriptions of the buildings follow.

The RPI Visitor Center, a 5,200-ft^2 office and police headquar- ters in Troy, New York. The building is designed to welcome visitors to the campus and serve as headquarters for campus police and other offices. It relies on a south-facing sunspace with mass walls and floor to supply warm air to the building through a system of plenums. Skylights with reflectors provide daylight and direct gain. Insulating shutters and curtains, and earth berming are also used.

Mt. Airy Public Library, a 13,500-ft^2 community library in Mt. Airy, North Carolina. The building is located on a hill next to City Hall, which is built of local white granite. While some direct gain through south-facing glazing is used, the strongest solar de- sign feature of the building is the set of south-facing, sawtooth clerestories and light baffles that line up in rows along the cen- tral portion of the building. The feature provides diffused daylight to the central areas of the building.

St. Mary's School Gymnasium, an addition of a 9,000-ft^2 gym- nasium to an existing school in Alexandria, Virginia. In response to varied times of occupancy, the delivery of radiant heat is phased to the interior of the building. This was accomplished by constructing the thermal mass in the concrete ceiling-to- floor Trombe wall in three different thicknesses.

Security State Bank, an 11,000-ft^2 bank in Wells, Minnesota. The building is used only during banking hours. It was designed to make direct use of solar gain through south-facing glazing, rather than having large amounts of thermal mass capture and store heat for later use. A large, south-facing clerestory with a baffle diffusion system provides abundant natural light.

The Essex-Dorsey Senior Center, a 13,000-ft^2 multipurpose sen- ior center in Baltimore, Maryland. The center was housed in two Victorian schoolhouse buildings until this major renovation connected them and added needed lounge and multipur- pose areas. A south-facing clerestory on the new wing pro- vides daylighting and aids natural ventilation.

Shelly Ridge Girl Scout Center is a 5,700-ft² two-story, open-plan community education facility located near Philadelphia, Pennsylvania. Warmth is delivered throughout the day by selectively using direct gain and a Trombe wall in this compact, high-mass building.

Two Rivers School, a 15,750-ft² elementary school outside Fairbanks, Alaska. The building includes an experimental passive solar classroom originally designed to be a prototype of a small rural schoolhouse responsive to Alaska's harsh climate, high energy and construction costs, and need to provide even tiny villages their own schoolhouses. In addition to other features, the prototype classroom is equipped with a special thermal shutter system over much of the south-facing triple glazing.

Blake Avenue College Center, a 31,900-ft² community college building in Glenwood Springs, Colorado. The center was sited on the steepest portion of a south-facing site. As a combination community college, community center, day care center, and senior center, a wide variety of functions had to be integrated into one building. A three-story, central atrium unifies the functions and collects solar heat, acts as a plenum for the cooling system, and is a bright central lighting core from which adjacent offices and classrooms borrow light.

Princeton School of Architecture building, a retrofit project of a 13,700-ft² architecture school building in Princeton, New Jersey. The problem of integrating new conservation and solar features in an existing building was solved through utilizing existing skylight openings for specially designed direct-gain heating and lighting roof monitors.

Johnson Controls Branch Office Building, a 15,000-ft² office located in Salt Lake City, Utah. The building is one of several branch offices of Johnson Controls, a large environmental controls manufacturing and distribution company. The building combines a sophisticated computer control system with relatively straightforward passive solar design using a combination of features for direct solar gain and enhanced distribution of daylight.

Community United Methodist Church, a 5,500-ft² educational addition to a community church in Columbia, Missouri. The addition is located in a climate with high summer humidity and only modest solar availability. The addition features clerestories with overhangs and insulating shades and thermal mass in a relatively simple but effective configuration.

Princeton Professional Park, a 64,000-ft² speculative office building located in Princeton, New Jersey. The building illustrates how an energy-efficient building can be designed within the strict cost constraints typical for speculative office development. A central atrium was designed to function as part of the heating, cooling, and lighting schemes, as well as part of the circulation between offices.

Kieffer Store, a 3,200-ft^2 addition to a retail store in Wausau, Wisconsin. A light and airy environment for retail shopping was created by using direct-gain sunspace for heating and lighting, and roof monitors.

Comal County Mental Health Center, a retrofit of a 4,800-ft^2 1930s school building in New Braunfels, Texas. In order to preserve the historic appearance of the building, the energy-efficient features had to be integrated with the structure without significantly altering the building's exterior. In this hot, humid climate, a variety of defensive cooling strategies including an evaporative roof spray system became the major features of this cost-effective retrofit.

Gunnison County Airport, a 9,700-ft^2 airport terminal building in Gunnison, Colorado. The terminal is located in an area with a harsh, cold climate and expensive electricity. It uses a large thermal storage wall in tandem with an air distribution system and automatic night insulation to meet the large heating load.

Philadelphia Municipal Auto Shop project, a retrofit of a 57,000-ft^2 warehouse-like auto maintenance facility in downtown Philadelphia. An innovative solar window heater module was developed to replace the large expanse of existing south-facing windows, which had been a source of large infiltration losses.

Walker Field Terminal, a 66,700-ft^2 airport terminal building. It is the largest structure in the program and is located in Grand Junction, Colorado. Much of the energy needed for heating and lighting is provided by the prominent series of stepped, south-facing clerestories on the roof.

Touliatos Greenhouse, a 6,000-ft^2 commercial greenhouse building located in Memphis, Tennessee. Using direct gain through vaulted skylights and windows in a double-shed design, this greenhouse depends on biomass decomposition for auxiliary heat.

Abrams Primary School, a 27,400-ft^2 elementary school located in Bessemer, Alabama. The primary design feature is a set of water-filled PVC tubes mounted below the roof monitors and used to store heat as well as to diffuse sunlight and prevent overheating problems from direct solar gain.

This book is organized to help readers learn from the experience with and analysis of these buildings. The concept of carefully analyzing the process of design, construction, and operation of a building to learn how it actually functions when occupied is simply to do systematically what architects and/or designers have done informally in the past: observe the successes of the past and the exemplary work of peers and learn from them. This book consists of four chapters to support that learning process. A brief discussion of those chapters follows.

Chapter 1: The Design Process describes the most important building design issues encountered in design, construction, and evaluation of the 19 buildings. The chapter is an overview, designed to distill the experiences of all participants in the design phase of the program and to identify the common, predominant patterns emerging from the design processes. Recommendations about how and when to consider climate-responsive design alternatives are included.

Chapter 2: Building Performance discusses how well the group of buildings worked in terms of cost, energy use, and occupant satisfaction. The patterns show that, in general, climate-responsive approaches can provide substantial energy savings at little, if any, increased first cost. Performance parameters that contribute to success or failure include occupant behavior, user control, fuel cost, and the skillful handling of design elements such as solar apertures, thermal mass, daylighting systems, and integration of those elements with conventional design issues. Other issues, such as climatic limitation and predominant building load are shown to be less important.

Chapter 3: Case Studies describes in detail eight of these climate-responsive buildings. Each case study introduces the particular design issues related to the building and presents the design process and construction details for the building. The case study characterizes the building's energy performance, construction and operational costs, and occupant response. Most importantly, it describes the interactions among these factors. Design and performance case studies are included for the following buildings:

- Mt. Airy Public Library
- Johnson Controls Branch Office Building
- Community United Methodist Church
- Security State Bank
- Shelly Ridge Girl Scout Center
- RPI Visitor Center
- Philadelphia Municipal Auto Shop
- Essex-Dorsey Senior Center

Chapter 4: Key Design Issues presents results of special, in-depth analyses performed to examine the sensitivity of building energy performance to a variety of design- and occupant-related issues. These include automatic-versus-manual control of lighting, effectiveness of different thermal mass configurations, interactions between thermal mass and thermostat setback strategies, energy versus impacts of different acoustic treatments, and the effects of occupant management of shading devices on building energy performance. The quantitative information presented in this chapter can be used to guide design decisions.

• • •

The authors of this book come from a variety of educational and professional backgrounds, as do the readers. Thus the reader will notice differences in emphasis, style, and tone among chapters. It is hoped that this diversity in style will enhance the readability of the book.

1
THE DESIGN PROCESS

This chapter describes the most important building design issues encountered in designing, constructing, and evaluating the 19 passive solar buildings that are the subject of this book. The buildings encompass a broad spectrum of building types, climate locations, and design strategies.

The three phases in the Department of Energy (DOE) Nonresidential Experimental Buildings Program were design, construction, and performance evaluation. In the design phase, a panel of technical experts reviewed the project designs. The objective of the review was to ensure that designs effectively integrated strategies for passive cooling, lighting, and heating with each other, the building, and the auxiliary mechanical and lighting systems. These reviews provided the designers valuable feedback from the earliest design stage—when the greatest opportunities exist for saving energy—to the final preparation of bid documents.

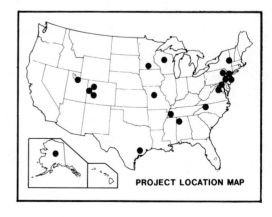

PROJECT LOCATION MAP

| PASSIVE SOLAR STRATEGY | | | | | | | | | | | |
| HEATING | | | COOLING | | | | | DAYLIGHTING | | | |
Sunspace/Atrium	Mass Floor	Mass Wall/Water Storage	Earth Contact	Natural Ventilation	Forced Vent./Night Flushing	Shading Mechanisms	Evaporation/Radiation	Windows (More Nat. Light)	Lightshelves	Clerestories/Skylights	Sunspace/Atrium
Two Rivers School		●						●			
Abrams Primary School		●				●				●	
St. Mary's School Addtn.	●	●			●					●	
Blake Ave. College Ctr.	●	●	●			●	●		●	●		
Princeton School of Arch.				●					●	●	●	
Mt. Airy Public Library		●	●		●	●	●		●	●	●	
Johnson Controls Branch		●						●	●	●	●	
Kieffer Store Addition	●	●				●	●		●	●	●	●
Princeton Prof. Park	●				●		●	●	●	●		●
Wells Security State Bank		●	●			●	●		●		●	
Community United Church		●	●		●	●	●	●	●	●	●	
Shelly Ridge Girl Scout Ctr.	●	●	●	●	●	●	●		●		●	
RPI Visitor Info. Ctr.	●	●	●		●						●	●
Essex Dorsey Senior Ctr.		●			●				●		●	
Comal County Health Ctr.		●	●		●	●	●		●			
Gunnison County Airport			●		`	●	●		●	●	●	
Walker Field Terminal Bldg.		●			●	●					●	
Phila. Municipal Auto Shop					●		●			●	●	
Touliatos Greenhouse		●	●	●	●		●		●		●	

SOLAR BUILDING DESIGN STRATEGIES

This overview distills the experiences of all design phase participants and identifies the common, predominant patterns emerging from the design processes. The observations and recommendations are intended to aid design professionals who have limited experience in the application of passive technology in nonresidential buildings. In 1979, at the outset of this program, most design professionals, including the 19 program architects, had limited experience. By the end of the program, the lessons they had learned greatly increased their understanding of passive commercial building design. The lessons are broad and apply both to passive technologies in particular and energy-conscious design in general. So that others may benefit, it is appropriate to document these lessons.

The contributors to this chapter recognize that design methods and procedures vary as widely as professional designers and the buildings they design. There is no single right or universal design formula to follow. Thus, the guidance presented in this chapter is broad and organized according to the traditional phases of the design process rather than the steps of a "how to" book. Building design occurs in the dynamic integration of various architectural issues; this chapter raises these issues and offers guidance on dealing with them—guidance rooted in both the buildings and design team experiences.

The three very broad and most important lessons to emerge from this program are:

- Consider energy-conscious design alternatives as early as possible in the design process.
- Support all design decisions with thorough analysis that addresses building efficiency in its broadest sense, which includes economics.
- Think of passive solar design as an architectural, mechanical, and electrical integration issue, not an "add-on" exercise.

Energy-conscious design must be viewed in a broad context. Building design is a problem-solving activity that integrates user needs, owner needs, and other requirements such as building codes. Energy is just one aspect of these and is rarely, if ever, the primary focus. It must be addressed, however, to achieve a fully successful building design.

SUMMARY OF PASSIVE SOLAR DESIGN GUIDELINES

GENERAL OBSERVATIONS:
- For a designer's initial projects, good solar design will probably take extra time and effort.
- Good energy-conscious design requires more than intuition.

PROGRAMMING AND PRE-DESIGN:
- Use the architectural and energy program for evaluating design decisions.
- Identify the building energy problem early.
- Use the base case building for evaluating design alternatives.
- Set the energy ground rules for the design team.
- Choose an appropriate design tool.

SCHEMATIC DESIGN:
- Choose simple design solutions that address the major parts of the energy problem.
- Pay close attention to system integration issues.
- Choose architectural features that have multiple functions.
- Develop potential amenities associated with passive solar features.

DESIGN DEVELOPMENT:
- Select a design tool that permits a refinement of the schematic solution.
- Integrate solar and conventional systems control strategies.

CONSTRUCTION DOCUMENTS:
- Bid documents should serve as performance specifications for evaluating product options.
- Call out and specify components carefully.

CONSTRUCTION AND BUILDING ACCEPTANCE:
- Monitor construction to ensure quality.
- Consider post-occupancy performance monitoring.

GENERAL OBSERVATIONS ABOUT SOLAR BUILDING DESIGN

For a designer's initial projects, good solar design will probably take extra time and effort. All buildings in the DOE program required more effort and a greater number of resources than typically needed to reach a final design solution. Program reporting accounted for a large proportion of the additional time, but design of these passive solar buildings also took an unusually long time. In most cases, the additional time resulted from having to "start over" or substantially revise an initial design concept.

COLORADO MOUNTAIN COLLEGE

Like many designers in the program, architect Peter Dobrovolny had just such an experience in designing the Blake Avenue College Center for Colorado Mountain College in Glenwood Springs, Colorado. Dobrovolny's initial schematic design relied on extensive use of direct-gain and Trombe wall strategies to address a perceived dominant heating problem. Review by a panel of experts and analysis by Lawrence Berkeley Laboratory (LBL) researchers, however, determined that it was necessary to substantially alter the design to address lighting and cooling energy problems, which were much more significant than the design team expected.

There are a number of important lessons to be learned from Dobrovolny's experience. First, and probably foremost, residential-scale, solar experience does not automatically translate to commercial-scale buildings; it pays to do an energy analysis in pre-design to make sure that one focuses on the predominant energy problem.

Second, computerized analysis is valuable in working with complex buildings. With the computer, iterative calculations to test new design strategies of the Colorado Mountain College building took only minutes to complete. Another lesson related to reducing design time is that simplifying the design analysis does not necessarily reduce analytical detail. For example, while the design team tried to perform its analysis to a high level of detail (it included 14 different building zones), the LBL analysis was simplified to only five zones without a significant loss of analytical detail. Apparently, extreme precision was not necessary.

There is also the painful but unavoidable lesson that learning a new subject, like learning a new building type, takes time and costs money. According to Dobrovolny, "Much more of the design time was spent learning new information and developing new methodologies. This process need not be repeated. Also, information gathered by observing this building will promote the development of rules of thumb to speed and improve design in the future. As a result, future passive efforts will be more refined and take much less time." In other words, the architect's time is likely to be much more profitable the second time around.

SIMPLE DESIGN TOOLS

Good energy-conscious design requires more than designer intuition. All designers rely on intuition—it is the stuff that prevents design from becoming rote. During the design reviews, Sarah Harkness, co-founder of The Architects Collaborative, characterized designer intuition as "informed experience." However, program architects initially found their experiences not as "informed" as they would have thought. Repeatedly, highly skilled professionals found their intuitive grasp of a building's energy problems off-target when tested by even the most rudimentary energy analysis techniques.

Realizing this, a few of the design teams began modifying their design process by starting with simple energy analysis whose level of detail increased to match the increasing level of detail in the designs. One such team was Harrison Fraker's Princeton Energy Group, which designed the Princeton Professional Park's speculative office complex. Following site analysis, the team used simple pre-design, energy analysis tools to identify the energy problem and to set a preliminary energy target by schematic design. These tools included hand calculators and a microcomputer for applying several analysis techniques: Solar Load Ratio, a thermal network analysis, and the simple bin method described in the ASHRAE *Handbook of Fundamentals*. None of these simple techniques could account for the energy effects of complex issues such as building mass.

These early analyses showed that internal heat gain and solar loads would probably supply all the building's heating needs during occupied hours. Also, these preliminary estimates suggested that a "reasonably" designed solar building could use significantly less energy than the owners had come to expect in previously designed buildings.

Based on this analysis and a literature search, the team developed a number of guidelines for its schematic design. They are:

- Insulation can be used to reduce conductive losses for heating from 10% to 25% and for cooling from 10% to 20% over conventional design.
- Passive solar heating (in the Princeton area) could provide 60,000 to 90,000 Btu/ft²/yr or reduce heating loads from 40% to 50%.
- Natural ventilation could reduce cooling loads by 10% to 20%, but only in the spring and fall "swing" seasons.
- A roof spray system could cut peak cooling demands by 5% to 10%.
- Lighting loads could be cut 40% to 50% using efficient ballast and daylighting strategies.

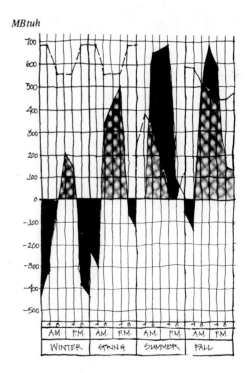

SAMPLE ENERGY ANALYSIS

15

SOPHISTICATED DESIGN TOOLS

As the team progressed into design development, it found that previously used tools often did not meet the needs for answering more specific questions. For example, the following design tools were either totally lacking or inadequate:

- Simple tools for calculating heating performance in buildings with high internal loads (as in many commercial-scale buildings)
- Tools for estimating annual daylight contributions
- Design tools (and performance data) for assessing indirect cooling with evaporative roof sprays
- Design tools (and performance data) for assessing cooling by natural ventilation.

Lacking available design tools, the team developed its own: a 12-node thermal network model for heating analysis (including analysis of the underslab rockbed) and a 14-node model for cooling analysis of stratification, evaporative cooling, and radiative cooling. These dynamic models took into account the effects of thermal mass. The team found it to be sufficiently accurate to calculate average monthly performance by extrapolating from average daily performance using modified degree days and an equivalent base temperature for the month.

The team based its lighting analysis on measurements of actual light levels in a scale model of the building. From these measurements, the team calculated daylighting factors and translated them into seasonal performance. This yielded auxiliary energy and cost requirements for lighting.

The levels of energy analysis employed by the Princeton Energy Group do not apply to all design projects. The point is that analysis is needed to make informed choices among energy design options. Energy analysis is critical for a team embarking on its first energy-conscious design projects, where intuition is not sufficient for good decision making.

Daylighting

The prominence of daylighting as a design solution to energy efficiency is a response to high electricity costs in nonresidential buildings. Measured in Btu's, lighting energy may be secondary to heating and cooling, but the cost of delivering light is two to three times greater than the cost of delivering heated or cooled air. Furthermore, unlike lighting in residential buildings, lighting in nonresidential buildings is a major end use.

Good daylighting demands that the designer have access to a palette of techniques, a vocabulary of daylighting strategies whose elements can be refined and confidently combined with other architectural elements. Daylighting apertures include clerestories (vertical glazing at perimeter walls), roof monitors (vertical glazing at interior spaces), skylights (horizontal glazing), atriums, and conventional windows. Distribution devices include light shelves, diffusing surfaces, and baffles. The designer must be aware of the differences between direct and indirect light, north and south light, and clear and translucent glass, and understand how these differences affect light quantity, color, and glare during various times of the day and year.

Several design principles emerged from the daylight designs. Vertical glazing was found to be generally superior to sloped glazing and definitely superior to horizontal glazing in internal-load-dominated buildings. Glazing sloped towards the sun admitted too much direct-beam light and was difficult to shade with overhangs. It caused glare and unwanted heat gain. Skylights admitted even more heat gains from the high, summer sun while creating complications for ceiling plenums and their contents. Except for dramatic light at entrances and lobbies, diffused light was best, with diffusion provided by walls, ceilings, or special diffusing grids. The Johnson Controls Branch Office used diffusing walls and ceilings, whereas Mt. Airy Public Library and Security State Bank used diffusing grids. Providing light to core areas was best achieved using roof monitors. Distribution to core areas was necessary for good perimeter lighting because light distributed evenly across the room reduces bothersome brightness contrast caused by a single-light aperture. Roof monitors faced south wherever there was even a modest heating load, and they worked best using distributed small openings rather than one large opening. Finally, light shelves were found to be expensive and did not demonstrate greater energy savings than did overhead daylighting systems.

A palette of aperture options

SKYLIGHTS

ROOF MONITOR

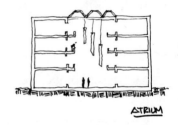

ATRIUM

LIGHT SHELF

CLERESTORY

SUNSPACE

17

It is best to use the architectural and energy program for evaluating design decisions. Just as an architectural space program is the basis for determining a building's spatial solution, the energy program is the basis for determining a building's energy solution. The energy program should describe performance—not simply identify a particular solution. The performance description will be used to assess design alternatives as they are developed. Careful attention to this performance description and evaluation criteria before beginning the development of design solutions allows the designer to identify at an early stage those alternatives having the highest potential for satisfying the building's architectural and energy requirements.

There can be no elegant solution to a misstated problem, so it is important to identify the building's energy problem early. Time spent in the programming phase to correctly identify the characteristics of a building's energy use is directly related to time saved during the design process because identifying the characteristics narrows the range of alternatives to be explored during the design process.

The architect/engineer (A/E) team must establish the nature, timing, and quantity of building energy requirements. For example, it asks: How important are heating, cooling, and lighting energy requirements? In what order? Do those requirements occur during occupied or unoccupied periods? Does the timing of those energy requirements coincide with the availability of solar or other environmental resources? Frequently, it is useful to establish the nonsolar base case building in answering these questions.

Analyzing a conventional (nonsolar) building—the base case—helps determine the building energy problems identified above and is useful in evaluating alternatives. Establishing a base case can be done in a variety of ways. Among those used by the designers in the DOE program were computer modeling of a hypothetical building without solar features; comparing a technical reference such as the Building Energy Performance Standards (BEPS) budget applicable to the building type and location; examining the energy-use records of similar buildings in the area; and assessing the last building developed by the same owner. Regardless of the option chosen, the objective is to identify the conventional building characteristics that the owner otherwise would have built.

The base case can then be analyzed to establish the energy problem. It can be used to quantify the magnitude and timing of heating, cooling, and lighting energy requirements. Internal heat generators such as computers or unusual ventilation requirements for a natatorium or gymnasium are an important part of this analysis. The anticipated use patterns of the building,

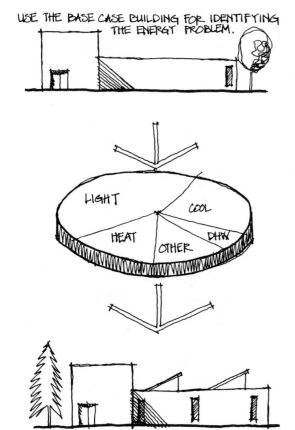

USE THE BASE CASE BUILDING FOR IDENTIFYING THE ENERGY PROBLEM.

including timing and number of people, should be estimated, and the probability of changes in these patterns assessed.

In constructing the base case, assume common architectural, space conditioning, and electrical systems. For example, an office building might make use of envelope requirements dictated by prevailing standards (such as ASHRAE 90), a variable air volume mechanical system, and lighting and equipment power levels of 2½ to 3 watts per ft².

It is important to distinguish among three commonly, but incorrectly interchanged, terms in making this analysis:

- *Loads.* These are the net heating, cooling, and lighting quantities that must be met by the building mechanical and electrical equipment. Traditionally, loads have been used for equipment sizing purposes. They are not very useful for energy decision making.
- *Energy Consumption.* This is the nonrenewable energy that must be purchased from utilities and supplied to the mechanical and electrical equipment to meet the loads. Because mechanical and electrical equipment operate with different efficiencies, their *energy consumption* may vary significantly from the loads.
- *Energy Cost.* This is the price paid to utilities, including demand charges, for supplying energy to the building. Because the costs of different fuels vary significantly, the proportions of the energy problem as seen from the perspective of "energy cost" may be quite different from that seen from the perspective of "energy consumption."

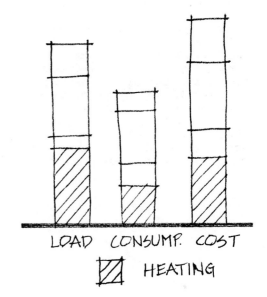

Distinguishing among "loads," "energy consumption," and "energy cost" is fundamental to correct decision making in developing an energy-responsive building. Under most circumstances, the energy cost will be the most useful basis on which to make decisions. For example, what is the financial result of reducing the amount of electricity that must be purchased for building lighting? Similarly, what is the value of an equivalent reduction in building heating requirements? The designers in the DOE program frequently found that the most appropriate solution for reducing loads or energy consumption differed significantly from that for reducing energy cost.

ENERGY GROUND RULES

Energy ground rules are the agreements among the client and design team members that describe their common objectives and identify assumptions that will underlie design decisions. It is important to set them for the design team.

The architect, as programmer, will most easily gain the support and cooperation of design team members by getting them involved at the earliest possible stage. Setting energy ground

Passive Cooling

Three strategies dominated the design of these buildings for low cooling energy. The first was the avoidance of heat gains by using shading and landscaping. Use of exterior shades (e.g., in Security State Bank and Blake Avenue College Center) and overhangs (e.g., in Mt. Airy Public Library) were the most direct approaches. Interior shading using blinds and light shelves was less effective. The second was natural ventilation/night flushing. Air flows must be direct; convoluted paths that wind through a building are a designer's fantasy. Also, it is difficult to combine natural ventilation with window shading if closing the shades reduces air flow. Third, well-controlled daylighting will reduce cooling since, lumen for lumen, daylight generates less heat than does artificial light. The designer's objective is to admit modest amounts of light distributed over large areas. Excessive light will generate excessive heat gains, and poor distribution will require more artificial light in interior areas than is otherwise necessary (which also generates heat). Achieving well-controlled daylighting was best met in the Mt. Airy Public Library, St. Mary's Gymnasium, Princeton Professional Park, and the Security State Bank.

rules also demands client involvement and input from all the architectural, mechanical, electrical, and structural disciplines. Although this may generally apply to conventional buildings, a solar building requires a design team that is more diverse and more specialized than that of a conventional building. To avoid assumptions that may lead to expensive redesign, the involvement of top management at this early stage is also important.

One example of an energy ground rule is: To achieve cooling comfort, passive means shall be considered before mechanical means. Suppose that A/E principals are ignorant of (or even disagree with) this requirement and suppose the architectural design relies on operable, southwest-facing windows to catch summer breezes. If the mechanical consultant designs for minimal infiltration, the electrical consultant specifies circuitry to handle maximum kW chiller load, and the owner requires closed windows for security purposes, the building will meet nobody's expectations for minimum energy consumption.

On the other hand, the most smoothly produced buildings in the program included those for which maximum agreement had been reached early in the process, or where one organization performed many functions. At Johnson Controls, for example, the owner was architect, engineer, control system designer, control system installer, and user of the building. Thus, coordination and startup problems were held to a minimum. Similarly, in the case of the Touliatos Greenhouse, the owner was energy consultant, general contractor, and user of the building. For other projects, close involvement of disciplines produced similar benefits by eliminating disjointed communication and belated agreement.

The primary objective shared by all program participants was reduced energy costs. A similar objective was to shield the building owner from energy-cost uncertainties because fluctuating, but rising costs are unnerving and make cash flow projections difficult for the owner who operates on a narrow margin. As the designer of the Community United Methodist Church said, "Building owners want solar because they want low energy bills." This sentiment is even less surprising given the fact that natural gas costs rose 70% during 1982 in the church's area and electricity costs rose even more. Of course, there are other objectives at play; some of them are discussed below.

INTANGIBLE ENERGY OBJECTIVES

The building owner may want to work toward certain societal goals related to relying on a sustainable energy resource or to working toward an energy-conservative planet. The architect of the Shelly Ridge Girl Scout Program Center said, "Using the natural energies was among the [Building Task Force members'] earliest thoughts. Their motives are philosophical and educational, but also include the pragmatic concern for minimizing operating expenses." This philosophical commitment sought to create a special building at Shelly Ridge which would demonstrate a sensitivity toward nature and natural resources and reflect the Girl Scouts' longstanding commitment to such issues. The building was also to reflect the Girl Scouts' role as an educator of youth, who are expected to experience a future of limited nonrenewable energy supplies. (Unexpectedly, the solar aspects fulfilled another, more tangible, purpose: They served as a positive selling point in the fundraising campaign.)

Having solar energy serve as a symbol was another common objective and presented an interesting aesthetics problem. Faculty at the Princeton School of Architecture said that the primary benefit of their solar retrofit was that it became an educational tool. It encouraged the students to develop a concern for energy resources, which would be important in their professional careers. Moreover, the Community United Methodist Church pastor explained, "The use of solar energy is a visible sign to the community concerning the stewardship of natural resources and the concern of the church for these resources." In addition, the Princeton Professional Park's developer pointed out that project members felt the passive solar aspects might speed necessary zoning approvals by making the project appear benign and, therefore, palatable to surrounding home owners.

Solar energy, in the form of sunlight for heating and landscaping for cooling, brings nature to building occupants, contributing to health and well-being. Clear glass provides views of blue sky, and operable windows admit fresh air; both improve the quality of the building environment. Gunnison County Airport owners wanted a natural atmosphere in their building, which is a gateway for outdoors-oriented tourists. The owner of Kieffer Store even went so far as to suggest that he could increase rent for solar amenities. But even if higher rent is not earned, the amenities bring other financial benefits. According to its designer, the clerestories at Princeton Professional Park "serve as an architectural amenity which gives the developer an intangible marketing edge over the competition for leasing space." Simply put, the energy savings pay for architectural features, and the environmental benefits become useful marketing tools.

FINANCIAL ENERGY OBJECTIVES

Solar energy can serve as a financial investment, an objective which requires the designer to weigh costs against benefits. In the DOE program, this objective applied to both profit and nonprofit owners who were explicit in their desire to maximize the return on their investment. The owners of Comal County Mental Health Center and Princeton Professional Park earmarked particular building funds for energy improvements. For Comal County Mental Health Center, a nonprofit organization, the funds came mainly from donations; for Princeton Professional Park, a private development, the funds were raised from investors. In both cases owners used the funds as an investment whose return would have to match alternative investment instruments.

FLEXIBILITY

In addition to setting energy objectives, the design team should resolve conflicts among objectives. Two objectives that can pose conflicts peculiar to low-energy buildings are energy savings and flexibility—flexibility in space planning, thermal comfort, lighting quality, and building schedule.

The process of optimizing energy performance requires the designer to make assumptions about expected building use and operation when projecting energy use. Some of these assumptions have room for change. Others allow no room for change unless energy performance is to be compromised. When actual building occupant behavior deviates from these assumptions, energy performance may not meet expectations; therefore, the architect who designs for such change usually must settle for increased energy consumption. At the outset, the design team must settle issues such as whether atriums will be used strictly for circulation and, therefore, can tolerate more extreme temperatures; whether daylighted meeting rooms can be used for slide presentations; and whether schools will always be used during the daytime, thereby minimizing the need for thermal storage.

At times, balancing these goals becomes a key design issue. Princeton Professional Park was designed for the speculative office tenant. Consequently, the duration and magnitude of internal loads were unknown. A variety of tenant requirements had to be planned for, thereby complicating the design process, since most of the strategies examined met some requirements but not others.

The Blake Avenue College Center expected primarily early-evening use five days a week. The atrium was to be used only as a transitional circulation space and, therefore, was allowed to float in temperature. After the building was opened, however, faculty and students used it extensively and adopted the atrium space as their central gathering place both day and night. Consequently, the owner decided to condition the space to the same comfort levels as the rest of the building and extended the operating hours by opening earlier in the morning and keeping the building open later into the evening.

At the Gunnison County Airport, a loft space designed as an overflow passenger lounge was converted into the home office of a small airline. The unplanned heat loads from the several CRTs and the host computer raised the temperature beyond a comfortable level. Rather than increasing air conditioning capacity, the owner simply replaced fixed windows with operable ones.

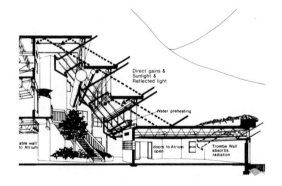

BLAKE AVENUE BUILDING
COLORADO MOUNTAIN COLLEGE

22

The Comal County Mental Health Center was programmed for a five-day work week. But soon after completion, the administration sublet space to a church group that uses the building on weekday evenings and weekends. Although the subsequent increase in energy use was understandable, the center may have missed the opportunity to justify even more solar measures than were originally incorporated since higher use creates greater potential savings.

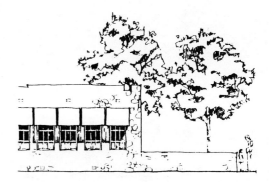

COMAL COUNTY MH CENTER

The DOE program abounds with examples of changed use and instances where reasonable assumptions were not borne out. The local community booked Alaska's Two Rivers School so extensively in the evenings that the janitor had to change his work schedule to begin after midnight, thereby interfering with night setback. Mt. Airy Public Library staff decided to open earlier because of the building's increased popularity. However, the building's thermal mass was sized for later occupancy, thereby requiring more purchased energy to warm the building even during daylight hours. The designer of the Princeton Professional Park assumed that tenants would select energy-conserving options rather than pay for higher energy use. The tenants, however, write off their energy costs as a business expense, and equipment depreciation is available only to the building owner. Thus, a number of tenants selected the conventional option of dropped ceilings with recessed fluorescent troffers over the daylighting option.

The lesson to be learned from these occupancy issues is that it is difficult to predict the user's behavior patterns. Therefore, the designer must consider a range of operating conditions when making assumptions leading to energy performance. If flexibility and energy performance are inversely related, the design team must decide upon an appropriate compromise. This will dictate the performance required of the solar thermal and lighting systems.

USER CONTROL

The dependability of the user in correctly operating the solar building is another issue that the design team must agree upon. At some point, the designer of every building must decide the degree to which its occupants and operator will have to flip switches, adjust settings, and replace expendable parts such as filters in order for the building to function properly. The two extremes are (1) very close manual control and (2) total automation. The trade-offs are like those of manual-versus-automatic transmission in an automobile: close control and low cost, but the requirement of an experienced, dependable driver versus higher cost and automatic operation, but the possibility of increased breakdowns and maintenance problems. Thus, the design team must settle issues such as, Should the users have to open and close windows according to a daily and seasonal schedule? Should occupants be responsible for turning on and off electric lights in the presence of varying daylight? What about controlling air movement with ceiling fans? Resolving these issues is even more elusive when nonresidential aspects of occupancy are involved; occupants are unpredictable when it comes to operating the building if they are not the owners paying the utility bills.

These issues require careful consideration since controversy surrounds the appropriate level of control. Many mechanical engineers caution against operable windows, saying that users who open them will be conditioning the great outdoors. Even when maintenance personnel are available to operate the building, one cannot assume they will readily accept that responsibility. Gunnison County Airport employed a full-time maintenance man to manipulate systems for the transient users. When he realized, however, that the tasks included closing doors, adjusting thermostats, and performing other functions that he felt people should do for themselves, manual-versus-automatic control took on a different meaning.

It is also a mistake to deny occupants all control. St. Mary's Gymnasium employed a time clock-controlled lighting system, which had to be overridden frequently by community basketball team members who played after hours. In another example, employees of the Security State Bank felt the need for more outside air in their tightly constructed building. Their solution was to circumvent automatic control by opening the air handler's outside air dampers even during winter months.

In spite of these complexities, the program produced a guideline useful in overcoming them: With proper design and an understanding of building users' behavior, manual controls can be sufficient. Specifically, if users are a small, easily educated staff, centralized, manual controls are sufficient. But if users are transient, indifferent, or uneducated about how to control their environment, it is best to specify automatic controls.

CONSTRUCTION

The final ground rule to be established relates to construction quality. Specifically, the design team should anticipate how much the builder will know about solar construction. If the architect can depend on a contractor who is experienced in, for example, earth-integrated construction, the architect will not hesitate to consider this option and will develop the construction documents to the appropriate level. The architect will assume the contractor knows the implications of proper waterproofing and structural design. Generally, if the contractor is not expected to understand the system, specifications must be tight and construction closely supervised to ensure job quality. On the other hand, if the contractor knows passive solar construction, an unanticipated quality of construction may be provided or the contractor may even suggest effective, lower-cost alternatives for critical subsystems. The St. Mary's Gymnasium project illustrates this situation. It was the contractor on the project who encouraged the idea of a two-story Trombe wall of precast concrete tees bolted to a steel frame. The system proved to be faster to erect, and provided a thermal capacitance that varied appropriately according to available thicknesses.

Identification of construction cost goals and the budgetary allowance for passive solar techniques should be established from the outset. If minimizing construction costs is of paramount concern, then it should be recognized that construction workers with lower skill levels may be employed and the design should be developed accordingly. For example, complex passive solutions requiring considerable care during construction should be avoided in favor of simple solutions with a lower margin for construction error. The plans for Princeton Professional Park specified a contractor-built HVAC control system that had 11 different modes of operation. The system was designed, tested, rejected, redesigned over budget, and finally redesigned and installed by another subcontractor, all of which resulted in a 15-month delay in installing the system. In other projects, motorized insulating curtains caused similar difficulties.

APPROPRIATE DESIGN TOOL

Even before schematic design, it is necessary to choose and use a design tool. At first this may seem peculiar, but if performance of the base case is to be quantified, the base case must be established using the design tool chosen for subsequent iterations in the design process.

The Building Design Tool Council, a national consortium of building designers established to provide guidance for energy design tool research, defines design tools as "any device which assists in the formulation and/or evaluation of energy-efficient strategies for new or existing buildings." This broad definition consists of a number of procedures varying in accuracy, cost, and ease of use, including workbooks, nomographs, calculator routines, physical models, microcomputer software, and mainframe computer programs. The problem for the solar building designer is to choose the right tool for the specific needs.

Designers participating in the DOE Nonresidential Experimental Buildings Program learned quickly which tools were appropriate. The best tools at early design stages are those that accept simple input. A tool that requires mechanical equipment part-load curves is often too cumbersome for pre-design and schematic design. Consequently, the design tool should incorporate reasonable default values if it does not require detailed input. For example, if an hour-by-hour building operating schedule is not required for simulating an office building, the design tool should assume an 8:00 a.m.–to–5:00 p.m. schedule for five days per week, not the 24-hour occupancy characteristic of a residence.

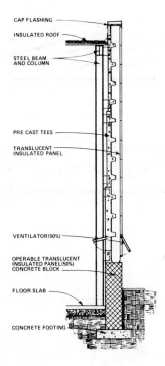

ST. MARY'S PARISH SCHOOL
Cross section through Trombe wall

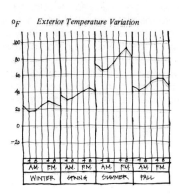

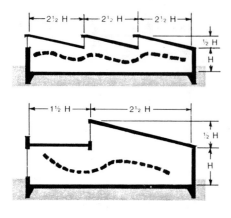

INTERIOR LIGHT LEVELS

Physical Models

A physical model is the best design tool for assessing the quantity and quality of light. Light performs in models exactly as it does in full-sized environments, provided the architectural surfaces and details are accurately replicated. These details include the scale and geometry of spatial elements, window openings, texture, reflectivity, transparency, and opacity of key finishes. Color is important if reflective properties are concerned. Transmission properties of glazing can be simulated or described by numerical factors if openings in the model are left uncovered.

The scale used for daylighting models can range from ¾ in. = 1 ft. (suitable for the study of single rooms) to ⅜ in. = 1 ft. (generally suitable for larger configurations). Smaller models are difficult to detail and are not recommended for room studies, although they may be appropriate for large spaces.

Using models in the design of the Security State Bank resulted in dramatic design changes. The models showed that in the early designs, uniformity of light had to be increased (by adding sidelighting); that the view was desirable; and that available daylight was overestimated. They told the designers that neither a fixed, nor an operable, shading/baffle system was best, and that a combination was optimum. Finally, they indicated the daylighting system could provide not only ambient light but the majority of task-lighting as well.

The design tool should be able to return results quickly. Output that takes more than several hours to generate interrupts the designer's work rhythm and concentration. Thus, microcomputer software, nomographs, and simple formulas are more dynamic than physical models and mainframe programs (which can be used later during design development to make refinements). To generate quick feedback, many program designers used a program called "Energy Graphics," a series of quick calculations whose output is provided in graphic form. Others used hand-held calculator programs such as TEANET, PASOLE, and PEGFIX.

Output should also display results in a simple, organized fashion that makes subsequent design directions obvious. Reams of computer output or tables predicting the performance of each pump and fan require the designer to spend time reducing output to a usable form. Graphic output is most easily grasped and will readily indicate where and when peak loads exist.

Finally, the design tool should be comprehensive, integrating the various energy end uses. Output that tells the designer that the clerestory reduces artificial lighting needs by 30%, but neglects the effects on heating and cooling creates more work since the designer still must calculate these effects. In 1981, most designers in the program used physical daylighting models to determine the quantity and quality of light. There were no programs to quickly measure heating and cooling interaction, so mainframe programs (BLAST, TRACE, TRNSYS) were used to do this.

The best design tools were described by one design team as those that "produced rapid energy snapshots of the project as it took shape on the designer's desk." Such tools led to design changes which, if postponed until design development, could not be easily incorporated. The designers of the Security State Bank switched from a high-mass to a low-mass structure on the basis of design tool feedback. The designers of Walker Field Terminal in Grand Junction, Colorado, dispensed with nighttime thermal storage once their output showed nighttime building loads lower than anticipated. Had these developments occurred later in the design process, major structural changes would have been more difficult.

SCHEMATIC DESIGN

It is important to choose simple design solutions that address the major parts of the energy problem. By examining the energy problem and available environmental resources identified during the programming phase, a palette of solutions can be identified. In this idea-generation stage, focus on solutions that appear to offer the best answer to the project's combined architectural and energy requirements. When a building element can be used to satisfy multiple functions, economy and overall building quality are improved. Solutions identified for development should be simple, realistic alternatives that avoid overly complex control requirements or that depend extensively on occupants' actions for success.

In this program, many different approaches were taken to arrive at schematic design solutions. In Princeton Professional Park, which is a medical office building, circulation requirements suggested a double-loaded corridor arrangement. This led to the development of a basic building cross-section, which used space for circulation as a solar atrium. In the Security State Bank, simple physical models were used to explore alternative building forms that incorporated daylighting without aggravating heating and cooling loads. In the Mt. Airy Library, daylighting roof monitors, which had been successfully used on a previous project, were adapted to the project's requirements.

Design alternatives should be carefully evaluated using either simple calculation techniques or quickly constructed physical models to gain an understanding of the relative success of the alternatives. Unless the project requirements are exceptionally unusual or complex, avoid the use of analytical techniques that require extensive, sophisticated inputs, or that are costly. At this stage in the design, the objective is to be sure that the potential design solutions meet the objectives established during the programming phase. Precise, quantitative results are not as important at this stage as is a general indication of energy results.

SYSTEM INTEGRATION ISSUES

Perhaps the easiest and most likely way to get in trouble with energy-conscious design is to consider individual system performance in isolation. All design strategies have implications for other building systems and functions. This is especially true for passive, conventional HVAC and lighting systems. In the program, every building faced this issue.

The St. Mary's School Gymnasium in Alexandria, Virginia, provides just one example of the attention required to address the complexity of interacting building elements. Successful operation of the entire heating system involves the simultaneous interaction of the Trombe walls, the two linear roof apertures, the thermal storage mass contained in the floor slab and walls,

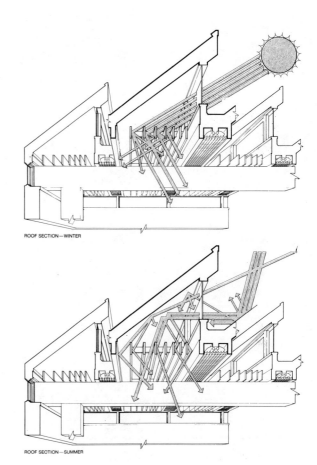

ROOF SECTION—WINTER

ROOF SECTION—SUMMER

DAYLIGHT ROOF MONITORS
MT. AIRY PUBLIC LIBRARY

and the mechanical system. Interior and exterior awning windows are provided for the various heating and cooling modes.

In the heating mode, solar apertures collect energy during the day, which is stored in the building mass or allowed to stratify at the ceiling. Heating units turn on only when preheated air at the ceiling is unavailable. In the summer, ventilation air is pulled from the north side and moves over the gym floor with the natural convection cycle induced by the rising hot air in the Trombe wall cavities. Roof fans assist the venting of warm air to the outside. When mechanical refrigeration is necessary (only for assemblies of over 20 people, according to the designers), interior and exterior awnings and windows are readjusted to check the natural convection cycle.

It is apparent that systems integration must receive close attention from the start, and that integration issues are not limited to mechanical systems. A given passive solar strategy can potentially affect virtually all building systems and functions from structure (massive-versus-light frame) to finish (color and texture). A highly effective daylight aperture can become just another source of glare if surface contrasts are incompatible. The designer must think through all implications so that final decisions do not become future problems.

MULTIPLE FUNCTIONS

Often the only way to economically justify passive solar features in a building design is to use them for several energy and/or physical functions. The Princeton Professional Park design provides a clear example of this strategy.

According to the park's architect, Harrison Fraker, the speculative office building developer's cost constraints meant that from the beginning only simple solutions would be investigated. "There just wasn't room in the budget for anything fancy like ice ponds and photovoltaics," Fraker observed. "We had to focus on simple things we could do to either the form or the envelope." "Our other principal discovery," Fraker explained, "is that the more applications we could find for one basic concept, the more cost-effective the concept became. Take our idea for an atrium. If we used it only as expensive circulation space, it was certain to get rejected. However, if we included it as part of the lighting scheme and part of the heating and cooling systems as well, the cost was a lot more justifiable."

POTENTIAL AMENITIES

Some aspects of certain passive solar strategies can be viewed as either liabilities or attributes. High ceilings and extra glazing can be seen as simply expensive or they can become valued features, depending on how they are treated. The award-winning Shelly Ridge Girl Scout Program Center in Philadelphia, Pennsylvania, is an excellent example of the thorough refinement of

Functioning Elements

Solar spaces such as atriums and "greenhouses" work best if they serve another important function. Not only do sunspaces add interest, they become more cost-effective if their benefits include more than energy reductions. For example, the RPI Visitor Center and Blake Avenue College Center use sunspaces not only as solar collectors, but also as organizing circulation elements. People enter into dramatic spaces illuminated by direct-beam sunlight creating light and shadow that change during the day. Princeton Professional Park is organized around a light- and heat-collecting spine that transforms what might have been a banal corridor into a tree-lined walkway, a major selling point for potential office tenants. Though amenities such as generous circulation or atmosphere cannot be easily assigned a dollar value, their practical and aesthetic benefits may make or break passive solar.

passive features into obvious building amenities. The designer was able to transform a mundane Trombe wall into an undulating building element, which created an interesting progression of spaces and heightened the sense of entry and arrival.

The solar wall, the dominant energy feature of the center, received a great deal of analytical attention and underwent quite a few design revisions. The first variation on the basic design sprung from a desire to integrate the building entrance with the passive solar elements. The logical entrance to the building was from the northeast or northwest, but a visitor entering from that direction would not be exposed to or involved with the solar wall. The design solution to the problem involved breaking the solar wall to permit an entrance sequence that brings the visitor through the solar space. The entrance sequence helps the visitor experience and understand the solar design as well as enjoy the scenic views to the south. A refinement of that concept produced a meandering solar wall that maintained the building's compact external surface area, and brought the heating element closer to the north walls for better heat distribution.

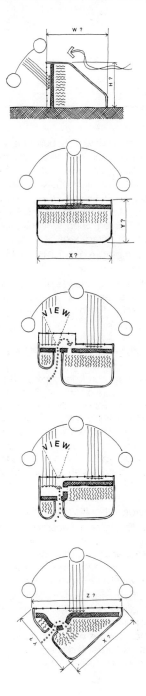

Design Revisions
SHELLY RIDGE GIRL SCOUT CENTER

Thermal Mass

Both high-mass and low-mass buildings work well, but each must be examined carefully with respect to climate and building use. High-mass buildings work well under the following conditions:

- Where there is extended evening and weekend use (e.g., Mt. Airy Public Library and Shelly Ridge Girl Scout Center). Such schedules can take advantage of stored heat.
- In sunny climates (e.g., Mt. Airy). Solar energy can charge the mass.
- With high-cooling load (e.g., Mt. Airy, Community United Methodist Church, and Comal County Mental Health Center). High mass absorbs heat gains.

Low-mass buildings work well under the following conditions:

- Where building hours follow typical 40-hour-per-week schedules (e.g., Security State Bank and Princeton Professional Park). In other buildings, night and weekend setback may contribute higher savings than will thermal mass, which dampens setback temperature savings. In general, setback is difficult in high-mass buildings because heating systems must recharge the mass before the buildings open. Occupants feel cold with cold walls and floors even though the air temperature is sufficiently high.
- In cloudy climates (e.g., Security State Bank and Two Rivers School). Solar energy should meet the instantaneous heating load before being stored in thermal mass. This makes storage less important with limited solar energy.
- High-volume buildings (e.g., St. Mary's Gymnasium and Philadelphia Municipal Auto Shop). High ceilings can be used to collect excess heat, which can be vented or ducted to floor level. The venting and ducting minimize heating and cooling loads.

DESIGN DEVELOPMENT

One of the objectives during the design development phase is to size components of both conventional and solar systems for the building. This makes determining the rate, quantity, and quality of energy flow important. For example, the Trombe wall may have stored a certain quantity of energy, but the rate at which that energy may be distributed and the temperature (or quality) of that heat are important determinants in maintaining thermal comfort. More sophisticated analytical techniques capable of addressing these questions are now appropriate. One must select a design tool that permits refinement of the schematic solution.

The potential for overheating, overcooling, or overlighting should also be examined at this stage. Such fine-tuning can often be achieved by properly sizing building components. For example, large quantities of concrete were exposed on the interior of the Mt. Airy Public Library to provide thermal mass, which would store heat and moderate internal temperature swings. Thus, the building does not overheat during warm afternoons. Some comfort problems have been reported on cold winter mornings, however, because it is impossible to heat the thermal mass quickly after it has cooled off at night. This underscores the importance of giving consideration to the overall result of sizing a particular element so that the solution to one problem (such as overheating) does not create another (such as sluggish morning warm-up).

INTEGRATING CONTROL STRATEGIES

Whether the sequencing of building operations depends on manual or automated control approaches, integrating various elements must be carefully planned. For example, if large amounts of thermal mass are incorporated in the building, consider minimizing night-setback temperature strategies that may make it difficult to quickly achieve thermal comfort on cold mornings. If daylighting is an important element of the design solution, consider the way in which artificial lights will be controlled. Manual control of artificial lights can be effective if a small group of highly motivated users retains control. In fact, in some buildings in this program, manual control of artificial lights proved more effective than automated dimming or switching devices would have been.

Try to avoid control operations that run counter to the occupants' intuition. For example, while closing fireplace doors may limit flue losses, it is not the natural response of people who wish to experience the fire's warmth.

The control sequences selected should be carefully documented for inclusion in the building's operating manual. Be sure to specify the signals to which building occupants are expected to respond, and explain the control sequences in clear, concise terms. Try to avoid control schemes that may conflict with each other. For example, Essex-Dorsey Senior Center used insulating panels to control heat loss, but, unfortunately, the panels restricted the amount of natural light. Similarly, blinds opened for solar gain cannot be expected to shield occupants from glare.

Finally, consider increasing temperature control tolerances in room and equipment thermostats. Since conventional heating systems address comfort requirements by short-term inputs of large quantities of high-temperature heat, excessive short-cycling to maintain tight temperature ranges can depreciate the slow, steady heat available from passive elements.

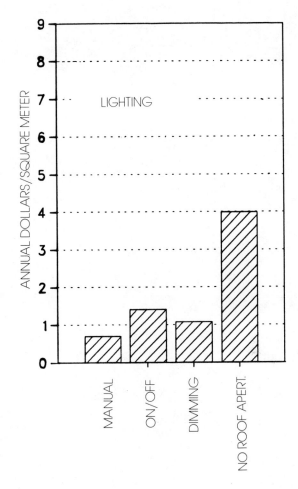

LIGHTING CONTROL ANALYSIS
MT. AIRY PUBLIC LIBRARY

CONSTRUCTION DOCUMENTS

Bid documents should serve as a performance specification for evaluating product options. Although plans and specifications may be tight, specific products should not necessarily be called out in all instances because a prescriptive approach denies the contractor the leeway to achieve maximum performance at minimum cost. More appropriate is a tight specification that spells out exactly how well the system should function. An example is "Thermostats shall provide temperature control within a 2°-F throttling range and accommodate both heating and cooling functions with an adjustable deadband of 8° F." When this performance criterion was initially omitted from the Gunnison County Airport and Blake Avenue College Center specifications, single-point thermostats were installed in swing spaces where energy savings depended on diurnal temperature swings.

Most building contractors will assume conventional building practice unless told otherwise, and even then they tend to do what they are accustomed to doing. Thus, call out and specify components carefully. A case in point is Gunnison County Airport where the electrician wired the exhaust fan to the boiler circuit because it was the most convenient circuit available. As a result, the exhaust fan would not operate in the summer when the boiler had to be shut down at the main breaker. Similarly, the Princeton Professional Park designer failed to specify how foil-faced batts would be installed between roof joists. The contractor, accustomed primarily to above-ceiling installation, did not tape the joints. The water vapor that passed through condensed on the metal deck and dripped back into the conditioned space.

The designer should make it a point to caution the contractor against altering conventional mechanical equipment to fit solar control specifications. In Mt. Airy Public Library and Princeton Professional Park, the designers originally intended to optimize building performance by opening the heat pump and monitoring the position of certain valves. Upon learning that this would invalidate the equipment warranties, they changed to a strategy of monitoring interior air temperature as an indication of heating and cooling energy use.

TEST, BALANCE, AND TROUBLESHOOTING

Although testing and balancing mechanical systems are usually specified for commercial-scale buildings, they are even more important when those buildings rely on passive solar systems. For example, when mechanical cooling is introduced into a building to supplement natural ventilation, the fans either reinforce or fight natural air flows. The competent designer will design to reinforce, of course, but testing and balancing will ensure that the design intentions are realized. For example, at Mt. Airy Public Library, zones that are lower in elevation require more heat and less cooling because air stratifies according to temperature. Because the exact quantities are difficult to establish during design, adjustments must be made during test and balance.

Systems other than the HVAC system may need fine-tuning; the designer should anticipate and provide for this. Automatic passive solar controls for night insulation, shading devices, and fans are cases in point. Before testing and balancing, the photocell-controlled awnings in the Security State Bank opened and closed every few minutes because of short-cycling. Although this is not easily quantified during design, a good test and balance would make the necessary refinements.

A fine line separates testing and balancing from troubleshooting startup problems, with one activity often flowing into the other. Troubleshooting usually extends into the building's breaking-in period, a duration of up to one year after the building is turned over to the owner. Difficulties during this time can be minimized if the designers specify sufficient ports for measuring fluids and thermometers for checking critical temperatures. Clear labels for switches, valves, and flow directions are also helpful, as are submeters for systems where problems leading to excessive energy consumption may lurk. For example, at Comal County Mental Health Center, all mechanical systems appeared to be operating properly immediately after installation. Each furnace put out its rated capacity when individually fired. But during the first heating season, the utility meter showed far less gas consumption than was suggested by a run-time meter put in during initial installation. The technical monitor hypothesized that perhaps something was limiting natural gas flow to the burners. Indeed, when the owner checked the gas piping against the drawings, he found the diameter was less than half the diameter specified in the drawings. (This, of course, results in a combustion that is too lean, and leads to a decrease in combustion efficiency.) In at least five other projects, such submetering led to the resolution of initial startup difficulties soon after they were detected.

TRAINING

Specifying training of building personnel is standard practice in nonresidential buildings, but specifications must be more explicit when energy performance is a measured criterion of the building's success. Such specifications should include designated training time and duration of the training, required attendees, topics to be covered (which include startup, short-term, and annual maintenance procedures and elementary troubleshooting), and technical assistance during the first few months of building shakedown. At the training, comprehensive operating manuals should be distributed. Like any other shop submittal, the manual should be approved by the A/E team. The manual should include cut sheets on each mechanical component, as-built mechanical drawings, and schematic diagrams of all major control systems. If the design intent is to have non-maintenance occupants operate the building, these occupants should be trained. At Princeton Professional Park, energy consumption was substantially lower in many of the rental suites following a user orientation session. At the Shelly Ridge Girl Scout Center, a similar session decreased energy consumption by one-half. These significant reductions underscore the need to specify training sessions and hold the contractor to providing them before final payment.

Retrofits

In retrofits, conservation measures should precede passive solar measures, and should be reflected in the base case. Cost-effective passive solar measures will probably be those that address a predominant heating problem since architectural lighting modifications are more difficult. Heat can be collected by components (as was done in the Philadelphia Municipal Auto Shop, Princeton Professional Park, and Princeton School of Architecture) or by building additions, usually in the form of sunspaces (as was done in Kieffer Store). The latter strategy can be more easily justified if the addition serves other useful purposes that can accommodate high temperature swings. Examples of such additions are atriums, entryways, and greenhouses.

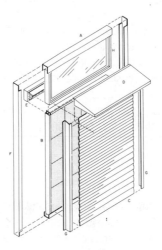

WINDOW RETROFIT
PHILADELPHIA MUNICIPAL AUTO SHOP

CONSTRUCTION AND BUILDING ACCEPTANCE

On-site inspections undertaken throughout the construction process are traditionally part of the design team's responsibility. There are a number of areas that merit special attention if the design team is attempting to achieve an energy-efficient building. Specifically, the architect should check the integrity of the building envelope. Air leakage is a common reason for buildings to fall short of their energy-efficiency potential. Areas that merit close inspection are the continuity of insulation and the integrity of air/vapor barriers. Both of these tend to receive less-than-careful attention from contractors not specializing in solar construction. In addition, the mechanical engineer should check ductwork for air tightness and proper insulation. Excessive leakage will make it difficult to balance the HVAC system. Furthermore, leakage occurring in the wrong areas could lead to excessive energy consumption. Finally, lighting equipment should be checked, especially for the correct ballasts and fixtures. Sometimes high-efficiency ballasts are specified, but not delivered. Also check that fixtures are installed in the proper places. A lighting strategy that mixes high-efficiency and regular fixtures can be confusing to or ignored by installers.

In the DOE program these lessons were best illustrated where contractors installed conventional materials and components that served solar purposes. At Security State Bank, specified glazing was replaced by glazing that did not have as high a transmissivity. The solar consultant for Gunnison County Airport performed lengthy calculations to optimize at 12 in. the Trombe wall thickness. When the wall was formed, however, the contractor found some existing 14-in. forms on site, so he increased the thickness by the extra 2 in. at no charge without realizing the thermal consequences. In most cases, though, careful construction was encouraged throughout the program. For example, the Community United Methodist Church is even tighter and more comfortable than predicted because of the builder's care and attention to detail.

POST-OCCUPANCY PERFORMANCE

Few buildings achieve maximum energy performance within a year of their construction completion. Buildings are not like store-bought products, which due to their mass production can be used immediately at rated capacity with full confidence. Clients do not fully realize this fact, and may blame the designer for normal startup problems.

The delicate integration of passive solar and conventional systems creates a greater need for post-occupancy monitoring and fine-tuning. Innovative systems such as the window insulating systems at Johnson Controls Branch Office or the window shading at Princeton School of Architecture and Urban Planning can be subject to short-cycling, damage by uninformed users, and maladjustment by contractors unfamiliar with the intended control strategy. In addition, occupancy may have changed since the system was designed. For example, at the Security State Bank a storage room was turned into an automatic check-canceling station with two operators. It is no surprise that the operators complained of air stuffiness until the ventilation system was readjusted.

All of these situations, which exemplify the necessity for fine-tuning, are reasonable for any building owner to expect within the first year of building operation. In the first year, all seasonal modes of operation will have occurred and problems will have been identified. The architect who offers post-occupancy de-bugging services is not trying to cover for bad design, but is simply attempting to make building shakedown less trying and minimize disruptions.

The DOE Nonresidential Experimental Buildings Program has generated a rich and diverse collection of lessons and experiences in passive solar design. What has resulted from this effort, and what kinds of issues pertinent to future design research have emerged?

Of the 22 buildings designed, 19 were constructed and yielded performance data, which are documented in a series of case studies and in a companion performance overview. Eight of the case studies and the overview are contained in this book. Analysis of energy savings, economics, and occupant satisfaction has shown the stakes are high. Overall performance has been excellent, with program buildings using 47% less energy than their conventional counterparts on an area-weighted average. Most did not cost more to build than nonsolar buildings of similar type. Occupant satisfaction was, in all cases, higher than average. Certain buildings' performances were particularly outstanding, demonstrating utility costs as low as $0.15/ft^2/yr. Others encountered architectural and mechanical problems that kept performance from going much higher than base case levels. In both instances, results could be traced back to the design, especially the design's flexibility for accommodating changing building uses.

Apparently, designers must ask a greater number of "what if" questions. Answering such questions, however, is not easy. Since 1980, little progress has been made on developing design tools that can be easily used for nonresidential buildings. Existing tools often require the designer to interrupt the creative process to generate performance feedback. One solution to this problem could be an energy design tool that piggybacks with computer-assisted design and drafting (CADD) systems.

From the schematic design on a CRT, an architect could be able to quickly retrieve heat gains, heat losses, natural lighting levels, shading factors, and the like for various climatic conditions and operating schedules. Results can appear graphically as overlays on the working sketches. Such an "energy/graphics" option could offer various levels of complexity corresponding to progressive design phases, each one requiring and yielding more detailed information. It could also allow the architect to focus on specific building components such as overhangs and Trombe walls when the particulars of shading, sizing, and timing need attention.

With more sophisticated design tools, architects can quickly answer questions identified in this overview as crucial. For example, what happens to the success of a particular schematic design for a school if: The administration decides to offer night classes? The building staff fails to operate the shading as instructed? A new building goes up across the street? A bid option of carpeting is accepted?

The issue of design tools is but one of the many issues that emerged during the DOE program. Program participants will agree that the program probably raised as many questions as it answered. Rather than providing definitive answers to the question, "How should a passive solar building be designed?," the program has shown there is still room for making the process more efficient and for making the product more successful.

2 BUILDING PERFORMANCE

The issue of energy performance of buildings is directly quantifiable and of great concern to building owners since it translates into dollars and cents. As an owner increasingly expects energy efficiency in his or her building, the designer must keep abreast of what is feasible, both technically and economically, for the climate and building type. This chapter gives both the owner and designer actual numbers on how the best buildings perform, thus establishing realistic limits and achievable goals for other climate-responsive, nonresidential buildings.

This chapter answers the questions: How well do the climate-responsive buildings work? Do they save auxiliary energy? Do they function as well as conventional buildings in terms of maintenance, operation, and comfort? What do they cost compared with conventional buildings?

In the following pages, the reader will find that there are positive answers to most of these questions, thus countering past assumptions that nonresidential buildings are unlikely candidates for passive solar technology due to their high internal heat gains, large volume, and rigid environmental conditions. The buildings in the DOE Nonresidential Experimental Buildings Program saved significant amounts of energy at little or no extra construction cost, which translates directly to lower building operating costs. In addition, user satisfaction was above average, and occupant operation and use of the buildings had a significant impact on auxiliary energy consumption.

The purpose of this chapter is to answer questions about how well climate-responsive, nonresidential buildings work and the circumstances associated with the best examples of building performance. While the actual performance of each building discussed reflects a complex set of interactions among building design, construction, and operation, the patterns of similarity that occur across a number of buildings provide useful guidance for future design and performance expectations.

KEY TO PROJECT CODES USED IN FIGURES

JC	Johnson Controls
TR	Alaska DOT
ED	Essex Dorsey
AS	Abrams Primary
MA	Mt. Airy
PA	Phil Municipal Auto
CO	Colorado Mt. College
CM	Comal County
CU	Community United Methodist Church
SR	Shelly Ridge GSC
GU	Gunnison Airport
KI	Kieffer Store
PS	Princeton School of Architecture and Urban Planning
PP	Princeton Professional Park
RP	RPI
SB	Wells Security State Bank
TG	Touliatos Greenhouse
WF	Walker Field
SM	St. Mary's Gymnasium

ENERGY PERFORMANCE

Two of the most frequently asked questions about climate-responsive buildings' energy performance are: Do the buildings really save significant amounts of energy compared to conventional buildings? and Where do they save energy compared to conventional buildings? This section addresses these questions.

The climate-responsive buildings participating in the DOE program used 47% less energy than their conventional counterparts. On an area-weighted average, new buildings submitting a year or more of monitored consumption data used almost half the energy that the conventional buildings would have used and significantly less energy than research for Federal standards determined to be economically feasible. They also used about 60% less energy than average U.S. nonresidential buildings. These data are based on comparisons with base case buildings.

For the DOE program each building team selected a base case, the "nonsolar" building the owner would have built had the decision not been made to go solar. The base case provided the teams a standard against which they evaluated the energy performance of the solar building. The base case would represent common practice in the local area and would be the basis of comparison for the passive design. For owners of multiple buildings, the base case was often the last building built. In other cases, the design team chose a building in the same area and collected construction and operating cost data. In all cases, the base case was reviewed and approved as reasonable by the project monitoring team. The base cases in the program ranged from pre-engineered metal classrooms to standard corporate architecture. In the case of retrofits, base cases were the existing buildings before retrofit. All base cases reflected the owners' budgets and standard construction practices in their areas.

The U.S. Buildings Energy Performance Standards (BEPS) program also used base cases as benchmarks. Estimated energy for the DOE program base cases approximated BEPS base cases within 10%, demonstrating good faith on the part of these designers not to artificially alter energy-use benchmarks to make actual measured savings appear greater.

Actual energy consumption is compared to base case predictions in Figure 2-1 and shows the aggregated decrease in energy consumption from the base cases. Figure 2-2 shows the range of decreases for the buildings participating in the program. The energy consumption of every building was either projected or actually measured to be substantially below that of its corresponding base case. Furthermore, when the actual energy consumption of new climate-responsive buildings (see Figure 2-1) is compared with the BEPS figures (see Figure 2-4), the average fell 14%. Only the retrofit projects exceeded BEPS budgets, which is not surprising because basic energy-conservative design practices, such as orientation on the site or appropriate aspect ratio, were often not considered during original design.

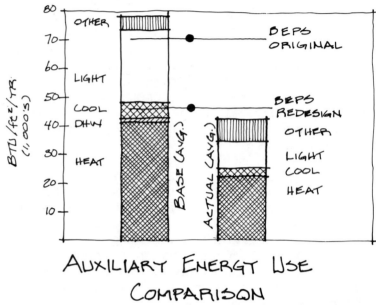

Figure 2-1.

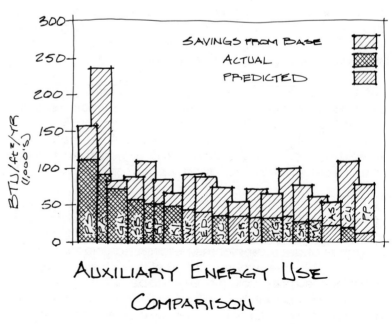

Figure 2-2.

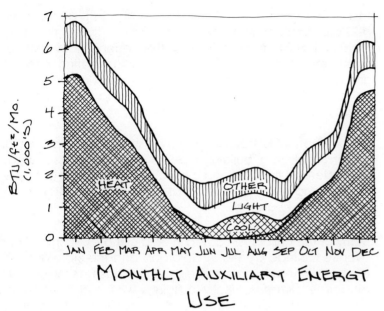

Figure 2-3.

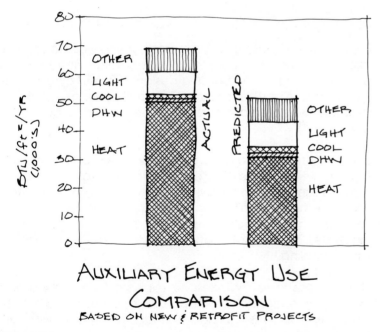

Figure 2-4.

NOTES

The Building Energy Performance Standards (BEPS) energy levels were determined by the U.S. DOE in 1979, based on a comprehensive survey of buildings designed between 1973 and 1976. These energy budgets represent the average building energy use by particular building type and location that was believed to be economically feasible to achieve. They do not include energy for computers and other plug-in appliances.

The primary difference between the design process in the BEPS program and in the DOE program was that in the latter, technical assistance provided to the designers covered not only energy conservation, but passive solar heating, cooling, and daylighting. This indicates that passive solar technology, not just conservation measures, contributed to the reduced energy consumption of these buildings.

The distribution illustrated in Figure 2-2 shows that no particular pattern of climate, building type, or energy savings strategy characterized the best and the worst performers. It did show, however, that retrofits could not attain the same reduction levels as the new buildings.

Many of the buildings located in cold climates, such as Blake Avenue College Center in Colorado and the State Security Bank of Minnesota, performed as well as those in sunnier, more moderate climates. Finally, buildings with design strategies aimed primarily at reducing heating, cooling, or lighting energy loads are distributed fairly evenly across the range of improved energy use compared to the base case predictions of energy use.

REDUCTIONS AND INCREASES IN ENERGY USE

Energy use for heating, cooling, and lighting was reduced by large amounts (see Figure 2-1). This is particularly interesting because over half the building designs focused on daylighting, and there had been some concern that using daylighting strategies would create increases in energy use for cooling or heating.

Solar heating was the focus of approximately 50% of the designs. There was some initial concern that energy use for cooling would increase in the fall months when one might expect solar apertures to collect unwanted heat gain from the low, southwest afternoon sun (see Figure 2-3). However, solar heating strategies were not accompanied by increases in energy use for cooling.

This demonstrates that despite expected internal cooling loads, nonresidential buildings are good candidates for daylighting and passive solar heating. Cooling loads were low because daylighting strategies reduced the need for auxiliary lights.

Auxiliary lighting energy use (and, therefore, associated heat gains) was 22% lower in summer months than in non-summer months largely because of the greater seasonal availability of sunlight. In June, July, and August, buildings submitting a full year of data reported, on the average, monthly lighting energy consumption of 57 Btu/ft². The artificial lighting reduction (22%) was less than the increased availability of natural light (34% to 60% depending on geographic location), because in most cases daylight hours extended past normal office hours in the summer. Thus, daylight could no longer be used to offset artificial lighting energy. In addition, cooling load was reduced because daylighting efficacy (90 to 150 lum/W) is generally higher than that of artificial light (25 to 100 lum/W for fluorescent sources).

Energy use for "other" building functions was double the predicted amount. "Other" energy users included (Figure 2-4) fans, pumps, task lighting, wall appliances, and office equipment. In modeling the base case, designers tended consistently to underestimate the demands of these energy users.

MORE ENERGY USED THAN PREDICTED

In the performance monitoring phase, actual building energy use exceeded projections by 20% on an area-weighted average. In only one case, the Johnson Controls Branch Office, was actual energy consumption significantly lower than predicted. Other buildings used as much as twice the predicted figure.

Figure 2-4 shows the breakdown of predicted energy use by function across all buildings. Heating energy use showed the most discrepancy: 31% higher than the original estimate, despite warmer weather with fewer heating degree days than usual in almost all cases. On the other hand, cooling performance beat initial estimates by 47%, buoyed by the concurrent increase in cooling degree days.

Discrepancies between the actual and projected consumption resulted from at least two factors: unanticipated building-use patterns and design tool limitations. Of the two, unanticipated building-use patterns probably contributed the most to the discrepancy. Project monitors reported numerous instances where building operation hours were extended because of the popularity of the building; where a greater number of people than planned used the building; and where storage spaces were turned into offices or classrooms, thus requiring space conditioning and lighting. Because predicting building-use patterns is so difficult, designers of climate-responsive buildings should anticipate post-occupancy changes by modeling their designs under a wide range of use patterns.

Many of the design tools used for predictions were originally intended not to provide specific energy-use estimates, but to give general design direction. Their precision, therefore, was limited. Some design tools were oriented primarily toward residential-scale buildings; others had primitive or no means to account for thermal mass effects, especially the interaction of thermal mass with building setback. In addition, they were weak in handling the dynamic interactions among heating, cooling, and lighting. As a result, the predictions were not accurate projections of actual energy use.

ECONOMICS

The purpose of this section is to review two key questions underlying the economics of using climate-responsive approaches in nonresidential buildings: (1) Do climate-responsive buildings cost more to build? and (2) Do they reduce annual operating costs? Based on the analysis, climate-responsive, nonresidential buildings cost significantly less to operate annually and can be built for about the same first cost as conventional designs.

Most climate-responsive, nonresidential buildings do not cost more to build than conventional buildings of the same type. Although a great deal of time has been spent in the past trying to isolate the incremental increase in first cost of solar buildings or energy-efficient components, it can easily be argued that, in the end, it is the total cost of a building that is of most con-

PASSIVE SOLAR COMMERCIAL BUILDINGS
PROJECT DESCRIPTIONS AND COSTS

	NAME	LOCATION	SIZE (FT^2)	TOTAL COST^1 ($)	COST/FT^2 ($)
	Two Rivers School	Fairbanks, AK	15,750	2,347,000	$149.00
	Abrams Primary School	Bessemer, AL	26,600	954,400	$ 36.00
	Community United Methodist Church	Columbia, MO	5,500	258,000	$ 47.00
	Blake Avenue College Center	Glenwood Sp., CO	31,900	1,874,000	$ 59.00
	Mt. Airy Public Library	Mt. Airy, NC	13,500	1,188,000	$ 88.00
	St. Mary's School Gymnasium	Alexandria, VA	9,000	655,400	$ 74.00
N	Johnson Controls Branch Office	Salt Lake City, UT	15,000	855,000	$ 57.00
E	Princeton Professional Park	Princeton, NJ	64,000	3,000,000	$ 46.00
W	Security State Bank	Wells, MN	11,000	704,000	$ 64.00
	Essex-Dorsey Senior Center	Baltimore, MD	13,000	850,000	$ 65.00
	Shelly Ridge Girl Scout Center	Philadelphia, PA	5,700	485,000	$ 85.00
	RPI Visitor Center	Troy, NY	5,200	423,900	$ 81.00
	Gunnison County Airport	Gunnison, CO	9,700	774,800	$ 80.00
	Walker Field Terminal	Grand Junction, CO	66,700	4,000,000	$ 60.00
	Touliatos Greenhouse	Memphis, TN	——	——	$ 12.00
R E T R O F I T	Philadelphia Municipal Auto Shop	Philadelphia, PA	57,000	479,000	$ 9.00
	Princeton School of Architecture	Princeton, NJ	13,700	123,000	$ 9.00
	Kieffer Store	Wausau, WI	3,200	57,500	$ 18.00
	Comal County Mental Health Center	N. Braunfels, TX	4,800	14,000	$ 3.00

^{1} Cont. Cost + Contractor O.H. + Cont. Profit — Arch Fee — Land Cost — Site Work

Figure 2-5.

46

cern to owners. Once a building budget is established, it is the goal of the design team to bring in a building that meets the owner's needs within the budget prescribed. The choice of specific building elements is left to the design team. It is the design team's responsibility to trade off various building elements to arrive at a cost-effective solution.

In this context, it was decided that the most valuable analysis of construction costs for the buildings in the DOE program would be a comparison of total building costs (per ft²) to typical conventional building costs. The cost per ft² of each climate-responsive building was computed from actual construction documents (see Figure 2-5). This cost was compared to a range of typical building costs (for similar building types) according to statistics compiled by either R.S. Means, F.W. Dodge, or both (see Figure 2-6). The comparison was performed for the actual year in which the building was built to

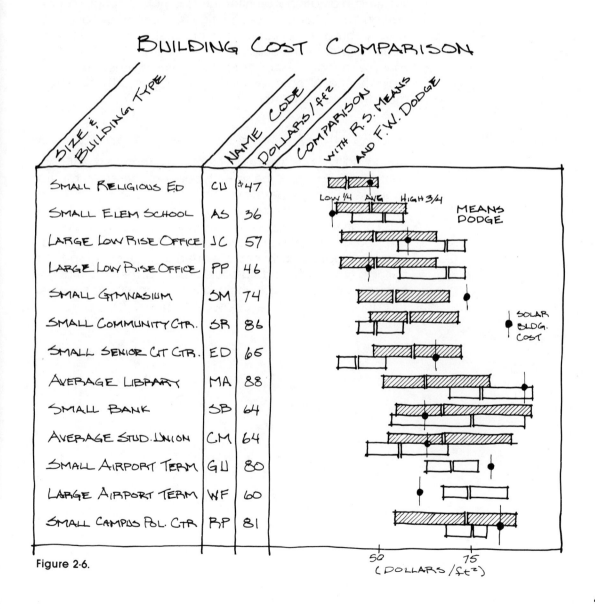

Figure 2-6.

reduce any effects of inflation, and was adjusted for building size and region where possible. In all, comparative data were available for 13 of the 15 new buildings completed in the Non-residential Experimental Buildings Program. Of the 13 buildings studied, 10 (75%) fell within or below the range of typical costs for conventional buildings of the same time. Specifically:

- Two buildings fell below the range of typical costs.
- Four buildings fell within the range of typical costs but below the median for either Means or Dodge.
- Four buildings fell within the range of typical cost but above the median.
- Three buildings fell above the range of typical costs.

The three buildings that exceeded the range of typical costs all fell within the owners' budget expectations. One of these was a national-award-winning building, and another was featured in a national architectural journal. Although a comparison to national average figures cannot account for specific building characteristics or amenities, the fact that three-quarters of the buildings in the program fell within a reasonable range of first costs for comparable buildings clearly indicates that climate-responsive buildings need not cost any more than conventional construction.

ANNUAL UTILITY COSTS

Annual utility costs were significantly less than costs for conventional buildings of the same type. Comparing climate-responsive building operating costs to conventional building operating costs is difficult because there is no national data base of annual operating costs by building type equivalent to the Means and Dodge data on construction costs. Nevertheless, some data do exist and are often quite good for specific building types. Where data could be found, it is clear that annual utility costs for passive solar buildings are significantly less than for conventional buildings. (See Figure 2-7.)

PASSIVE SOLAR COMMERCIAL BUILDINGS
PROJECT DESCRIPTIONS
AND
ANNUAL UTILITY COSTS

	NAME	LOCATION	SIZE FT^2	STUDY PERIOD	ANNUAL UTILITY COST			ANNUAL UTILITY COST ($/FT^2)
					ELEC. ($)	GAS ($)	TOTAL ($)	
N E W	Community United Methodist Church	Columbia, MO	5,500	11/82-10/83	236	569	805	0.15
	Blake Avenue College Center	Glenwood Sp., CO	31,900	07/82-06/83	27,388	2,340	29,728	0.93
	Mt. Airy Public Library	Mt. Airy, NC	13,500	01/83-12/83	6,119	No Gas	6,119	0.45
	Johnson Controls Branch Office	Salt Lake City, UT	15,000	04/82-03/83	7,249	1,219	8,468	0.56
	Security State Bank	Wells, MN	11,000	06/83-07/84	3,938	430	4,368	0.39
	RPI Visitor Center	Troy, NY	5,200	06/83-06/84	6,249	NA	6,249	1.20
	Gunnison County Airport	Gunnison, CO	9,700	09/81-08/82	8,159	No Gas	8,159	0.84
R E T R O F I T	Kieffer Store	Wausau, WI	3,200	06/82-05/83	386	399	785	0.25
	Comal County Mental Health Center	N. Braunfels, TX	4,800	09/82-08/83	1,161	515	1,676	0.35
	Philadelphia Municipal Auto Shop	Philadelphia, PA	57,000	08/83-07/84	19,279	◇31,176	50,455	0.89
						◇Gas and Oil		

Figure 2-7.

A full year of utility cost information now exists for 10 passive solar nonresidential buildings in the program (see Figure 2-8). These are actual energy cost data, taken from monthly gas, oil, and electric bills (excluding such extraneous costs as water or sewer charges, which are often found on such bills).

Comparative data were taken principally from four sources, according to the building type in question:

1. *Nonresidential Building Energy Consumption Survey (NBECS).* This survey of over 5,000 nonresidential buildings conducted by the Energy Information Administration (at DOE) was based on a carefully selected statistical sample of the U.S. nonresidential building stock. It combined personal interviews with building operators and actual fuel bills collected from utility companies. From the data given, it is possible to compute an average total utility bill per ft^2 by building type either by region or building size. Unfortunately, it is not possible to obtain both simultaneously. Although this data base is not equivalent to Means or Dodge (it exists for only a single year, 1979), it is clearly the best national data base across all building types.

2. *Building Owners and Managers Association (BOMA).* Each year, BOMA publishes the *Exchange Report,* which includes a summary of office building operating costs for specific cities across the United States. In many cases the data are further subdivided by location (e.g., urban vs. suburban) and sometimes by size. This is clearly one of the best data bases for office buildings, but is limited to this single building type. Because data are specific, the number of buildings in any one category may be quite small. For this reason, any single datum can be skewed by one or two uncommon buildings.

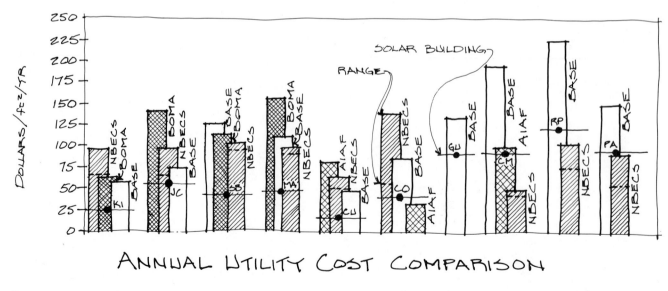

ANNUAL UTILITY COST COMPARISON

Figure 2-8.

3. *American Institute of Architects Foundation (AIAF)*. Under contract to DOE, the AIAF prepared a summary of all available data on energy costs in elementary and secondary schools. This report confirmed that few states report summary energy costs by ft^2 for schools. There are, however, a few states that offer this data. Maryland and New Jersey have particularly high-quality data on energy cost per ft^2. Their figures were used for comparison to school and school-like buildings in the program.

4. *Base Case Comparison (BASE)*. Each design team participating in the DOE program was required to prepare a "Base Case Building Profile" as part of the design process. Of the four comparisons used in this analysis, this is probably the best because of the effort made to find a reasonable comparison for the passive building actually built. Of the 10 buildings studied , the total annual utility cost for each of them fell well below the base case alternative (see Figure 2-8). The best performing building was 68% below its base case. The poorest performing building was 8% below its base case. The average across all 10 buildings was an energy cost 51% less than that of the base case. (See Figure 2-8.)

If one looks beyond the base cases to all the data base comparisons made for this analysis, the conclusions are only modestly different. The best performer costs 80% less to operate than an average building of its type. The average reduction in cost (all buildings against all data bases) is 33%.

It is only fair to point out that, in some cases, the passive solar building spends more on energy per year than a comparative or average building. This is especially true when the passive building is compared to national average figures in the NBECS data base. In each of these cases, it could be argued that the base case more accurately represents local climate and utility cost characteristics. On average, gas prices have increased 30% and electric costs as much as 150% since the NBECS data were collected. In all comparisons, the base case is significantly higher than the average figure. As one would expect given typical rate increases, it would be an interesting study in itself (though beyond what is possible here) to investigate these discrepancies and recompute the NBECS average costs. If NBECS were eliminated from the comparison, average savings across all remaining comparisons would be 48%.

A few numeric artifacts should not, however, distract from the key message of this analysis — that passive solar, climate-responsive buildings can spend significantly less on utilities than conventional buildings. Half the buildings studied use less than $0.50/ft^2/yr for utilities, and 9 out of 10 use less than $1.00. The average savings across all the buildings studied were from 30% to 50%. In fact, the lowest-cost building in the program (a church school and community center in Missouri) spent only $0.15/ft²/yr for utilities. That translates to a total annual utility bill for both electricity and gas of $806.

OTHER COST-RELATED ISSUES

In a data base of 10 unique buildings, it is impossible to find a large enough number of similarities to be statistically accurate when commenting on any particular design feature. Nevertheless, several cost-related issues have been identified which merit mention at least by anecdote. As more climate-responsive buildings are designed and built, these issues should be studied further.

Back-up systems or multiple systems can be unnecessarily costly. In the experimental climate-responsive designs, there was reasonable cause for concern about whether or not systems would work as well as predicted. For this reason, designers were cautious and included either full-scale back-up systems or designed multiple system options that could meet heating and cooling loads in case the experimental system failed. In all cases, these systems meant added first-cost for equipment and added operating and maintenance costs over the life of the building. As climate-responsive design concepts continue to prove themselves, confidence in their effectiveness will continue to grow. As this occurs, redundancy can be eliminated, thereby increasing cost-effectiveness of the overall design.

Since nonresidential-quality, movable insulation is not generally available, its application and use can be a source of cost problems. Movable insulation is a key part of many designs used in the DOE program. In most cases, however, high-quality, movable insulation systems were not commercially available at the time of construction. Designers worked hard to develop special or site-built systems, but the end results were mixed. In at least five cases, there were either delays in the original installation, problems with operation once installed, or poor enough performance that the original systems had to be replaced. All of these situations had a more or less negative effect on cost.

This is not to say that movable insulation should be removed from passive solar designs altogether — performance would clearly suffer from this approach. It is to say that designers should take special care in designing these components, should learn from past mistakes, and should identify products that can be expected to perform in a nonresidential environment.

Climate-responsive designs may add value by increasing building amenity, but this can be verified only by anecdote. As can be seen from the occupant analysis in this chapter, there is no doubt that most occupants enjoy climate-responsive buildings. In several cases there is a significant increase in building use. One owner claims that productivity is up because employees like the space in which they work. In one school, children said they like the passive solar area better, and in another school a principal reported that teachers are doing better.

If, and it is a big "if," any of these conjectures could be quantified, they would have a very significant impact on the economic analysis of a building. In most cases, a change of only one or two percentage points in the productivity of employees would overwhelm annual savings in utility costs. Payroll per year in most buildings outweighs utility costs ten to hundreds of times. If a connection does exist between the quality of spaces that result from passive solar design and the productivity of occupants, and if it can be identified, the cost of the type of design reported in this analysis would be small by comparison to their value.

Such an analysis was clearly beyond the scope of this project. Nonetheless, findings here suggest that climate-responsive design and the effects of daylighting in general should become an important part of future research on productivity.

OCCUPANCY

User-related issues underlie how well these energy-efficient buildings worked. Occupancy evaluation focused on occupant impacts on building energy use and user satisfaction with the building environment (particularly as it related to the building energy system design). For the buildings to be considered successful, occupant impacts on energy use must have been positive and users must have been satisfied with the building.

For each building, monthly measurements of building energy use, collected either by manual (submetered) or automatic data collection equipment, were compared to predicted energy use, and discrepancies between the two were analyzed. Possible reasons for differences include poor predictions, design errors, construction mistakes, unusual weather patterns, and a variety of occupancy factors.

Occupancy issues were assessed in a number of ways. Full-time and part-time building users were asked each month to complete a questionnaire. As part of the monthly reporting, building operators and managers answered a number of questions about operations and occupancy. Site visits and observations occurred at most buildings. Interviews were conducted with architects, building program personnel, building managers, and selected staff on an as-needed basis.

OVERALL SATISFACTION

Overall satisfaction with the buildings was quite high. Figure 2-9 illustrates the month-by-month overall satisfaction reported by building occupants on a 6-point scale. Although satisfaction fluctuated slightly for each individual building, the pattern indicates a high degree of satisfaction with *all* buildings in *all* seasons of the year.

The popularity of some buildings led to longer operating hours and significantly increased occupancy levels. Figure 2-10 indicates the differences in both amount and pattern of occupancy between those predicted by the designer and those actually occurring in the occupied building. The only building that was occupied at a lower level than predicted was Johnson Controls Branch Office, because the company hired fewer people to staff the office than predicted.

Most users liked the appearance of the buildings and felt that the design had a positive effect. There was a statistically significant relationship between liking the building and knowing it was a solar design.

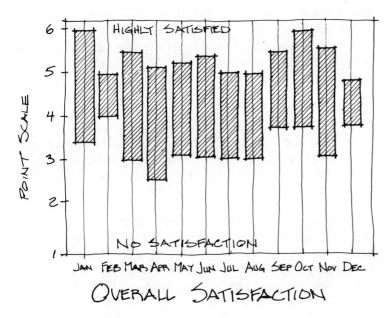

OVERALL SATISFACTION

Figure 2·9.

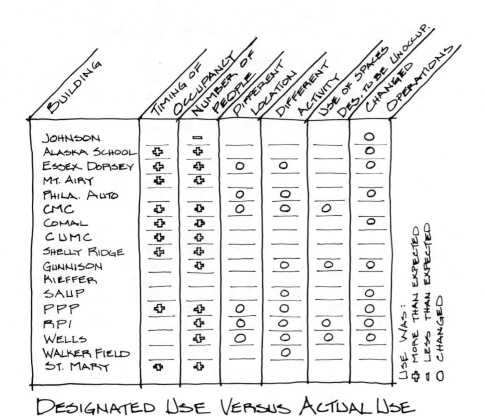

BUILDING	Timing of Occupancy	Number of People	Different Location	Different Activity	Use of Spaces Des. to be Unoccup.	Changed Operations
JOHNSON		=				O
ALASKA SCHOOL	+	+				O
ESSEX DORSEY	+	+	O	O		O
MT. AIRY	+	+				
PHILA. AUTO			O	O		O
CMC	+	+	O	O	O	
COMAL	+	+				O
CUMC	+	+				
SHELLY RIDGE	+	+				
GUNNISON		+		O	O	O
KIEFFER						
SAUP				O		O O
PPP	+	+	O	O		O
RPI		+	O O	O	O	O O
WELLS		+	O	O	O	O O
WALKER FIELD				O		
ST. MARY	+	+				

USE WAS:
+ MORE THAN EXPECTED
= LESS THAN EXPECTED
O CHANGED

DESIGNATED USE VERSUS ACTUAL USE

Figure 2·10.

Perceived thermal comfort was high, averaging 74%. Most occupants said they were comfortable most of the time. Thermal comfort was reported highest during the spring, and most complaints were reported on winter mornings. A repetitive pattern of "too cool" mornings and "too warm" afternoons occurred in many instances, especially in high-mass buildings. Ventilation strategies for cooling in several buildings experienced numerous operational problems and interfered with the ability to provide comfort effectively. These findings are discussed further in the sections on thermal mass and natural ventilation and analyzed in detail in Chapter 4, "Key Design Issues."

Satisfaction with lighting was consistently high. Daylighting was used in 100% of the designs and was usually well received. Users spontaneously mentioned delight with daylighting in the buildings using a wide variety of natural lighting solutions. Artificial lighting and daylighting were well integrated in the buildings, providing acceptable lighting conditions almost all the time. Fewer than 5% of the respondents complained of "too dim" or "too bright" conditions, regardless of time of year, time of day, or building location. Glare problems reported in several buildings were usually associated with perimeter rather than overhead light sources. Careful, broad distribution of indirect daylight emerged as the most successful.

In most cases, lighting energy use was lower than predicted, regardless of whether lighting controls were automated or manual. Daylighting alone sometimes provided 100% of the illumination needs. The issue of manual versus automatic lighting controls was analyzed in detail for two of the buildings. The results are presented in Chapter 4.

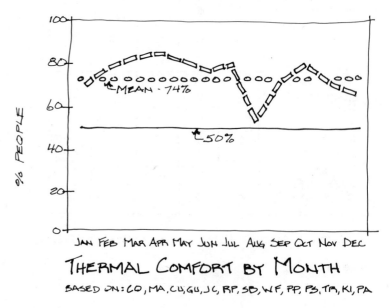

THERMAL COMFORT BY MONTH

BASED ON: CO, MA, CU, GU, JC, RP, SB, WF, PP, P3, TR, KI, PA

Figure 2-11.

56

Complaints about acoustics occurred in the majority of buildings. Many buildings had acoustic problems associated with ineffective sound isolation and ineffective absorption of sound. Four types of perceived acoustic problems were examined: disturbances caused by overhearing sounds, difficulties hearing during telephone or other types of conversations, and difficulty concentrating. Concentration and conversation problems were most frequent. Users reacted to these acoustic problems by complaining, installing acoustically absorptive materials, or adding public address systems.

Acoustic problems were related to the fact that many wall and floor surfaces were primarily designed to provide thermal storage mass and, therefore, were constructed of acoustically nonabsorptive materials. Open plans designed to enhance convective currents and broadly distribute light interfered with sound isolation. In addition, increases from the number of occupants originally anticipated created additional sources of sound.

There were few perceived air quality problems. The only consistently perceived air quality problems were those associated with stuffiness in areas that had not originally been designed for occupancy. Infiltration problems occurred in a number of the buildings shortly after move-in, but most of these were construction problems that were quickly remedied.

OCCUPANCY PATTERNS: PREDICTED VERSUS ACTUAL

Actual occupancy patterns differed significantly from those predicted in most buildings. Findings showed that there were many differences between predicted and actual occupancy patterns and building operations. Most likely, these changes strongly influenced actual building energy use, although the exact impact cannot be determined. Actual occupancy differed from predicted occupancy in four major ways: timing, location, number, and type of activity. Because the buildings were very popular, people used them many more hours per day than predicted. Moreover, occupancy began earlier in the day, lasted longer into evening hours, and included significant amounts of weekend use. This situation caused energy demands that had not been anticipated in design. Spaces that had been designed to be unoccupied, such as storage areas and mezzanines, were frequently pressed into use, influencing their energy use and comfort. Because these areas were not designed to provide comfortable conditions for occupants, users of these areas experienced some discomfort; thus, in trying to achieve comfort, more energy was used than designers had anticipated.

In addition, more users than predicted occupied the buildings. In one case, almost twice as many users occupied the space. This popularity put unanticipated demands on the building energy systems. Spaces that had been designed to provide thermal comfort conditions appropriate for one set of activities became uncomfortable when other types of activities took place. For example, when a sunspace was temporarily filled with blackboards and used as a classroom, the area became uncomfortably warm. In addition, the adjoining offices, which depended on borrowed light from the sunspace, were affected because the blackboards blocked their light source.

Changed building operations influenced building energy use. Building energy-use predictions were based on fairly specific operational assumptions. Each design team specified an operational protocol, which was used as the basis for its energy-use predictions. Assumptions ranged from straightforward instructions specifying when to switch a system from summer mode to winter mode to fairly complex and subtle directions indicating the sequence of actions to be taken if the building became too warm during spring and fall. For some buildings, operational protocols were explicitly transferred to the building users through written instructions; in others, through a verbal briefing to the building users. In still others, the building operation remained in the hands of an on-site building manager.

Building operations differed from those initially planned for a number of reasons. Changed use sometimes made planned operations inappropriate. In some cases the use patterns had been so significantly altered from those predicted that operations had to change in order to provide comfortable conditions.

Instructions were sometimes inappropriate. To be effective, operational instructions must respond to the needs, education, motivation, interests, and sophistication of the building users. Sometimes in these buildings, only a few users received instructions; sometimes the user population changed and the new occupants never received instructions; or sometimes the language, format, and distribution of written information was too sophisticated for the building users.

Instructions were sometimes not transferred. The question of who has responsibility for effectively transferring operational instructions often is not explicit. As a result, communication of useful information from the design team to the building users and managers sometimes does not occur.

Building operations were sometimes complex. Some buildings had numerous operation and control options, each of which was appropriate only for certain situations. The complexity sometimes overwhelmed unsophisticated users.

Appropriate actions were sometimes unfamiliar. When correct building operation depended on users taking unfamiliar actions, they often did not take the actions or they performed them incorrectly.

The relationship between operational actions and comfort was sometimes too indirect. Users sometimes could not understand the relationship between the actions they were supposed to take and comfort conditions because the effects were indirect or because the actions seemed counter-intuitive (e.g., closing glass fireplace doors to keep the building warmer). On the other hand, controls or operational components which were familiar and located close to users were used correctly.

Following instructions sometimes did not result in comfortable conditions. In these situations, building occupants tried a variety of other means to achieve comfort. Actions ranged from adding portable electric heaters, fans, and lights to blocking off light sources to reduce heat gain, darken a room, or achieve privacy.

Operations that solved one comfort problem sometimes contributed to a different comfort problem. In several cases, glare-control devices, solar-gain controls, and ventilation systems were poorly combined. As a result, for example, user attempts to control thermal problems interfered with the ventilation strategy and attempts to control ventilation caused problems with the lighting strategy.

RESULTS AND IMPLICATIONS OF
SELECT DESIGN STRATEGIES

Design options were limited, but easier to assess for retrofits. Of the 19 building projects reporting performance data, 4 were retrofits of existing buildings: Comal County Mental Health Center (New Braunfels, Texas), Philadelphia Municipal Auto Shop (Philadelphia, Pennsylvania), Princeton School of Architecture and Urban Planning (Princeton, New Jersey), and Kieffer Store (Wausau, Wisconsin). Because the number of retrofits is limited, it is difficult to make broad generalizations with confidence.

Compared with new buildings, retrofit design options were limited by lack of control over siting, massing form, glazing, thermal mass, and other issues usually addressed in early design phases. Thus, their performance level was also limited. However, it was easier to quantify the level because first costs and energy savings were clearly identifiable. In each case, the first costs, which were easy to isolate, became the total project costs. First costs tended to be low, between $3 and $18 per ft^2. In addition, the energy savings could be isolated directly. In each case, savings were the difference between the base case's and the DOE program building's utility bills. The level of savings was largely a function of the original building; projects with the more inefficient original buildings achieved more savings. In all cases, savings were significant, ranging from 14,700 to 137,700 Btu/ft^2/yr during the periods in which buildings were monitored.

Occupant satisfaction in retrofit projects could be more accurately measured because users could compare comfort and operation directly with that of their old building. Generally, occupants were more pleased with the retrofits than with their old buildings.

Lacking design options, it was difficult to achieve amenities available to new construction projects such as quantity and quality of light, or visual interest afforded by atriums. The best solutions focused on integrating conservation measures with solar and efforts to reserve daylight. Conservation measures to reduce heating, cooling, and lighting loads such as those taken in Comal County Mental Health Center often precluded more expensive solar measures. Where existing windows created glare, such as in the Philadelphia Municipal Auto Shop, solar components to mitigate glare, reduce heat loss, and retain light were custom designed.

DAYLIGHTING

Daylighting solutions in these buildings saved energy and contributed to comfortable lighting conditions. Daylighting was used as a design strategy in all buildings in the DOE program and was relied on heavily in over half. Six types of daylighting solutions were used: windows to reduce artificial lighting needs (78% of buildings), light shelves (48% of buildings), clerestories (39% of buildings), roof monitors (35% of buildings), sunspace and borrowed light (13% of buildings), and skylights (13% of buildings). This section summarizes the experiences associated with these daylighting strategies.

Daylighting resulted in significant cost and energy savings while contributing to user comfort. Approximately 55% savings over base case lighting energy use was achieved through these daylighting strategies. The energy savings, discussed in greater detail in an earlier section, were *not* achieved "at the expense of" user comfort or energy use for heating or cooling.

Successful daylighting designs shared a number of characteristics. The most important aspect of the successful use of daylighting was distribution. If daylight was well distributed, a visually comfortable and largely glare-free environment was attained. The most successful design solutions had the following characteristics:

- Glare and contrast were controlled.
- Beam daylighting was not allowed to enter an occupied space directly. Baffles, diffusing reflecting surfaces, and/or diffusing glazing were used to break up beam lighting.
- Occupants were not able to see the light source directly from the spaces they usually occupied.
- Light was admitted high on the wall plane or at the ceiling plane.
- The view was retained.
- A number of smaller roof apertures (clerestories and roof monitors) were used rather than a few large openings.
- Roof monitors and clerestories were designed with south-facing glazing.

Satisfaction with the lighting environment was quite high. In most buildings, daylight provided ambient or background illumination, with artificial lighting used to provide task-specific lighting. However, in three buildings — Mt. Airy Library, Security State Bank, and St. Mary's School Gymnasium — daylight provided the majority of the required task lighting. Daylight is a principal contributor to the increased amenity of passive buildings. Fewer than 5% of the occupants complained about "too dim" or "too bright" conditions, across all buildings and types of daylighting design. The many spontaneous comments about the delightful qualities of the daylighting attest to user satisfaction.

Manual controls for artificial lighting can be operated successfully by building occupants. Correct manual lighting control can result in both energy savings and acceptable lighting levels. Special studies carried out by Lawrence Berkeley Laboratory (LBL), summarized in Chapter 4, conclude that in the two buildings they studied in detail, users operated manual lighting controls in a more energy-efficient manner than simple automated control systems would have done. One reason is that occupants were satisfied at illumination levels lower than those recommended by industry standards, which are used by automated control systems. Although this is insufficient evidence on which to draw general conclusions, it indicates that occupants can use lighting controls effectively under some conditions.

Integration of daylighting and artificial lighting can be successful. The most successful integrations of daylighting and artificial lighting occurred when the following were true.

- Switching of any kind was unnecessary for extended periods (e.g., whole days).
- Zoned switching could supplement variations in distribution of daylight according to need in the space.
- Zones were laid out parallel to the daylight source rather than perpendicular to the daylight source.
- Multilevel switching could supplement available daylight as necessary.

THERMAL MASS ISSUES

Despite the fact that passive solar, climate-responsive buildings are often thought of as being dependent on high-mass solutions, the buildings in this program can be divided into three groups, each using a different type of thermal mass solution. High-mass buildings, such as Mt. Airy Public Library, Community United Methodist Church (CUMC), Alaska Two Rivers School, and Comal County Mental Health Center, used distribution of large amounts of thermal mass to store, delay, and diffuse heat energy throughout the building. Another group of buildings used localized thermal mass (such as Trombe walls), where the location of the mass was designed specifically to supply the heating and/or cooling energy needs of a particular area of the building. This group included Shelly Ridge Girl Scout Center, St. Mary's School Gymnasium, Johnson Controls Branch Office, RPI Visitor Center, CUMC, and Gunnison County Airport. The third group used low-mass design solutions, appropriate to factors such as timing of occupancy and climate. Low-mass buildings included Security State Bank and Princeton Professional Park.

High mass does not appear to be a contributing factor to the energy-efficient functioning of these buildings, and it does not appear to solve thermal comfort problems.

High-mass construction is not necessary to achieve significant energy savings. The effective use of mass depends on understanding the interrelationships among several factors: occupancy schedule, type of building use, type of energy problem, and the way mass is distributed throughout the space.

High-mass solutions are often associated with acoustic, thermal, and mechanical system integration problems. Acoustic problems appear because exposed hard surfaces of thermal storage material cannot easily absorb sound. Thermal regulation of timing and amount of "heat delivery to space" is difficult to predict because most design tools cannot yet handle effectively thermal mass effects. In addition, the processes by which thermal mass is charged by mechanical systems and/or natural passive systems are not well understood. Moderate amounts of well-distributed thermal mass are apparently sufficient to solve most thermal problems.

Localized mass can be an effective strategy to provide delayed heat to specific building locations. Several buildings successfully used localized thermal mass to provide comfort conditions, while saving energy at little incremental construction cost.

The Security State Bank and Alaska Two Rivers School are low-mass buildings that used little energy and provided comfortable conditions for building users. Because these buildings had daytime occupancy patterns, they required early morning warm-up and had no need for delay of heat delivery to the space. The designs took advantage of direct-gain strategies for heating.

NATURAL VENTILATION

Natural passive ventilation was an integral part of the cooling strategy in a number of buildings. While it is impossible to know exactly how well the natural ventilation systems performed, problems with various approaches can be identified.

A number of designer assumptions about the paths that interior ventilation currents would take in order to cool effectively and/or ventilate the space were found to be inaccurate. For example, in some buildings, currents were assumed to turn corners or travel along indirect pathways to create comfortable conditions and save energy; these expectations were not substantiated.

Conflict between shading devices and apertures impeded ventilation flows. A variety of natural ventilation sources were employed in the buildings, usually in the form of an operable window or door. In order to be effective, these sources had to remain unobstructed. However, in a number of buildings, these ventilation sources were covered by shading devices, which impeded the inflow of air. These shading devices were being used to control glare, darken space to show slides or films, and reduce solar heat gain.

Manually operated ventilation control strategies can work. Controls are most effective when they are familiar, close to the affected user, and simple to understand and operate. For example, clerestory windows that opened by pull chains were used effectively. On the other hand, users did not understand the proper operation of Trombe wall vents and used them inappropriately or not at all.

CLIMATE DEPENDENCY

Climate-responsive buildings succeeded in a wide range of climates, from very cold to hot and humid. During the planning of this program, there was particular effort made to achieve a geographic and climate spread across the range of projects. The success of the buildings is distributed across the entire range (Figure 2-12). Specifically, buildings reporting a full year of data are located in very cold areas with cloudy winters (i.e., Fairbanks, Alaska and Troy, New York); cold, sunny areas (i.e., Gunnison, Colorado and Salt Lake City, Utah); moderate areas (i.e., Colombia, Missouri); and hot, humid areas (i.e., Mt. Airy, North Carolina and New Braunfels, Texas). Urban areas (i.e., Philadelphia) are also represented. This distribution provides substantial evidence that passive solar, climate-responsive architecture is not limited to sunny areas with large diurnal temperature swings such as the Southwest.

Energy performance was not dependent on climatic variables. There is essentially no pattern of heating energy performance by heating degree day (HDD). Btu/ft^2/HDD is a good measure of the energy performance of buildings be-

HEATING BTU'S PER HEATING DEGREE DAY
NOTE: (R) indicates retrofit project

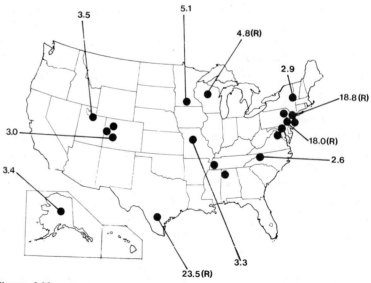

Figure 2-12.

cause it equalizes auxiliary energy without regard to building size or heating climate. Data show the performance parameter to be relatively independent of heating degree days. The range is between 2.6 and 4.0 Btu/ft^2/HDD, about half that of the base case values.

There is essentially no variation of heating energy performance by horizontal solar insolation. One would expect the buildings in sunnier locations such as Colorado and Utah to perform significantly better than those in not-so-sunny locations such as Alaska and upstate New York. The data, however, on the newly constructed buildings in the program show a fairly constant value near 3.5 Btu/ft^2/yr/HDD.

Most of the passive solar techniques used were very reliable and did not increase building maintenance requirements. Most project teams spent a considerable amount of time during the design process refining the passive solar techniques that would be used in the buildings and making them as simple as possible. This proved to be time well spent. Projects that made use of simple solutions and did not place unusual requirements on building occupants for successful operation were well accepted, performed satisfactorily, and were not difficult to maintain. In many cases, the building maintenance personnel responded very favorably to these buildings because they were easy to understand and operate.

By contrast, some techniques that were used required daily adjustment or used complex motorized controls; these proved frustrating to building personnel and sometimes created maintenance problems. For example, a few projects used operable insulating shades, which were not durable enough for nonresidential applications. The shades required substantial maintenance by building personnel and usually were used less regularly than originally intended.

People were willing to perform routine operations if they were easy to understand, were not disruptive to other building operations, and the effects could be seen or felt. In some projects, for example, the designers' desire to have operable windows open during the night to promote natural ventilation and cooling conflicted with security requirements. The designers' intentions were quickly abandoned by building staff and maintenance personnel. On the other hand, adjustments that were necessary only on a seasonal basis were usually well accepted. For example, when Trombe wall vents needed to be adjusted only in the spring and fall to accommodate change from the heating to the cooling season, adjustments did not usually become a problem. In a few projects, multiple mechanical distribution devices with sensitive construction tolerances were used; these almost always caused problems. Passive devices that were difficult to install or seemed counterintuitive to construction personnel were usually built incorrectly and, in some cases, were sabotaged by construction personnel. For example, in one project the auxiliary electric resistance space heaters were wired to operate continually, because the electrical contractor did not believe the passive techniques would provide sufficient heating. When the problem was discovered through performance monitoring it was easily corrected.

Occupants are often the most complex elements in nonresidential buildings. In buildings where occupants and maintenance personnel could easily understand the reason for including passive features and the way in which they were intended to operate, few problems existed. When people either misunderstood or disregarded the building's passive elements, problems inevitably arose. In some projects, for example, occupants placed plants and books on the light shelves, compromising their function as daylighting devices. In other projects, building users routinely turned on artificial lights even when they were not needed. This problem was most easily overcome by orientation sessions in which the designers explained the intended use of the building, and building occupants became familiar with the way in which the passive systems were intended to operate. When a level of confidence and trust developed on the part of building occupants, daylighting and passive heating or cooling devices were well accepted.

SYSTEM INTEGRATION

Passive heating, cooling, and lighting techniques must be carefully coordinated with conventional HVAC and lighting systems. Because passive and conventional systems usually shared the requirements for maintaining space comfort and adequate lighting, the highest cost and energy savings were realized when the designers carefully thought through the integration of those systems and the building personnel carefully carried them out. In particular, the best buildings were designed to avoid competition between passive and conventional systems intended for the same purpose.

If artificial lighting systems are not dimmed or shut off when adequate daylight is available, the energy savings potential will be lost, and worse, the spaces may overheat or experience high electrical demand charges. Similarly, mechanical heating systems that maintain comfort by providing short bursts of high-temperature air may overpower the radiant heat provided by Trombe walls or other passive heating devices. This occurs because the conventional systems are usually controlled by thermostats, which respond to dry bulb temperature, while the passive systems may rely on the steady flow of a moderate quantity of radiant heat. Mechanical cooling systems should also be considered when juxtaposed with natural ventilation systems or techniques making use of building mass and circulation of cooler night air.

In most projects, this interface did not prove problematic. In fact, in many projects the mechanical heating or cooling systems were shut off for large portions of the year because the passive techniques were capable of maintaining adequate space comfort.

In some projects, however, problems arose. For example, in a project that used a large atrium space with a significant amount of exposed concrete to provide thermal mass, the designer intended to allow for a swing in space temperature to store adequate amounts of heat in a space primarily used for circulation purposes. However, the mechanical controls subcontractor installed single setpoint thermostats, which automatically switched from heating to cooling based upon deviation from the setpoint. This conflicted with the intended temperature swing and, until corrected, eliminated potential energy savings. Similarly, in other projects where a significant degree of thermal mass was exposed on the interior of the building, night setback of the space temperature was employed. This was a problem in some cases because the building was hard to heat in the early morning. People felt too cool because of the presence of radiant surfaces, which had discharged their heat during the night and had to be recharged during the day. An easy solution was developed by minimizing the night temperature setback so that morning startup operations could be accommodated by the solar and mechanical heating systems.

Manual controls were sometimes more energy conserving than automated devices. This was particularly true in buildings where users perceived they had a a greater level of control over the interior environment. Frequently, the users voluntarily set temperature or lighting conditions below those assumed by building designers. For example, in the Mt. Airy Library and the Community United Methodist Church, which both used manual control of artificial lights to achieve savings, the manual controls were actually more effective in producing energy savings than automated dimming or switching devices. This was experimentally verified by Lawrence Berkeley Laboratory researchers who carefully monitored the use patterns in both buildings and compared the measured results of manual control of the artificial lights to predicted performance for automated controls. One of the reasons for the success of the manual controls was the willingness of occupants in both buildings to work at lower lighting levels than those recommended by industry standards. This voluntary action by building occupants is apparently connected to the high degree of personal control users perceived in those buildings.

CONCLUSIONS

The DOE Nonresidential Experimental Buildings Program has provided the largest data base of cost, energy, and occupant performance of nonresidential buildings to date. Patterns that have emerged show that passive, climate-responsive technology generally can provide substantial utility cost and energy savings at little, if any, increased construction cost. Performance parameters contributing to success or failure include occupant behavior, user control, fuel cost, and the skillful handling of design elements such as solar apertures, thermal mass, and daylighting systems and their integration with conventional design issues. Of minor concern are climatic limitations and predominant building load; passive buildings can perform well in a wide variety of climates to reduce heating, cooling, and lighting needs. Climate-responsive design does not place unnecessary constraints on comfort or on building aesthetics and, in fact, can enhance both. The greatest potential for failure lies in poor or complicated controls and designs that do not anticipate changing uses; but, even in the worst cases, these buildings can perform as well as conventional buildings.

The DOE program's results and the results from other successful solar buildings need to be disseminated to building owners using techniques and channels normally used by them. Amenities such as user satisfaction and marketability need to be quantified and described in language understandable to these decision makers. Increased worker productivity should be documented and aesthetic benefits highlighted so that passive solar is not overwhelmed by connotations associated with "alternative energy."

Evaluators uncovered several questions that potentially limit the acceptance of passive, climate-responsive design. One area insufficiently investigated is the design and performance of large nonresidential buildings. Only 3 of the 19 DOE program participants had floor areas over 50,000 ft², but almost half of the 1984 nonresidential building floor area exists in buildings in the United States larger than this. The retrofit of existing buildings also deserves greater attention. About two-thirds of commercial buildings existing in 1980 in the United States will still be in use in the year 2000 and, therefore, will require a large fraction of future building energy. Reducing this energy involves issues different from those surrounding new buildings. Existing buildings often are not oriented properly. In addition, they have greater internal spaces inaccessible to solar heat and daylight, are built with heavy construction materials such as brick and concrete, are located on urban sites shaded by neighboring buildings, and have historic perservation covenants restricting design alternatives. Although these issues make retrofit more difficult, potential savings are often greater than for new buildings because old buildings tend to be energy wasters.

Additional research is needed in the development of design tools. Design tools are procedures convenient to the designer for accurately measuring potential energy savings during the design process. Tools that exist today are either cumbersome (i.e., they require extensive computer input and take a long time to return results) or are unsophisticated in their approach to integrating the many energy flows in a building. Many simple programs, for example, do not give credit to cooling energy when daylighting reduces heat gain from artificial lights. Energy design tools need to be integrated with those in non-energy areas of architecture, so that the architect can develop building designs on a computer screen and instantaneously see the implications for energy consumption, construction cost, handicapped access, fire protection, and structure.

These topics point to another area in need of further research: whole-building analysis. It is not enough to conduct research in separate architectural disciplines; as is true in design, the disciplines must be integrated. Whole-building systems research identifies the optimum integration of architectural, mechanical space conditioning, and electrical systems with passive solar technologies. The need for further research was underscored in the DOE program, where designers had little basis for answering questions such as: How well will open floor plans facilitate natural convection cooling? How consistently will occupants naturally keep lights off in daylighted spaces? To what extent is thermal mass necessary to store heat in buildings where lighting is the main energy load or where heating is not needed at night?

More research is also needed in the areas of advanced glazing products and daylighting techniques. In addition, controls must be further refined, especially automatic and manual controls that integrate solar and conventional heating, cooling, and lighting systems. These components are sufficiently far from market readiness that their research would benefit from public support.

3 CASE STUDIES

MT. AIRY PUBLIC LIBRARY

"Big buildings in big cities aren't the only places where 'back to nature' designs are cropping up," wrote Mark Dodosh in the July 23, 1980 edition of the *Wall Street Journal*. Dodosh was referring specifically to the new passive solar library in little Mt. Airy, North Carolina (population 7,000). The new facility, which has an 80,000-volume capacity, has been hailed as one of the finest and most modern libraries in the United States. (See Figure 3-1a.)

When Mayor W. Maynard Beamer dedicated the new municipal building a few years ago, he told the group that the city's next number-one priority would be a new public library. Early in 1980, with the help of a Department of Energy (DOE) contract, the Mt. Airy Board of Commissioners decided to replace the existing library with a larger and better facility.

Figure 3-1a. Mount Airy Public Library.

71

Finally, after 52 years, the city would have a new public library, the first built expressly for that purpose. According to the citizens of Mt. Airy, it was worth the wait. The old mansion that housed the library had become cramped and worn with use. Not only had the immediate community outgrown the library, but the Mt. Airy branch of the regional library system consistently attracted more patrons from outside the community than any of the nine other libraries in the system.

The new library, completed in April 1982 is regarded as a multi-purpose cultural center by the city. Clad in locally quarried white granite, it is located on a southward-sloping 1.3-acre site next to City Hall and other downtown institutional and cultural facilities.

ARCHITECTURAL DESIGN PROBLEM

The most critical design program objectives for the library were related to the flexibility, openness, and accessibility of the design. The flexibility requirement had two components. First, the library had simultaneously to accommodate different user groups without creating conflict among them. Because people of all ages would use the library, a children's area, a record and tape collection, a repository for local history, reference and periodical areas, and an adult reading room all had to be integrated within a relatively small plan. Workrooms, card catalogs, rest rooms, entry and display areas, other miscellaneous support functions, and, of course, room for thousands of books also had to be accommodated — all in 13,500 ft^2.

The flexibility requirement also demanded that the building provide space for special events such as seminars, films, colloquia, and childrens' groups. This meant that at least part of the library would have to be accessible when the library itself was closed. This area is aptly called the "multipurpose room," an integral part of the library that may also function as a separate facility.

The design objective for "openness" was based on two requirements: (1) free circulation throughout the facility (possibly a reaction to the cramped quarters in the old house) and (2) the library staff's need to have visual control over all library areas and materials including the entry, stacks, and other public areas. Since a solid granite substrate limited excavation on portions of the site, the single-story floor plan was stepped down in three levels, which enhanced the openness of the design and increased the effectiveness of visual surveillance from the lending desk.

"Accessibility" pertained mostly to building code requirements including site planning and accommodations for cars, pedestrians, and disabled people (particularly those confined to wheelchairs). A ramp for handicapped persons and book carts provides easy access to all three levels.

EXPECTATIONS FOR REDUCING ENERGY USE

The principal energy design objective was to reduce the annual energy consumption (i.e., electricity) by 70%. If this objective were achieved, energy costs—a high priority item with the Commissioners — would be only one-third the costs normally incurred.

The design team and the Commissioners believed from the outset that a solar building, constructed with attention to conservation measures, was the best approach to meet the energy performance objective. The design team applied basic rules-of-thumb and manual calculation methods during the early design stages to establish the 70% energy savings objective. The team simulated the energy performance of a similar sized, conventional building (the "base case") to determine that about 56,000 $Btu/ft^2/yr$ in energy use was typical. After simulating the same building with various passive solar strategy combinations and studying scale models of the initial designs, however, the design team knew that the Mt. Airy Library would use much less than 56,000 $Btu/ft^2/yr$.

The analyses enabled the design team to break down the component parts of the new library's energy end-use loads. They found that lighting, cooling, and mechanical equipment (mostly fans) would use the most energy over a typical year. In the final design stages, the computer projected that the selected passive solar and conservation measures would reduce energy use by the following:

- Lighting by 82%
- Heating by 63%
- DHW by 56%
- Cooling by 47%
- Ancillary equipment (mostly fans) by 31%.

The floor plan (Figure 3-1b) was a major factor in meeting the energy design objectives. The preliminary floor plan was refined throughout the design process so that it would meet all the design requirements. Because the floor plan was stepped down into three levels and segmented into separate "wings," (see Figure 3-1c) the design team was able to take full advantage of the southern exposure and existing shade trees to help meet energy performance requirements.

INTEGRATION OF DAYLIGHTING, PASSIVE HEATING

After carefully analyzing projected energy needs, the design team determined that lighting was the largest end-use requirement and the best place to start. Because the library was

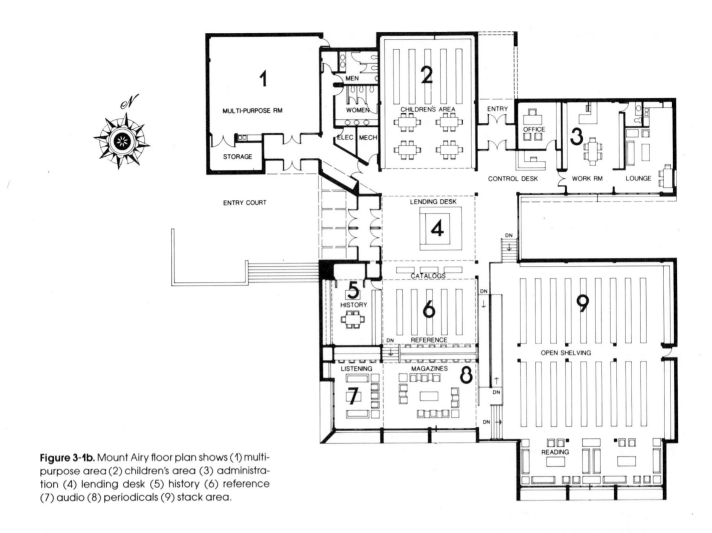

Figure 3-1b. Mount Airy floor plan shows (1) multi-purpose area (2) children's area (3) administration (4) lending desk (5) history (6) reference (7) audio (8) periodicals (9) stack area.

Figure 3-1c. Short stairs and ramps connect the spaces in the tri-level, one-story floor plan. Note recessed light baffles in ceiling.

primarily a facility used during the day, the design team looked to develop a daylighting system that could meet most daytime lighting needs. The team developed a scheme that would complement the architectural design and define various areas within the library. Because the direct rays of the sun could damage library materials, the team developed a system that admits glare-free, diffuse light to all major library areas, while preventing direct-beam illumination of the stacks.

The final design also included south-facing windows (see Figures 3-1d and 3-1e), which provide side lighting and a view. As shown in Figure 3-1g, a typical window unit in the south wall consists of a light shelf (above the viewing frame) that reflects sunlight onto a light-colored ceiling, distributing diffuse light to the adjacent area. The light shelf prevents direct-beam illumination of any of the interior areas. The window units used throughout the building are double-glazed. Overhangs are necessary on the south-facing windows to prevent summertime overheating. The design team predicts that all south-facing glass will be entirely shaded from April 21 to August 21 each year, but that by December 21, full sunlight will reach the building interior.

Figure 3-1e. Typical window unit. Light shelves and overhangs prevent the direct rays of the sun from entering this reading area along the south wall next to the stacks.

Figure 3-1d. Periodical shelves and reading area next to south-facing windows with light shelves.

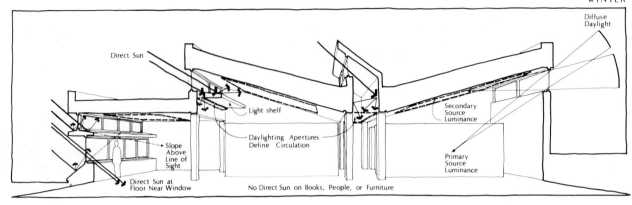

Diffuse
Daylight

Direct Sun

Light shelf

Secondary
Source
Luminance

Daylighting Apertures
Define Circulation

Slope
Above
Line of
Sight

Primary
Source
Luminance

Direct Sun at
Floor Near Window

No Direct Sun on Books, People, or Furniture

SUNLIGHTING

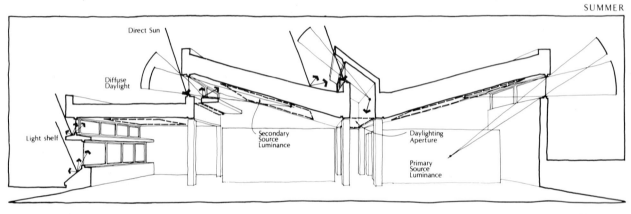

SUMMER

Direct Sun

Diffuse
Daylight

Light shelf

Secondary
Source
Luminance

Daylighting
Aperture

Primary
Source
Luminance

DAYLIGHTING

Figure 3-1f. Cutaway diagram of the stacks area. Illustrates why no direct sun strikes books, people, or furniture.

The daylighting system is designed to provide more than half the winter heating needs, as well as most of the year-round lighting needs. The considerable masonry mass of the concrete structure stores enough heat to moderate auxiliary heating energy requirements throughout the day. Although heating occurs directly through the apertures, glare and "hot spots" in the well-insulated building and the adverse effects of ultraviolet light on the book collection are avoided by baffles. The baffles are positioned to absorb the ultraviolet light and scatter the sun's direct rays before they reach occupied spaces. (See Figures 3-1h and 3-1i.)

During the summer months, the clerestory glazing is in shade. However, light-colored gravel on the flat areas of the roof reflects sunlight into the clerestory space above the ceiling. The baffle system below each clerestory further diffuses natural light throughout the space below.

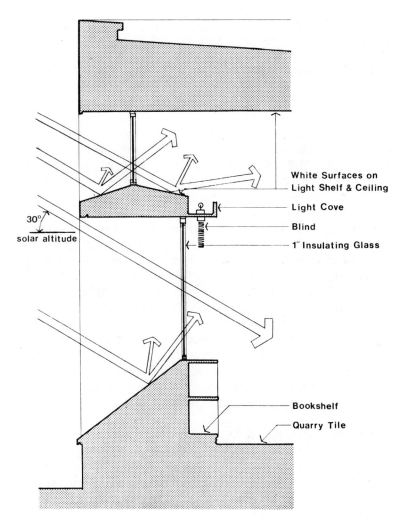

White Surfaces on
Light Shelf & Ceiling

Light Cove

Blind

1" Insulating Glass

30°
solar altitude

Bookshelf

Quarry Tile

Figure 3-1g. Light shelf design—winter solstice.

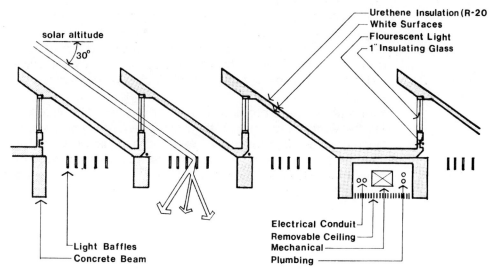

Urethene Insulation (R-20
White Surfaces
Flourescent Light
1" Insulating Glass

solar altitude
30°

Electrical Conduit
Removable Ceiling
Mechanical
Plumbing

Light Baffles
Concrete Beam

Figure 3-1h. Clerestory design—winter solstice.

77

Figure 3-1i. View of the light baffle system from the main floor.

AIR-TO-AIR HEAT PUMPS SELECTED OVER WATER-TO-AIR UNITS

Normally, water-to-air heat pumps operate more efficiently than air-to-air units for several reasons. First, water-to-air heat exchange is simply more efficient than air-to-air heat transfer. Second, the water supply temperature is usually higher during the winter than the ambient air temperature. Consequently, the water-to-air heat pump operates more efficiently than the air-to-air unit. This higher overall efficiency allows the system to operate at or near its rated capacity for longer periods and, therefore, less back-up heating is required.

For the Mt. Airy project, however, a water-to-air heat pump system would have introduced costly complications. The amount and quality of the discharge water may have required the client to file for both federal and state discharge permits. The water-to-air system required 70 to 100 gallons per minute per ton (2-2.5 gpm/ton). Discharge of such a large amount of water may have required an Environmental Protection Agency permit, if the system discharged into a stream. If the system discharged into the city storm drains, the water temperature would have been high enough to require a state permit. Moreover, discharging into the sanitary sewers would have required expensive effluent treatment.

The system water supply also was a concern. Municipal water would cost a minimum of $1,100 per month ($0.725/1,000 gal.). Although this is not exorbitant for a commercial building, it is quite high for a small library. The alternative was to use well water. The groundwater in Mt. Airy, however, is generally hard and corrosive. Residents are constantly faced with deterioration of both copper and galvanized pipes. Corrosive well water would have required treatment before use in the heat pump system, adding an initial cost and yearly maintenance fees to the basic system costs. To determine if there was an adequate supply of noncorrosive water at a reasonable depth on the library site, a test well was required. However, the cost of drilling through granite for perhaps hundreds of feet and the high probability that the groundwater was corrosive led the client to specify an air-to-air heat pump system.

Even without these problems, it may have been difficult to justify the water-to-air units on the basis of energy cost savings. Since considerable savings will result from the library's passive systems, the more efficient water-to-air heat pumps may not have been as cost-effective as they would have been in a conventional building.

Overall, the Mt. Airy Library has met or exceeded all expectations of its designers and users. The attractive, crisply detailed, white granite structure was recognized by a design award from the North Carolina chapter of the American Institute of Architects (AIA). Perhaps even more important, the library has earned high grades from employees and visitors. Year-long occupancy surveys indicate that over 90% of the full-time staff is very pleased with the library, and more than two-thirds said they prefer the design and appearance of Mt. Airy to other libraries with which they are familiar.

Library patrons have also expressed satisfaction with the new building. Over twice as many people as originally anticipated use the library each day, and management has expanded operating hours from 53 to 66 hours per week.

REDUCED ENERGY USE, LOWER UTILITY BILLS

The library's energy use has been extremely low, as have its utility bills. In its first year of operation, energy consumption was about 40% lower than that of a base case facility, i.e., a similar building in the same climate, without solar energy features. Mt. Airy's energy use also was approximately half as much as a relatively energy-efficient BEPS building. Figure 3-1j shows the major end-use energy requirements of the all-electric building for the 12 months from November 1982 through October 1983.

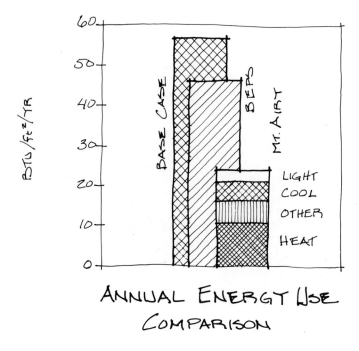

ANNUAL ENERGY USE
COMPARISON

Figure3-1j. Annual energy use comparison. Cooling and lighting energy consumption are very low..

Heating dominated end-use consumption, accounting for more than two-thirds of the total annual energy use. Cooling energy use was very low for the year, with July and August accounting for more than 70% of the cooling load. Daylighting system performance far exceeded expectations. Lighting energy use was very low, especially for a library where lights normally constitute a large portion of energy use. The lighting energy consumption for the year amounted to less than one-eighth of the total building energy use.

An efficient lighting system (i.e., fluorescent general lighting and incandescent task lighting) works with the passive solar design to keep lighting energy use low. Other conservation features are integrated into the building design to help control heating and cooling energy consumption. The library is well insulated, with R-20 walls and ceilings and insulated double-pane glazing. Air lock entries reduce infiltration losses, and a zoned system of heat pumps efficiently maintains comfortable temperatures.

Energy costs over the test year were more than 50% less than a comparable conventional building, and over 40% less than the BEPS energy levels, as shown in Figure 3-1k. At $.06/kWh, this translates into a total first-year cost savings of $7,120 over a similar nonsolar building and $4,750 over the BEPS building.

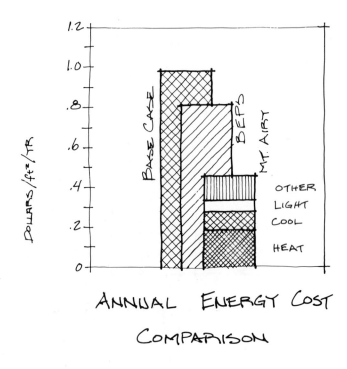

Figure 3-1k. Annual energy costs comparison. (Electric rate: $0.06/kWh or $17.50/MMBtu)

CONSTRUCTION COSTS

The Mt. Airy Public Library is a one-story, concrete-frame and masonry structure with a built-up steel roof. According to Means and Dodge construction cost reports, the average 1982 cost of a conventional public library of similar construction was $79/ft^2$. Mt. Airy final costs were higher, at $88/ft^2$. But a simple cost comparison with industry data on conventional libraries of standard construction can be misleading. For example, the white granite cladding, tile floorings, and cast-in-place concrete frame of the Mt. Airy Library are not typical of most libraries. The degree of attention to interior finish and detail in the Mt. Airy Library is also atypical. In short, the construction and finish of the Mt. Airy Library are of superior quality, and its energy-efficient design is hardly conventional.

Four innovative libraries were examined as a potentially more meaningful comparison group. The libraries, listed in Figure 3-1l, are superior quality, "nonconventional" buildings. They are similar to the Mt. Airy Library in that they are constructed of concrete and/or steel and have unusual structural, design, and finish characteristics. They range in cost from $54/ft^2$ to $138/ft^2$, and average $96/ft^2$. While four buildings are too small a sample for a statistically valid cost comparison, the range of costs suggests that $88/ft^2$ is well within the range for a high-quality, innovative library. It was also within the owner's budget.

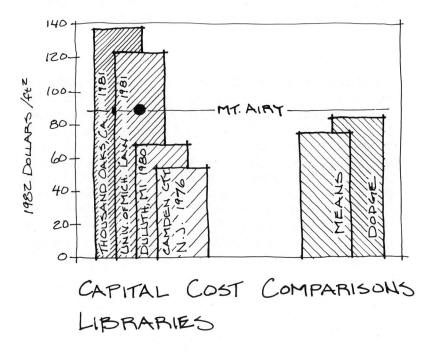

Figure 3-1l. Capital costs comparisons for libraries. Library costs exclude A/E fees, land, sitework, and interior furnishings.

DAYLIGHTING SYSTEM

Lighting quality and levels are very good. The daylit interior provides an ideal environment for browsing, recreational reading, and serious study. The titles of books on all the shelves are clearly readable in any part of the library without the aid of artificial light during most of every day. All library staff reported that the natural light was sufficient for normal activities including reading, at least part of each day.

The relatively few complaints about glare (excessive brightness and contrast) attest to the success of the daylight distribution scheme. Glare was no more a problem in this building than in any other. Occasionally, the staff complained that low sun angles in the winter resulted in sunlight entering the reading areas along the south and east walls and the staff workrooms on winter and early spring mornings. Most of these bright spots can be controlled by properly adjusting the miniblinds.

The daylighting system not only provides quality ambient lighting, it results in very low lighting energy use. Because the library is primarily a day-use facility, the daylighting system was designed to meet most daytime lighting needs and, therefore, save the most in energy costs. The result is very low lighting energy use, which is not usually associated with a library. The building consumed 2,800 Btu/ft^2/yr (less than 1 W/ft^2) compared to the 20,000 Btu/ft^2/yr typically required for commercial buildings. This represents an 86% reduction in lighting energy use, with the lighting load amounting to less than 12% of total building energy use. By contrast, for the base case the lighting load made up almost two-thirds of total energy use.

SHADING, SUNLIGHT DIFFUSION

The glazing area in the building is 3,000 ft^2, or more than 20% of the floor area. Two-thirds, or 2,000 ft^2, is south-facing glass. Ordinarily, this glazing area might be considered excessive, even for a passive solar building. Too much glass could lead to overheating problems and place increased demands on air conditioning equipment. The daylighting system in the Mt. Airy Library, however, takes advantage of natural light while preventing direct-beam radiation from causing overheating during the spring and summer months. Occupants rarely complained of being too warm. In fact, only two complaints were reported in June, the first particularly warm month of the year, even though the air conditioning was not turned on until July.

The daylighting system is designed for maximum possible dispersion and distribution of direct sunlight. Although various techniques are employed to diffuse the beam sunlight, the essential concept in each technique is basically the same (see Figure 3-1f). The sunlight is received directly on a reflective diffusing surface (e.g., the light shelves and roof monitor ceilings). It is then reflected off another light-colored diffusing surface (e.g., the stacks area ceiling and the light baffles below the roof monitors) before entering the space. This technique effectively attenuates the beam sunlight and also substantially reduces the amount of radiation entering occupied levels of the library. As a result, incoming radiation is evenly diffused and evenly distributed throughout the building's major spaces to heat and light surfaces.

The daylighting system had little apparent effect on heating and cooling loads. Computer simulation results of the Mt. Airy Library and its nondaylight counterpart (i.e., without roof apertures) clearly show a negligible solar contribution to heating and cooling loads. Several different factors could possibly account for this somewhat surprising result.

In order to increase solar heat gain during the winter, the large solar apertures admit considerably more sunlight than necessary for lighting purposes. Some excess heat is stored in the tiled concrete floor slab, while the rest immediately heats the space. The heating benefit compensates for increased conductive heat losses through the glazing and decreases the heat load in milder months.

During the summer, virtually no beam radiation enters the glazing. Light diffused through the large windows continues to provide daylighting, but not enough to cause overheating. Because natural lighting has a higher luminous efficacy (lumens/watt) than electric lighting, the effective use of daylighting rather than electric lights reduces the amount of heat entering the space. Although some excess radiation is admitted, cooling loads are not measurably affected.

MANUAL LIGHTING CONTROL

The impressive lighting energy savings were achieved with totally manual lighting control. The designers' manual control strategy was at odds with the trend of installing sophisticated computerized lighting control systems in commercial buildings. It was also counter to conventional wisdom, which dictates that automatic controls are necessary because occupants cannot be expected to operate the lights in an energy-efficient manner. Nevertheless, the manually controlled lighting system at the Mt. Airy Library works well.

For the most part, lights remain off when there is sufficient daylight. The library staff willingly accepts the responsibility of managing the lighting system. Informal staff orientation and periodic reminders appear to be sufficient to achieve generally effective lighting management. The staff uses switches, centrally located at the circulation desk, to control the library's lights. Because responsibility for the lighting system rests with the full-time staff, their training in proper system operation has resulted in conscientious and consistent control.

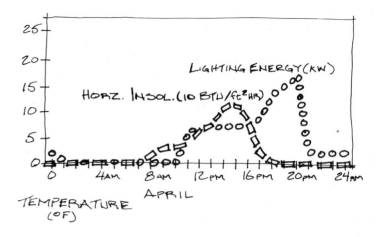

Figure 3-1m. Lighting pattern chart for overcast day.

One reason for the manual system's effectiveness is that to be turned on, the lights require a conscious action on the part of employees. Thus, under normal conditions lights are never turned on during the day because by the time the building is typically occupied (late morning) natural daylighting is usually sufficient to make electric lighting unnecessary. The savings realized on normal days as a result of the staff's "inaction" offset the additional costs the manual system creates on cloudy days, when the lights are turned on and tend to stay on even if the sun comes out later in the day. Figure 3-1m illustrates lighting patterns on an overcast day. The lights are activated at 10 a.m., and are not turned off when the sun appears at 2 p.m. So the fact that the staff takes no action to turn off the lights can penalize conservation on cloudy days, but on most days the fact that the staff never turns the lights on works to improve energy efficiency.

Manual lighting controls may be more effective for libraries than other commercial buildings. In libraries, constant high lighting levels are not as crucial to productivity or safety as in, for example, office buildings, stores, or factories. Library patrons may tolerate a wider range of lighting conditions than most other commercial building occupants. Moreover, they are free to move to parts of the building where lighting levels fit their individual preferences.

The research team analyzed in detail the relative merits of automatic and manual control systems in this building. The team found that the quality and distribution of natural light admitted by the large roof apertures and centralized control combine to make manual control of electric lights not only inexpensive, but effective.

The level and quality of natural light are sufficient enough to do away with the need for electric lights even when illumination levels are below the common standard. The analysis revealed that, with manual control, there are significant periods when no lights are turned on, even when lighting levels are below 50 foot-candles, as shown in Figure 3-1n. Nonetheless, both patrons and staff indicate that lighting is satisfactory on these occasions. The data in Figure 3-1n indicate the number of hours in which different levels of illumination are provided by roof apertures, and the amount of supplementary lighting energy required for the daylit building relative to a building not lit by daylight. The table summarizes data from November 1982 through February 1983. Manual control data are obtained from actual measurements, while automatic control results are simulated.

When natural light levels are from 2 foot-candles to 50 foot-candles, only about one-fourth to one-half of the lighting energy typically used in an interior not lit by daylight is required in the Mt. Airy Library. Thus, during the monitored four-month period, the manual control strategy reduced electric lighting energy use by almost 80%. The continuous-dimming, automatic controls were almost as good a judge of adequate lighting below 50 foot-candles as the library staff, except during periods of very low light levels. Although the automatic dimming strategy is more sophisticated, it is also more costly. The automatic on/off system is unable to discriminate between differences in lighting levels from 2 foot-candles to 50 foot-candles and it is not intended to do so. On the other hand, both automatic control strategies performed significantly better than the manual control system at lighting levels above 50 foot-candles. Various factors contribute to the stronger performance, but the most influential factor is probably the "default condition."

The research team also analyzed the impact of various control strategies on energy use. The results indicate that in this building manual controls led to substantially less lighting energy use

Daylight Illumination Provided by Roof Apertures (fc)*	2-20	20-30	30-50	50-100	>100	Totals
Number of Hours at Each Level	65	97	162	214	248	786 hours
Relative Energy Use (%):						
. Manual Control	55	43	24	19	7	22.2%
. Automatic Continuous Dimming	85	45	25	0	0	17.7%
. Automatic On/Off	100	100	100	0	0	41.2%

* U.S. standards for lighting in offices and libraries are typically 50-70 foot candles (fc). For the purposes of analysis, 50 fc was chosen as the minimum acceptable illumination level. The automatic controls simulated were "on/off" controls (where the lights are fully on when the illumination from daylighting drops below 50 fc) and "continuous" controls (that provide just enough artificial light to maintain the minimum 50 fc).

Figure 3-1n. Table comparing auxiliary lighting control strategies. It reflects energy use for one-fifth of the library's annual operating hours. Manual controls outperformed automatic controls during most of the year.

than either of the automatic control strategies, as shown in Figure 3-1o. Nonetheless, any of the strategies can reduce lighting energy use by 65% to 85%, a lighting energy cost savings of $0.08 to $0.10/ft²/yr.

The "no-roof aperture" scenario in Figure 3-1o is based on the assumption that lights would be on over the entire 3,500 hours per year the library was open, requiring 27,700 kWh each year. The daylighting system, however, allows lights to be turned off during a substantial number of those hours. As a result, regardless of the control strategy chosen, two-thirds or more of the lighting energy used in interior spaces served by the roof apertures can be saved. This finding presumes the involvement of reasonably conscientious staff (in the case of manual controls), and that automatic controls are never overridden.

EXTENSIVE MASS, TEMPERATURE SWINGS

Extensive glazing and thermal mass, and their integration with the HVAC systems, had some unexpected impacts on heating and cooling energy use and thermal comfort.

Thick, solid concrete-block walls, a concrete-and-steel roof structure, and tiled concrete floors provide considerable thermal mass. More than 25,000 books stored in the library (there is space for 80,000) add to that mass. The amount of mass and the extensive, exposed surface area of that mass act throughout the year to attenuate the effects of outdoor temperatures on the building's interior. In fact, the large internal mass responds more slowly to ambient conditions than the designers intended.

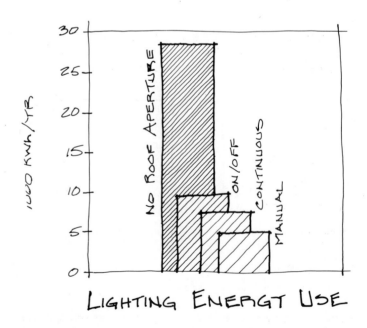

Figure 3-1o. Lighting energy use estimates for various control strategies.

The slow nighttime decrease in the indoor temperature indicates a very strong thermal mass influence during the winter. On winter nights with relatively constant ambient temperatures, it appears that the period of time required for the building to return to a given temperature without any energy inputs (i.e., the thermal time constant) is quite large. That is, when the building is losing heat at a constant rate, it takes about five days for the mass to discharge its heat fully to the indoor air. By contrast, the thermal time constant of a typical house may be four to eight hours.

Sunny weather on winter days seems to have little effect on building temperature. Figure 3-1p shows a day in December with almost no sunshine when heat pumps run all day. Figure 3-1q shows a sunny day in December. The heat pump serving

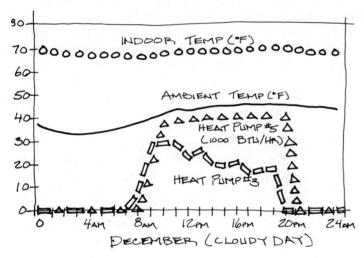

Figure 3-1p.

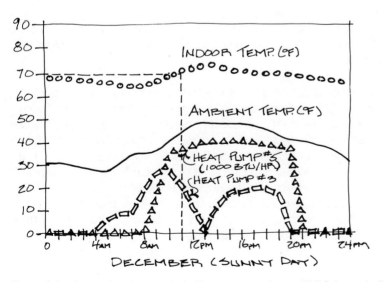

Figure 3-1q. December (sunny day). Slow warm-up keeps HVAC in coolest zones running on sunny winter days, and indoor temperature does not reach 70°F until 11 a.m.

the stacks continues to operate, and the heat pump in the administrative area shuts off for less than two hours. The total heating consumption was almost identical for the two days. The main reason appears to be that the thermal mass is damping out most of the instantaneous effect of the insolation. The thermal mass temperature remains essentially constant, changing only on a monthly time scale. In December, for example, the mass temperature may be about 67° F, close to the monthly average indoor air temperature.

The building's mass affects both comfort conditions and energy use during the heating season. Because the library is extremely massive, the building tends to remain quite cool until late spring. The relatively low mass temperature (i.e., 67° F to 68° F) lowers the radiant temperature, making occupants feel cool on winter mornings, particularly cloudy ones. In addition, the low mass temperature makes it difficult to warm the building in the morning. As shown in Figure 3-1q, even on a sunny winter day with all the heat pumps running at capacity, the air temperature does not reach 70° F until 11 a.m. The reason is that much of the heat-pump output is recharging the cool mass. This energy quantity is approximately equal to the heat loss that occurs during the night.

Simulations of building response to thermostat manipulation showed that raising the thermostat setting in the heating season does not significantly increase the radiant temperature, which remained uncomfortably low throughout the day. The thermal inertia of the building is simply too great to boost the radiant temperature quickly on cloudy days regardless of thermostat strategy. In order to keep the space comfortable, building operators must discontinue night setback or raise the air temperature 3° F to 4° F higher than originally intended. Both measures, however, substantially increase energy consumption and the annual peak heating load. The high heating loads generated by the thermal mass on cold, cloudy days prevent the building from reaching thermal equilibrium until late spring.

Thermal mass also dominates the cooling season performance. Figure 3-1r shows a day in May when the heat pumps were not used for any heating or cooling. Despite a 30° F ambient temperature swing and very strong insolation, the indoor temperatures do not fluctuate significantly. Even in the afternoon, when the ambient temperature is high enough to prohibit any heat loss, the indoor temperature does not rise in response to the solar gains. This is attributable to two factors: (1) the window and roof monitor designs, which effectively block direct radiation when the sun's angle is high, and (2) the thermal mass, which absorbs the solar energy without changing the temperature.

The main benefits of the building's large thermal mass occur during the spring and fall, when the mass keeps indoor temperatures stable and comfortable without any assistance from the mechanical systems. This effect is illustrated in Figure 3-1r for spring weather conditions. The same effect is shown in Figure 3-1s for a week in the fall, when cooler temperatures begin to arrive. As shown in Figure 3-1s, the summertime mass

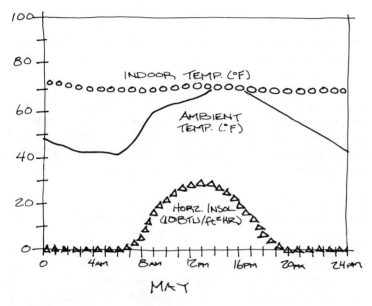

Figure 3-1r. Spring temperatures. Despite an ambient temperature swing of 30°F, indoor temperature remains fairly stable.

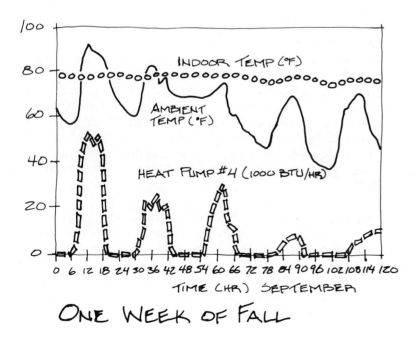

Figure 3-1s. Fall temperatures. Indoor temperature begins to track ambient temperature after five days of early fall weather as building mass cools.

temperature of 76° F begins to decrease, causing the indoor temperature to decline slowly on a steady course toward its midwinter level of about 67° F. Despite the swing-month benefits, the undesirable effects of thermal mass on winter mornings suggest that less mass, or less coupling between the mass and indoor air, could result in better overall comfort and performance.

COMPENSATING FOR STRATIFICATION

There is a substantial amount of glass in the building, which contributes to low radiant temperatures. The roof monitors, in particular, create a unique stratification and heat loss condition. The monitors trap the warmest air in the building. Their configuration, together with the baffles below them, helps prevent effective mixing of the trapped air. This situation increases heat loss that results from the higher temperature differences between the trapped warm air and cold outside temperatures.

Another unexpected stratification effect relates to the different levels in the library. The administrative wing and children's areas are 4 ft. above the reading areas and 6 ft. above the stacks level. This floor plan (see Figure 3-1b) encourages the formation of convective loops, where cooler air drifts down to the lower levels, and warmer air rises to the upper levels of the building. This condition forces the heat pump units serving the lower levels to operate at their limits for longer periods of time.

Almost every midwinter day, the heat pump in the stacks area runs all day, supplying the majority of the building's heat because this area is the lowest in the building (approximately 4 ft. below the main level). As a result, the heat from this zone rises to the other areas, while cool air from the floor of the children's, lending, and reference areas flows into the stacks. The temperature stratification in the building is clearly apparent in Figure 3-1t. On a sunny winter afternoon, the temperature at the ceiling of the children's area is 9° F warmer than at the floor; at the clerestory, 20° F warmer. At night, the temperature at the clerestory is actually colder than elsewhere because of the proximity to the glazing, which radiates heat to a cold night sky.

The way stratification affects comfort is reversed in the cooling season. Figure 3-1u shows a day in June when auxiliary cooling is necessary. The temperature is still constant at 76° F, but the heat pump serving the history, reference, and periodical areas must run most of the day to maintain this temperature. In the stacks, however, the heat pump only operates on extremely hot days.

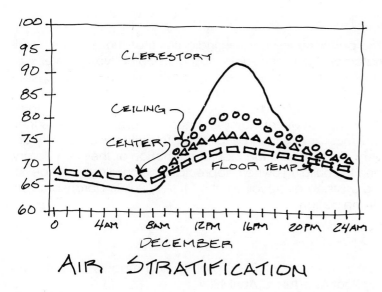

AIR STRATIFICATION

Figure 3-1t.

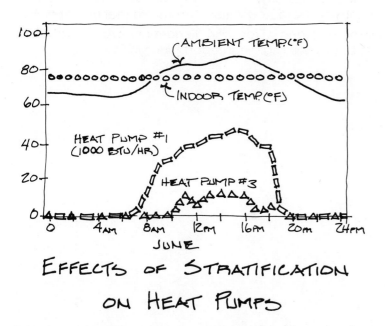

EFFECTS OF STRATIFICATION ON HEAT PUMPS

Figure 3-1u. Effects of stratification on heat pumps. Stratification makes the heat pump in Zone 4 work harder to maintain a 76°F temperature, while the heat pump in isolated Zone 3 idles during the day.

SUMMARY

The performance analysis indicates that the daylight-dominated design succeeds in most of its objectives. It saves substantial amounts of energy, and distributes diffused light throughout the library in a way that is easy on books and readers. Library staff and users are very satisfied with the new facility except on winter mornings when the library's extensive thermal mass keeps the interior chilly. The citizens of Mt. Airy are very pleased with the look and function of their new library, and the building owners appreciate the building's low operating costs. By all accounts, the Mt. Airy Public Library is a very strong design.

BIBLIOGRAPHY

Adegran, M. et al. 1984. "Total Building Impacts of South-Facing Roof Apertures," April 1984.

Andersson, B. et al. 1984. "Energy Effects of Electric Lighting Control Alternatives in Response to Daylighting," July 1984.

Architectural Energy Corp. 1984. "Mt. Airy Public Library Site Handbook: Data Acquisition System Information," April 1984.

Swisher, Joel, and D. Frey. 1984. "Performance Analysis of the Mt. Airy Library Building: Final Report," June 1984.

PROJECT SUMMARY
MT. AIRY PUBLIC LIBRARY

Building type: Public library

Floor area: 13,450 ft^2

Location: Mt. Airy, NC

Owner: City of Mt. Airy Board of Commissioners

Design completed: January 1981

Construction completed: April 1982

Occupancy: 127 occupants; 90 people for 66 hrs/wk (max.)

Construction costs: $88/ft^2

Annual energy use: 323 MMBtu/yr (24,000 Btu/ft^2/yr)

Climate:
3,971 heating degree days/yr
1,183 cooling degree days/yr

Insolation: 1,344 Btu/ft^2/day (annual average)

Energy costs: Electricity, $17.50/MMBtu ($0.06/kWh)

Solar design elements:

Clerestory daylighting and direct gain (1,160 ft^2 aperture area)

Light shelves with reflectors and overhangs for daylighting and indirect gain (250 ft^2 south-facing window area; 1,288 ft^2 total window area)

Natural ventilation via operable view windows
Thermal mass in floors, roof, and walls
Light-diffusing baffle system below clerestories
Active solar DHW (50-ft^2 collector area)

Other energy elements:

Fluorescent general lighting and incandescent task lighting (average ½-2 W/ft^2)

Zoned, 32-ton total air-to-air heat pump system with electric resistance supplemental heat (COP 2.0)
Infiltration control by air-lock vestibules at entries
1-in. double insulated glass
2-in. perimeter insulation
Building envelope shading with deciduous trees
Light-colored roof and exterior building materials (granite-clad walls)

Architect:
J. N. Pease Associates, Charlotte, NC
Mazria/Schiff and Associates, Albuquerque, NM

Monitoring period: August 1982-March 1984

Data collected:
Horizontal solar radiation
Diffuse solar radiation
Outside air temperature
Indoor air temperature
Energy consumption
Electrical demand
Lighting energy use
Wind speed
AC supply voltage

Data acquisition system: Aeolian Kinetics PDL-24 with 22 data channels to monitor temperatures, purchased energy use, and weather variables.

JOHNSON CONTROLS BRANCH OFFICE

When you arrive at the newest Johnson Controls Branch Office in Salt Lake City, Utah, you don't have to turn on the lights. Johnson Controls' Facilities Design Group (the company's internal architectural team) has incorporated automatic sensors to turn lights on and off for you — depending on the amount of available daylight in each office. The new office building combines relatively straightforward passive solar design with a sophisticated computer control system. The result is a building that consumes less than half as much energy as a similar conventional office building. (See Figure 3-2a.)

Johnson Controls, Inc. has devoted substantial effort in using the design, construction, and operation of its own facilities as testing laboratories for new control equipment. Because the firm has undertaken an ambitious growth program (e.g., Johnson Controls' Facilities Design Group leader, architect Doug Drake, designs and manages the construction of four to five new branch offices each year), the company has had to develop a highly structured and efficient design process. The bottomline for decision approval rests almost entirely on the cost-effectiveness —construction and operating — of proposed structures.

Drake's group had fine-tuned the basic design of all Johnson Controls branch offices to a point where more cost-effective savings were very difficult to achieve. Despite this, Johnson Controls management wanted to see if they could go further by employing passive solar techniques. The DOE Nonresidential Experimental Buildings Program provided an opportunity to try passive solar design in the Salt Lake project.

A variety of passive heating, cooling, and daylighting concepts were tested for both feasibility and cost-effectiveness. The Facilities Design Group had been focusing on the use and control of daylighting for all upcoming projects. Designers estimated that the Salt Lake branch office would use one-third less energy than Johnson Controls expected for this type of building the previous year. Energy savings over older Johnson Controls branch offices would be even more dramatic — more than 50%. Total energy use for the new Salt Lake office would be 51,000 Btu/ft^2/yr compared to 108,000 Btu/ft^2/yr in older offices.

LIGHTING AND HEATING COST SAVINGS

The most cost-effective features of the new design for the Salt Lake branch office, according to Johnson Controls officials, would result from the use of daylight. Johnson Controls had used high-efficiency luminares (fluorescent lamps and bal-

Figure 3-2a. Johnson Controls Branch Office. Visitors to Johnson Controls Salt Lake City office get a good view of the building's south-facing glass.

lasts) to conserve energy in its branch office designs as a matter of course for several years, but lighting remained the largest energy cost. Johnson Controls estimated that the total cost for heating, cooling, and lighting the new office would be less than the cost of lighting alone in its existing buildings.

Attempts to employ daylighting and passive heating techniques, however, could have an adverse effect on cooling loads in a building. Generally, as daylighting is introduced into a building, cooling loads decrease. (Daylight has a high luminous efficacy, meaning it can provide a given amount of light to a space with less heat than could normally be produced by fluorescent fixtures.) Unfortunately, it is often difficult to get just the right amount of daylight into a space because of the cost and complexity of daylight control. Most naturally lit buildings, like the Johnson Controls office, tend to err on the side of extra daylight, which in turn can cause modest increases in cooling loads.

When compared to a highly energy-efficient base case design (a nonsolar design very similar to the recently built Johnson Controls facility and located near Grand Rapids, Michigan), analysis indicated that the Salt Lake branch office would actually require 10% more energy for cooling. However, the additional cost for cooling —approximately one-half cent/ft^2/yr— would be substantially offset by heating and lighting cost reductions of about $0.04/ft^2 and $0.21/ft^2, respectively.

CHANGES IN BASIC DESIGN

The design team, including Don Watson, Fred Dubin, and Bill Lam, initially investigated passive heating, cooling, and lighting techniques. Their analysis suggested that passive heating options like massive thermal walls or greenhouses would add too much to the building's capital costs without producing significant energy savings over the already tight base case. Similarly, evaporative cooling, a feasible option in Utah's dry climate, could eliminate the need for chillers, but annual cooling energy consumption would remain about the same. The design team, therefore, decided to keep heating and cooling demand low with conservation measures like air-lock doors, extra insulation, and some earth berming. They focused their attention on using passive solar concepts to provide inexpensive natural lighting.

Watson and Lam constructed physical models to measure both the amount and quality of available daylight. The estimated energy savings from increased use of daylight caught management's attention. As a result, the final design relies heavily on daylighting in virtually all occupied spaces (see Figure 3-2b).

Figure 3-2b. A view of the lighting model interior showing illumination from the clerestory above.

Reliance on daylighting had an immediate effect on space, structural, and facade design concepts for the facility. In order to employ combined daylighting and passive solar heating to the desired extent, the Salt Lake branch office incorporated about twice as much glass as other Johnson Controls offices — about 1,200 ft² of glass for 10,000 ft² of office/sales space.

The offices were placed on the building's south side for maximum light and heat. The warehouse space, where light and heat are less critical, was placed on the darker north part of the building. Also, an "open office" approach was used to enhance daylight distribution (see Figure 3-2c). Unlike most modern buildings, minimum ambient daylight levels were used to help determine the final shape of the building. The daylight solution dictated a maximum allowable depth of 60 ft. in each space.

In addition to increased glazing and open planning, the Salt Lake facility required higher ceilings than other Johnson Controls offices. The higher ceilings were needed to facilitate the distribution of daylight. The reflective, sloped ceiling of the single-floor structure ranges from a height of 10 in. at the south wall to 13 ft. 6 in. at the interior edge of the clerestory spine. (See Figures 3-2d and 3-2e.)

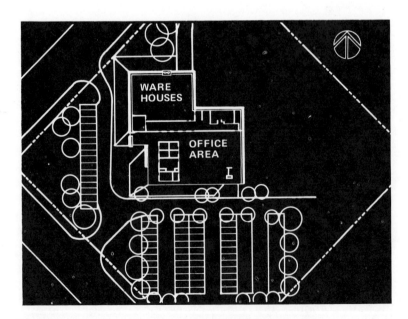

Figure 3-2c. A site/floor plan showing the location of offices in the south half of the building and the warehouse area in the darker north side.

Throughout the design process, particular attention was given to the effects of daylighting on defining design details. For example, it was found that positioning a major heating-and-cooling distribution duct in the clerestory could reduce interior daylight levels by as much as 50%. A dark north wall could have a similar effect. In the final design, light colors were used on all wall surfaces to reduce contrast.

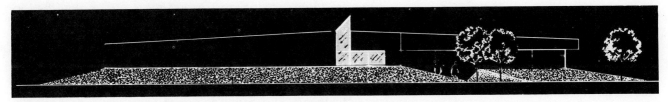

Figure 3-2d. A west elevation of the building showing its simple design, punctuated by a central clerestory.

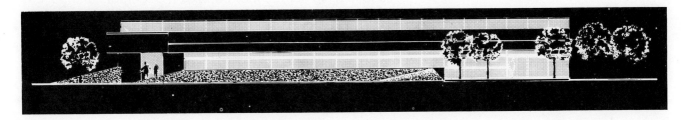

Figure 3-2e. The building's south elevation.

LIGHTING CONTROLS

Because of its passive solar design, virtually all of the building glass is located in two south-facing bands — 60% on the south facade and 40% on a south-facing clerestory (see Figure 3-2f). The south-facing clerestory serves as a circulation spine along the north wall separating the office area from the warehouse. All glazing is "managed" with movable night insulation and fixed or movable shading.

Operation of the glazing management system integrates architectural features, mechanical devices, sensors, and controls. Glass on the south facade is divided into two sections by a mirrored light shelf located approximately 2 ft. below the top of each window. The upper section of glass, the "daylight aperture," is unshaded and uses the mirrored upper surface of the light shelf to bounce light onto the ceiling of the office. The lower section of glass, called "view glass," employs a unique bottom-up interior shade to control glare and perimeter daylight levels. The mechanical shades are automatically raised and lowered in unison in response to photocell sensors. Fluorescent task lights at individual workstations are also computer controlled.

With these control devices, ambient light levels at the center of the office space can range from a low of 60 foot-candles in June to a high of 270 foot-candles in December, without any artificial lighting. Light levels are not, however, uniform throughout the space. Light levels at the north and south walls of the office are about three times higher than at the center throughout the year, ranging from 200 foot-candles in June to about 850 foot-candles in December.

As is the case in all attempts to advance the state of the art in building design, problems that required additional work were encountered during design and construction. For example, the only shades readily available were designed for residential applications. They did not fit the design module and were not durable enough for commercial use, which increased maintenance costs and reduced overall cost-effectiveness.

The HVAC control system was also substantially more complex. The Salt Lake branch office is equipped with a JC-8510 mini-computer for automated control of heating, cooling, and lighting. Typically, a building the size of the Salt Lake facility would not require so large a computer. But the JC-8510 is necessary because of the additional requirements to adjust artificial lighting levels automatically (adjustments are usually left to occupants in other buildings) and the facility's planned experimentation program. The controls automatically maintain a 30 foot-candles illumination level at the work surface.

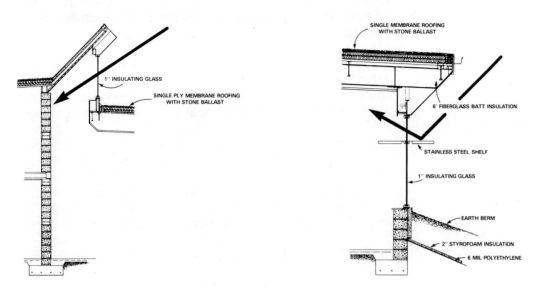

Figure 3-2f. Details of the clerestory and south-facade glazing illustrating how light enters the building.

After two years of occupancy, both owner and occupants declared the building a success. In fact, the best features of this prototype building were incorporated into six other branch office buildings.

Owner and user response to the new offices was enthusiastic. From the perspective of whole-building performance, including occupant reactions, total energy use, and total costs, the building is a successful example of energy-efficient design.

The one-story floor plan is typical for Johnson Controls offices, with a total of 15,000 ft² of space. Two-thirds of the building is devoted to engineering, sales, management, and support. About 5,000 ft² is dedicated to warehouse space for component inventory storage and systems assembly, as shown in Figure 3-2g. Employees are pleasantly surprised by the building's

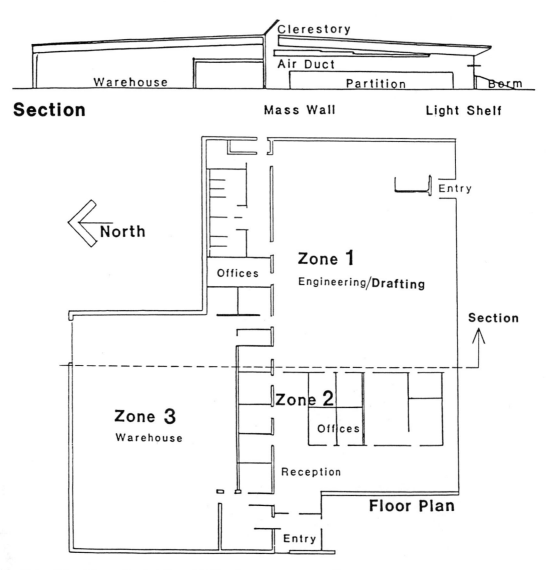

Figure 3-2g. Johnson Controls Branch Office floor plan. It shows the three major functional and HVAC zones.

atmosphere, appearance, and energy efficiency. Three-fourths of the full-time users are highly satisfied with the building; none are dissatisfied. Moreover, most visitors are favorably impressed. Johnson Controls reports that visitors as well as employees appreciate the design. In addition, management notes increased professionalism, improved morale, and higher productivity among employees. The facility won the 1984 Utah Governor's Award for Excellence in Energy Innovation.

Management is sufficiently enough impressed to have included many of the passive solar and other energy-conserving features in five of the six branch offices constructed from 1981 to 1983. The transferred energy design elements include clerestories, exterior insulation, earth berms, and light shelves (see Figure 3-2f). The company plans to continue use of the more successful energy design strategies in branch office construction. The energy-efficient approach may also be used in the company's manufacturing facilities.

ENERGY USE AND UTILITY BILLS

The data to be presented are based on performance monitoring results for the test year, October 1982 through November 1983. The heating fuel is natural gas.

Energy consumption in the new Johnson Controls offices is slightly less than half of a base case building (i.e., a similar building in the same climate without solar energy features or special conservation measures). As shown in Figure 3-2h, the office building uses about the same amount of energy as a relatively energy-efficient BEPS building.[1]

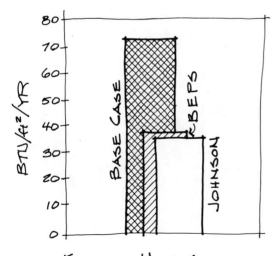

ANNUAL ENERGY USE COMPARISON

Figure 3-2h. Annual energy use comparison. The office building uses half the energy of a base case building and about the same as a comparable BEPS design.

Space heating accounts for more than half the total annual energy use, as shown in Figure 3-2i. Despite the 6,000-heating-degree-day climate, the Johnson Controls building uses less than half the space heating energy of the base case. Auxiliary heating is provided by a central VAV air handler and perimeter baseboard hydronic system. This system is used primarily for morning warm-up.

Fans use the second largest amount of energy, accounting for about one-fourth the annual energy consumption. The principal fans are in the VAV system, which is used to circulate both heated and cooled air year-round.

The most substantial savings over the base case are realized in lighting and cooling. The Johnson Controls lighting load is a very low 4% of total annual energy use, which is less than 7% of the base case lighting load. The principal reasons for the savings are the effectiveness of the clerestory and south-facing windows and an energy-efficient electric lighting/automated control system.

Cooling energy use is an even smaller portion (about 1%) of total energy use than is lighting. Factors contributing to this low cooling requirement are part of a combined passive/mechanical strategy. It includes two-stage evaporative cooling, night flushing of the building mass, high levels of thermal insulation, and well-designed overhangs. Typically moderate humidity levels and mild summers (900 cooling degree days) enhance the effectiveness of the overall cooling strategy. The Johnson Controls building consumes only 8% of the cooling energy used by the base case.

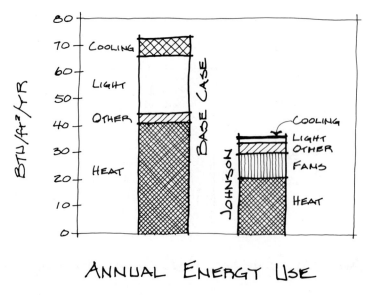

ANNUAL ENERGY USE

Figure 3-2i. Annual energy use. Lighting and cooling energy consumption are very low relative to the base case, indicating that both the daylighting system and the cooling load reduction strategies are effective.

Year-long energy-use patterns are shown in Figure 3-2j. Although space heating is about 60% of annual energy use, it is low in absolute terms for a 6,000-heating-degree-day climate. The office building uses only 3.55 Btu/ft^2/heating degree day under better-than-average insolation (1,600 Btu/ft^2/day). As shown in Figure 3-2j, fan operation is relatively stable throughout the year. Lighting is a low portion of monthly energy use, as is cooling.

Energy costs are about the same as for the BEPS building and about half the costs of a comparable conventional building, as shown in Figure 3-2k. Annual energy cost differences be-

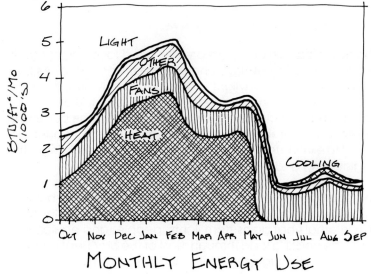

MONTHLY ENERGY USE

Figure 3-2j. Monthly energy use. Although heating energy use is more than half of the annual budget, it is relatively low in absolute terms for a 6,000-HDD climate.

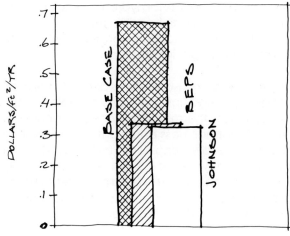

ANNUAL ENERGY COST COMPARISON

Figure 3-2k. Annual energy cost comparison. Energy costs reflect energy use, with the Johnson Controls offices costing at least $0.34/ft^2/yr less to operate than the base case building.

tween the base case and Johnson Controls building are shown in Figure 3-2l. The largest savings over the base case are in lighting, cooling, and heating. At $0.06/kWh and $2.86/MMBtu for gas, the annual average savings are $0.34/ft^2 or $5,125/yr.

ENERGY EFFICIENCY

The one-story masonry structure costs $57/ft^2 in 1982 dollars. As shown in Figure 3-2m, this is well within the reasonable cost range for similar office buildings at similar locations. The building is 50% higher in cost than the lowest average 1982 cost for a similar structure and 25% less than the highest average construction costs.

FULL RANGE OF SOLAR BENEFITS

The major passive elements are designed for daylighting, direct-gain space heating, and evaporative cooling. As previously described, daylight is admitted to the building, both through south-facing, grade-level windows on the office wing and through the clerestory windows that bisect the building in the east-west direction. On clear days, daylighting is often sufficient to eliminate the need for ambient electric lighting in the engineering and reception areas.

The south windows and clerestory also provide the building with direct solar heat gain during the winter. The solar gain, plus internal heat gains from lights, people, and equipment, carry the heating load through most of the day. Heat entering the building through clerestory windows is captured by return air grilles mounted high on the wall, which distribute the heat throughout the building.

The auxiliary heating system, which primarily provides morning warm-up, consists of a perimeter hydronic radiator system and a heating coil in the VAV air handler. The warm air system is used exclusively for rapid morning warm-up, while the perimeter system may run longer into the day.

The building temperature usually floats all night until the warm-up cycle begins. This setback strategy is possible because the building has a large, thermal time-constant, achieved by a combination of thermal mass and night insulation. Insulating shades that are closed mechanically by being lifted from the bottom of the window reduce night heat loss through the large southern glazing area. The building's interior has a large area of exposed concrete, which slows the night cool-down process and absorbs daytime heat gains to prevent overheating.

Cooling is accomplished both mechanically (with a system that has both direct and indirect evaporative cooling cycles) and passively, with both night flushing with outdoor air and a roof spray system to reduce summer conductive gains through the roof. Indirect evaporation with 100% outdoor night air is effective in reducing the indoor temperatures by 5° F before morning occupancy. As the cooling load increases during the day due to the ambient loads and internally generated heat gains, the direct evaporative coolers and roof spray system are used.

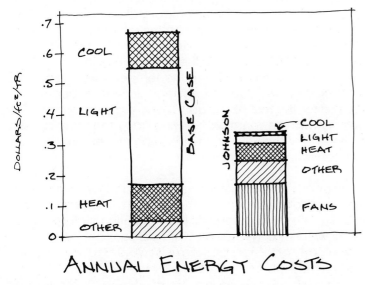

Figure 3-2l. Annual energy costs. The largest energy cost savings over the base case building are for lighting and cooling, while space heating costs are low as well.

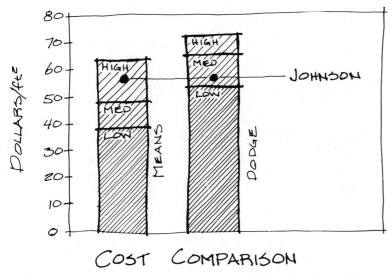

Figure 3-2m. Capital cost comparisons. Energy efficiency is achieved at reasonable first cost, based on industry estimates for similar buildings. (LOW = 25% of the comparable buildings cost $38 ($54) or less to build; MED = 50% were below $48 ($65); HIGH = 25% cost $65 ($72) or more).

105

The glazing overhangs and thermal insulation (R-30 roof, R-20 walls) are effective in reducing the cooling load. Even without the use of the mechanical cooling systems, the indoor temperature usually remains below 80° F on sunny weekends where the ambient temperature is above 90° F.

LITTLE OVERHEATING

The typical winter operation of the building is depicted in Figure 3-2n. The building is in the night setback mode until 7:00 a.m., at which time the interior temperature drops to 66° F. The boilers are fired at this time and both the hydronic perimeter system and the VAV air handler are activated. The boilers stay on until about 8:30 a.m. when the daytime interior air setpoint temperature is reached. When the temperature is reached, the boilers and the hydronic system circulation pumps are turned off for the rest of the day. The solar gains through the clerestory and the south-wall glazing carry the heating load until the end of the workday, while the ambient temperature varies between 28° F and 36° F.

Outside air control prevents winter overheating (i.e., temperatures even slightly above the thermostat setpoint) by direct solar gain. The air handler supplies ventilation air throughout the day while mixing return air with outdoor air. The position and use of one of the air handling unit's (AHU#1) dampers used to control the indoor temperature is shown in Figure 3-2n. The temperature in the engineering/drafting area (Room 12) rises

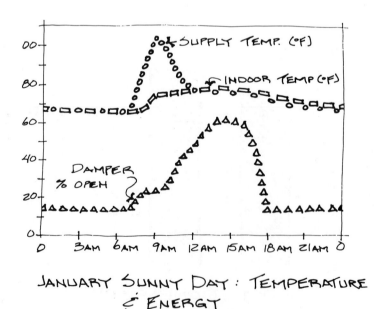

JANUARY SUNNY DAY : TEMPERATURE & ENERGY

Figure 3-2n.

above the comfort setpoint after 9:00 a.m. principally because of direct solar gains. Adjusting the intake damper so that a greater proportion of the cool outdoor air is admitted to the space removes excess heat. This procedure continues until 5:00 p.m. when the damper is returned to the minimum outdoor air position.

Although this system functions well on average winter days, some inefficiency occurs on very cold and sunny winter days. During cold, clear days, boiler gas consumption for the hydronic perimeter auxiliary heat is significantly greater than usual. Auxiliary heat is supplied to the building at the same time that the VAV system's dampers are supplying outdoor air to reduce overheating in the drafting room. A combination of solar and internal heat gains and heat losses from the perimeter hydronic system causes the overheating. Because the water-circulation-loop pipe is uninsulated, the pipe's heat loss adds some heat to the space. The building returns to normal night setback operation at 5:00 p.m., as it would on an average winter day.

The overheating encountered on a sunny day is not evident on cold, cloudy days. In fact, researchers found that the additional auxiliary heating requirements typical for cloudy winter days could be significantly reduced if the insulating shades on the south windows were left open to admit light from the sky and other reflected sources of solar heat.

CLERESTORY DAYLIGHTING

Daylighting is provided to the engineering/drafting area through the clerestory and south-wall glazing. Electric lighting consists of overhead ambient fixtures arranged in three banks along the east/west axis and task lighting at each workstation.

Electric light usage for both sunny and overcast March days is shown in Figures 3-2o and 3-2p, respectively. On a typical sunny day, the northern-most bank of uplights (those closest to the clerestory) remain off throughout the workday. The south bank of lights closest to the windows is usually turned on for a half-hour around 8:00 a.m. The center bank of lights is usually on for about two and one-half hours in the morning and in the afternoon. Therefore, on a sunny March day, there is sufficient daylight to keep all of the uplighting off for about four hours in the middle of the day.

The effectiveness of the clerestory is particularly apparent on a cloudy day. Figure 3-2p represents electric lighting needs on a March day that was overcast until about 3:00 p.m. All three banks of lights are turned on at first occupancy. The middle lights are on until after 5:00 p.m., while the south lights are only on half the time after 3:00 p.m. The north lights are on for two and one-half hours at the beginning of the day. They are then switched off for four hours and operated intermittently after 3:00 p.m. This four-hour "off" period demonstrates the effectiveness of the clerestory for daylighting even on an overcast day.

Although the overall daylighting system is effective year-round, the contribution of both the clerestory and the south window/light shelf combination depends on the time of year. Data collected for January, April, and July indicate that less

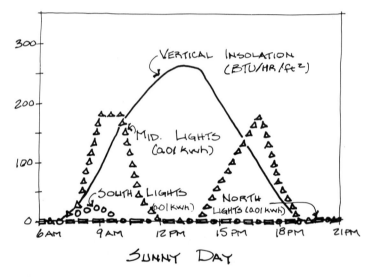

Figure 3-2o. Sunny March day: daylighting levels. On a sunny March day, the daylighting levels are sufficient to keep most ambient electric lighting off for four hours in the middle of the day.

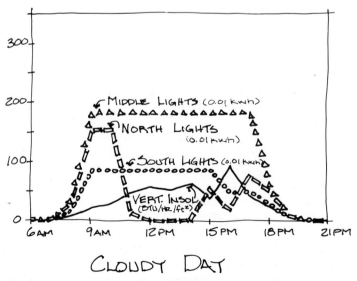

Figure 3-2p. Cloudy March day: daylighting levels. During a cloudy March day the north lights remain off for four hours and the south lights are on only half the day, indicating that useful daylight is available even in overcast conditions.

108

ambient lighting energy is consumed by the central bank of lights in the engineering/drafting zone in January than in April and July. The lighting energy-use pattern on sunny days in January indicates that some of the daylight to the middle zone is contributed by the clerestory and some by the light shelves. On overcast days, daylighting sufficient to keep the uplights off in the middle zone is received only through the clerestory. The clerestory effectively distributes daylight within the building during all January days. In January, the uplights are never off for an entire day because the days are shorter than in other months.

As the solar altitude angle increases in April and July, the daylighting effectiveness of the clerestory in the north zone is only marginally affected, while daylight penetration into the middle zone is significantly reduced. However, the low sun angles and more forward, scattered, and diffuse sunlight contribute to the effectiveness of the light shelves. Data for July in the south zone indicate a very small daylighting contribution from the light shelves or the south-wall glazing.

On balance, the clerestory appears to provide more useful daylighting than the south-wall glazing with light shelves. The clerestory configuration allows daylight to be reflected from above into the offices. The light shelves, however, reflect light into the space at a lower angle, resulting in generally less effective daylighting. The light shelves are more effective in January, for example, than in April and July because the sun angles are lower in winter. Sloping the exterior shelves inward might result in deeper light penetration and more daylighting when the solar altitude is high.

REDUCED SUMMERTIME ELECTRICAL LOADS

The performance of the Johnson Controls building during a sunny, six-day period in July 1984 is shown in Figure 3-2q. The effectiveness of the thermal insulation and overhangs is indicated by the fact that the interior temperature fluctuation during the weekend period varies between 74° F and 79° F, while the ambient temperature rises above 90° F with full sunshine. All mechanical systems are off during the weekend except the small air handler, which operates for three hours on Saturday morning. These data suggest that the overhangs on both the clerestory and the south-wall glass are effective for eliminating direct solar gain. The roof insulation reduces the heat gain due to ambient and solar temperature effects. As a result, the building remains within a generally acceptable summertime comfort range during this period of extreme ambient conditions without the assistance of any mechanical system.

The temperature and energy-use patterns for three typical weekdays are also shown in Figure 3-2q. The typical weekday cooling strategy is to turn on the indirect evaporative coolers with both air handlers at 2:00 a.m. using 100% outdoor air. This lowers the indoor temperature by 4° F or 5° F by 4:30 a.m. The procedure for a typical day is illustrated in Figure 3-2r. In order to maintain comfortable indoor conditions, the direct evaporative coolers and air handlers are operated with full outdoor air during the occupied period when the ambient temperature is too high to provide effective indirect cooling.

Total electricity use during the six-day period shown in Figure 3-2q is depicted in Figure 3-2s. Data indicate that a 3-kW-to-4-kW power consumption level exists in the building during unoccupied periods. The average daytime power level of 26 kW is typical of most weekdays in July. The Monday electrical load is somewhat higher because the heat stored in the building's thermal mass during the weekend shutdown period must be removed. A consistent power consumption pattern is evident in the building. For typical weekdays, the breakdown of the daytime power level of 26 kW includes 4-kW baseload; 10 kW for the cooling equipment and air handlers; 2 kW for ambient lighting; and 10 kW in internal gains attributed to building operation and activity.

Hourly data analysis shows that 40% of the total power is consumed by cooling and air-handling equipment, and that the load attributed to the space conditioning equipment is approximately equal to the building's operation load.

The daily average indoor temperatures during July were relatively constant at 74° F to 75° F. Data show that total daily energy use in the Johnson Controls building is neither a function

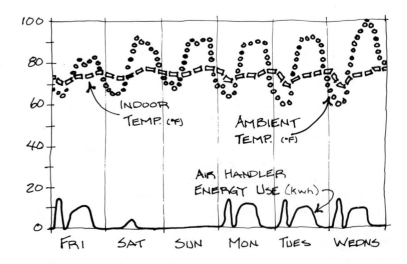

SUNNY DAY: TEMPERATURE & ENERGY

Figure 3-2q. Weekend and weekday summertime energy consumption. The building stays fairly comfortable even with ambient temperatures above 90° F.

of changes in the total daily insolation, nor of changes in the daily average ambient temperature. The total daily energy values for July are in a range between 278 kWh/day and 382 kWh/day for all weekdays over a wide range of total daily insolation values (i.e., 700 Btu/ft²/day and 1,200 Btu/ft²/day).

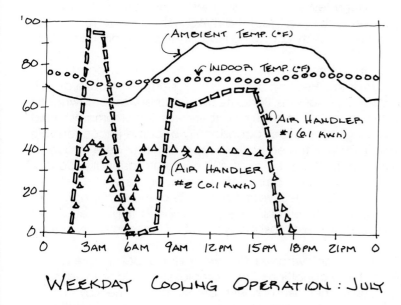

WEEKDAY COOLING OPERATION: JULY

Figure 3-2r. Weekday cooling system operation during mid-July.

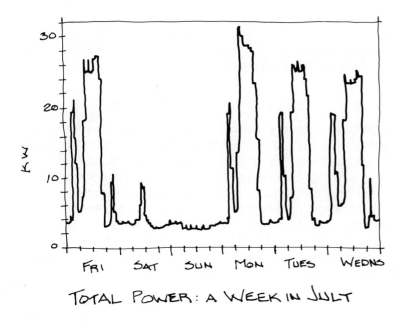

TOTAL POWER: A WEEK IN JULY

Figure 3-2s. Total electric power consumption for six days in July.

AUTOMATED SYSTEMS

Only one-fifth of the building users reported stuffy, too-warm or too-cool conditions, which indicates that the building was generally a satisfactory environment in which to work relative to a conventional office building. The complaints, however, provide insight into what operations could be improved to enhance both thermal and visual comfort. Weather conditions during the test year were sufficiently different from the long-term records used to set the HVAC systems to warrant exploring the possibility of adding flexibility in occupant control.

Occupants have very little control over thermal conditions in the building. Heating and cooling systems were calibrated to seasonal conditions. Because the weather was somewhat different than anticipated (e.g., there was higher summer humidity), some employees occasionally became uncomfortable. About 20% of the employees reported they were frequently too cool or too hot. About 40% were occasionally too cool during the winter. Complaints about coolness were distributed evenly over the test year. About 17% of the occupants complained of occasional or frequent overheating. Overheating was reported in almost every month of the monitoring period.

The occupants who were too warm responded in several ways to ambient conditions. For example, some did nothing, some discussed their feelings with others, and some slowed their work pace. The higher-than-expected summer humidity during the test year reduced the usefulness of the directive evaporative cooling system.

Those who were too cool responded by doing nothing, donning warmer clothing, covering vents, drinking hot coffee, or using portable electric heaters. Generally, despite user adjustments to individual comfort needs, occupant response had very little effect on energy loads.

PREDETERMINED LIGHTING QUALITY, LEVELS

Employees have significantly greater control over the building's levels and quality of lighting than over the HVAC systems. As a result, there are fewer reports of dissatisfaction with ambient lighting conditions. Building users are conscientious about operating manually controlled lights, recognizing the impact of lighting loads on energy savings. Solutions to occasional glare and dimness are straightforward and easily implemented. Individual adjustments of the visual environment include adding desk lamps, turning on ambient lighting and closing the insulated shades and turning on more lights.

Occasional glare is reported by 15% of the occupants. Both natural and electric lighting are cited as causes. Apparently, glare caused by natural light is an occasional problem near the south-facing windows, but only during two winter months when the sun angle is low.

About one-fifth of the employees in the engineering area report that the natural light levels are too low. Nearly all members of the engineering staff use desk lamps.

SUMMARY

Passive solar strategies for space heating, daylighting, and cooling are used successfully in the new Salt Lake branch office building of Johnson Controls. In addition to the energy efficiency of the building, the environment is pleasing, and both employees and management enjoy the building. The best energy-efficient features have been used in six additional Johnson Controls branch offices.

Analysis of the heating season's thermal performance indicates that the building effectively uses passive solar gains. The daylighting contribution of the passive systems is substantial. The light shelves on the south windows, however, appear to be less effective than the clerestory windows. Heat gains during the cooling season are reduced by high thermal insulation levels, window overhangs that block direct solar gain, and an effective roof spray system. The two-stage evaporative cooling system together with night flushing of the building substantially decrease the energy required for cooling.

Occupant satisfaction in the building has been very high despite occasional individual complaints of glare and/or dimness and thermal discomfort. These complaints appear to be no different than those experienced in conventional office buildings. To a significant extent, occasional reports of thermal discomfort are attributable to unanticipated weather conditions. The automated system has functioned very well, although users indicate that a greater degree of control is desirable.

PROJECT SUMMARY
JOHNSON CONTROLS BRANCH OFFICE

Building type: Office building/warehouse

Floor area: 14,900 ft^2

Location: Salt Lake City, UT

Owner: Johnson Controls, Inc.; Milwaukee, WI

Construction completed: March 1982

Occupancy: 50 people; 45 hrs/week

Construction costs: $57/ft^2

Annual energy use: 36,000 Btu/ft^2
(72,900 Btu/ft^2 for base case)

Climate:
6,000 heating degree days
900 cooling degree days

Insolation: 1,600 Btu/ft^2/day (annual average)

Energy costs:
Natural gas, $2.86/MMBtu
Electricity, 6.0¢/kWh

Solar design elements:
Increased south glass
Clerestory for direct-gain office wall and preheating return air
Enhanced daylight distribution through a reflective light shelf (south glass), high ceiling and light interior colors
Automated solar shades and glazing insulation

Other energy elements:
Earth berming
Air-lock entries
JC-8510 computer for all HVAC, daylighting, and task lighting controls
3-in. polyurethane exterior wall insulation
2-cycle evaporative cooling system
High-efficiency back-up fluorescent lighting (1.5 W/ft^2)
Variable air volume (VAV) HVAC system with economizer cycle
Roof spray system

Architect: Doug Drake; Johnson Controls

Solar designer: Donald Watson; Guilford, CT

Monitoring period: October 1982-September 1983

Data collected:
Energy consumption of blowers, electric lights, hot water, natural gas, miscellaneous circuits
Horizontal insolation
Wind speed
Indoor temperatures
Ambient temperatures

Data acquisition system: A Johnson Controls JC-8510 Energy Management System was installed to control and monitor the energy-related features of this passive solar building. This microprocessor-based system was used to collect weekly and monthly performance data during the first year of operation between April 1982 and March 1983.

In December 1983, an Aeolian Kinetics PDL-24 data acquisition system was installed in the building to collect hourly data. The results of detailed energy performance analyses presented in this report were determined using the hourly data collected on the PDL-24 system during the period of January 1984 through August 1984.

COMMUNITY UNITED METHODIST CHURCH CLASSROOM ADDITION

In early 1979 officials of the Community United Methodist Church in Columbia, Missouri, decided the church needed more space for educational and community activities. When they began to consider a classroom addition energy prices were soaring, so they decided to pursue the possibility of building as energy efficient a structure as possible given their budget. The solution was a passive solar classroom building which has been occupied since the fall of 1981. (See Figure 3-3a.)

Figure 3-3a. The new classroom building at Community United Methodist Church.

The basic design problem called for adding 5,000 ft² to 8,000 ft² of classroom space to a site constrained by four existing buildings. The buildings had each been built at a different time with no real plans for future expansion (see Figure 3-3b). In addition, neither the previous buildings nor the expected new classroom space had been scrutinized for energy use. In fact, before architect Nicholas Peckham became involved, the new classrooms were going to be housed in a steel building.

EXPANDED ANALYSIS

With the help of DOE funding, Peckham expanded his usual pre-design energy analysis to include both solar consulting advice and computer analysis. Both ASHRAE formulas and the PASOLE computer program — run by Dr. William Miller at the University of Missouri — were used to investigate energy issues. As the building progressed through design, energy analysis intensified and the annual energy-use goal for the building continued to decline: from 74,000 Btu/ft² as a steel building, to 32,500 Btu/ft² at schematic design, to 15,800 Btu/ft² at final

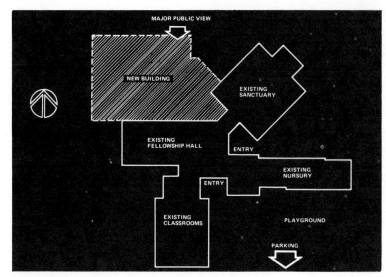

Figure 3-3b. Plan of the new classroom building.

design. Although Peckham admits that this level of energy analysis is atypical for most 5,500-ft² buildings, he says much of the additional cost was due to learning new solar design concepts. He freely admits that the project's team of experts produced a better design than any one of the experts would have produced alone.

Based on energy analysis and review by DOE technical support, it was decided that heating was the basic problem to be addressed. In addition, cooling would have to be addressed since it would be required during summer occupancy. The analysis led to a number of key design decisions. First, it was decided to tie the new classroom building to the north wall of the existing Fellowship Hall (Figure 3-3b). This would not only reduce high energy losses through north glass on the Fellowship Hall, but would reduce losses through the south wall of the new classroom building. Although this location limited solar access for the new building, it was the least disruptive to the rest of the site.

Second, a simple, direct-gain sunspace was chosen as the principal solar heating strategy over a more complex Trombe wall design that included rock bed storage. It was decided that in such a small building with a limited budget, a more complex system could not be justified. In addition, extensive mass was not required to store heat for extended periods of time. The decision to locate north of an existing building together with the decision to pursue a direct-gain strategy suggested that the main solar feature of the building should be a clerestory.

Finally, careful analysis of site temperatures indicated a typical daily temperature swing of up to 20° F. This suggested that night ventilation would be a reasonable cooling strategy. The energy analysis also eliminated a number of solar or solar-related strategies. In addition to rejecting both the Trombe wall and rock-storage ideas discussed above, the design team decided not to pursue either active or passive solar domestic hot water heating. The building's hot water requirements were simply too low to justify the initial investment. The idea of using a complex vestibule door to reduce infiltration of outside air was also eliminated because primary access would be from the existing building complex.

CLERESTORY DESIGN

As shown in Figures 3-3c and 3-3d, the final design for the new classroom building consists of three equal bays of 20 ft. by 80 ft. each on an east-west axis. Each bay is covered by a sloped

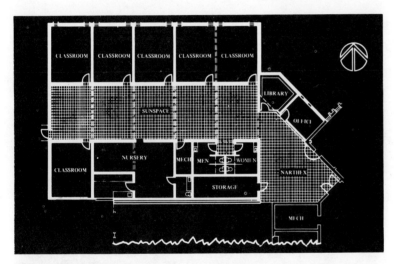

Figure 3-3c. Building plan showing three equal bays — each 20 by 80 ft. on an east-west axis.

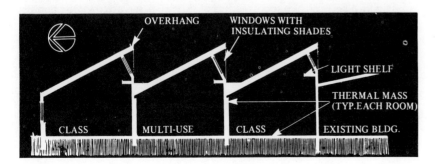

Figure 3-3d. Building section.

117

ceiling and a south-facing clerestory window. Classrooms, a nursery, and support facilities are located in the north and south bays, while the central bay serves as both a corridor and multipurpose room. The number of windows is limited on the north wall of the building, and windows are eliminated altogether on the east and west.

As finally designed, the clerestory provides two fixed glass panels and one operable window above each classroom (see Figure 3-3e). As can be seen in a photograph taken during construction (Figure 3-3f), window glass was tilted inward to face the winter sun more squarely and reduce reflection. This tilting creates a slight overhang above each clerestory, which is useful in shading glass from the higher summer sun. As shown in Figure 3-3d, a light shelf was built below each clerestory to enhance the reflection of light onto the light-colored, sloped ceiling.

Figure 3-3e. Each classroom module of 15 by 20 ft. served by three panels of glass — two fixed and one which can be opened for ventilation.

In the winter, light enters through the clerestory and is absorbed in the massive north wall of each bay and in the floor slab (see Figure 3-3g). The design team modified an early plan to have mass on all four walls of each classroom by reducing mass to a single block wall on the north of each bay. The result, about 50 lb. of mass for each ft^2 of floor space, is sufficient to meet short-term heat storage needs and much cheaper than the original plan. Insulating shades (with Llumar glazing) on clerestory windows reduce nighttime losses and are useful for shading during summer months.

Figure 3-3f. Shadow lines on the framing for one clerestory illustrating how low winter sun will strike future glass.

Figure 3-3g. North wall of the multipurpose room showing massive block walls and floor used to store solar heat.

After the first year, data on the addition's energy performance showed an impressive 75% energy savings. Since that time, the energy savings have continued to mount. After a second full year of data, and some fine-tuning of the building's systems and operational procedures, there is a clearer picture of the classroom addition's energy performance.

The overall performance of the addition has met expectations. Both the parish and community have responded enthusiastically. From the perspective of whole-building performance (including general occupant reactions, total energy use, and energy costs) the building has been a success.

GOOD MARKS FOR DESIGN

The Church Board of Trustees says it appreciates the way in which the addition ties together the other church buildings on the site. The Board indicates that it would build another solar building should the need arise. The pastor, Charles Buck, also says he is pleased with the addition and believes most of his parish is too. "Our new solar addition has been a real asset to the church," Pastor Buck explains. "The costs of operations are minimal, and the open design and structure allow a church like ours to be put to good use. The use of solar energy is a visible sign to the community concerning the stewardship of natural resources and the concern of the church for these resources."

Nearly all of the people who regularly use the building are pleased with its appearance. Originally, four out of five of the full-time staff said they found the addition attractive because of the solar design. After several months, however, most church members and other regular users started to forget the special features of the no-longer-new solar building. In addition, 9 out of 10 regular occupants said they were highly satisfied with the classroom wing. Although occasional users (those who visit the building about once a month) were less excited about the way the building looks, about a third of them liked the addition's appearance more than other buildings of its kind.

REDUCED ENERGY USE, UTILITY BILLS

Energy use in the addition has been extremely low, as have utility bills. Energy consumption is less than 20% of a base case — a similar building in the same climate without solar energy features. As shown in Figure 3-3h, the addition uses less than half the energy of a relatively energy-efficient BEPS building. The data that follow on the classroom addition are based on performance monitoring results for the 12 months, November 1982 through October 1983. The heating fuel is natural gas.

Heating dominates end-use consumption and accounts for more than 80% of the total annual energy use, as shown in

Figure 3-3i. Lighting, the second largest energy end use, is less than 10% of annual energy use.

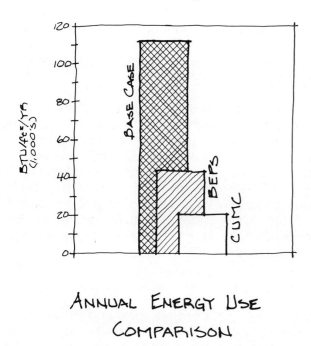

ANNUAL ENERGY USE
COMPARISON

Figure 3-3h. Annual energy-use comparison. The classroom wing performs remarkably well, particularly compared to the base case (an elementary school).

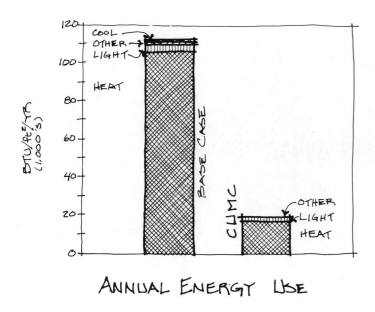

ANNUAL ENERGY USE

Figure 3-3i. Annual energy use. Heating and lighting account for over 90% of total energy use, while the connected cooling load is negligible.

Despite the hot, humid summers in Columbia, Missouri, the total annual connected cooling load is almost negligible because the conventional vapor-compression, central air conditioning system is rarely used. Almost all cooling is restricted to the sensible component of the cooling load and is provided by ceiling paddle fans and a central exhaust fan, accounting for 3% of the total annual energy use. Water heating (DHW) accounted for about 4% of the connected load. Energy-use patterns for the test year are shown in Figure 3-3j.

Energy costs are almost 85% less than a comparable conventional building and over 50% less than the BEPS building, as shown in Figure 3-3k. Annual energy cost differences by end use are shown in Figure 3-3l. The largest savings over the base case are realized by reduced heating and lighting needs (85% and 66% less, respectively). Energy costs for DHW and other uses (principally fans) are about the same as the base case. At $0.08/kWh and $3.67/MMBtu for gas, this translates to average annual savings of $0.39/ft² over the base case and $0.15/ft² relative to the BEPS building.

VERY LOW ENERGY USE

Factors contributing to low energy use and utility bills include design and occupancy characteristics. The passive solar design and conservation measures (e.g., high insulation levels) are responsible for a substantial proportion of the energy savings.

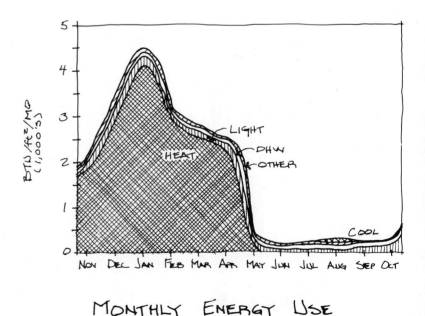

MONTHLY ENERGY USE

Figure 3-3j. Monthly energy use. Less than one-tenth of the total annual energy budget was used during the six months from late spring through fall.

The major passive solar elements are direct-gain heating and daylighting. The 750 ft² of south-facing clerestory window area provide direct solar gain in the winter without the usual conductive losses and indirect daylighting in the summer. The glazing is mounted at a 26° angle from the vertical, providing an overhang for shading the windows in the summer, as shown

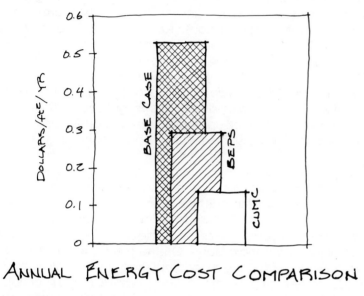

ANNUAL ENERGY COST COMPARISON

Figure 3-3k. Annual energy cost comparison. Even the BEPS building, which is equipped with some solar features, costs more than twice as much to operate as the church addition.

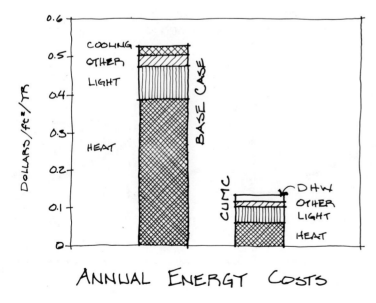

ANNUAL ENERGY COSTS

Figure 3-3l. Annual energy costs. Average annual energy costs are very modest compared to the base case, primarily because lighting loads are low and gas is a relatively inexpensive heating fuel.

in Figure 3-3m. An interior light shelf below the clerestory windows is used to reflect sunlight onto the ceiling in the summer for even daylight levels.

Thermal storage is provided by considerable mass in the concrete floor slab and dark masonry walls on the north side of each building module (Figure 3-3d). These dark walls are designed to absorb solar gain admitted by the clerestory windows. The thermal mass is also used for summer cooling. Natural cooling is provided by night ventilation of the thermal mass with a large central exhaust fan that pulls cool night air through the operable clerestory windows. Large paddle fans in each room are used in the winter to destratify warm air at the ceiling and distribute it throughout the space. The paddle fans also provide localized cooling in the classroom spaces. Auxiliary heating is provided by a conventional 95,000-Btu/hr gas furnace. The back-up cooling system consists of a standard, vapor-compression central air conditioner.

The conservation measures incorporated into the building are as important to winter energy savings as the passive features. The building has 12-in. batt insulation in the ceilings and 6-in. batt insulation in the walls. Additionally, the walls include rigid insulation on the outside of the frame structure. All windows in the building are triple pane. On the south-facing clerestory windows, triple-glazing is accomplished with two glass panes and one sheet of a selectively transparent film. The floor slab is also insulated from the ground. A low air-infiltration rate (estimated at 0.25 air changes per hour) has been attained by minimizing the number of outside entrances and exits from the new building, and by carefully installing an air/vapor barrier on exterior walls and ceiling. By minimizing the north-facing window area, the design further reduces both the air-infiltration rate and conductive heat loss. In addition, the joining of the south wall of the classroom wing to the existing Fellowship

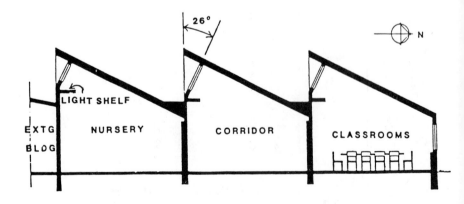

Figure 3-3m. Overhangs providing relief from the direct rays of the summer sun. Light shelves distribute daylight evenly throughout the space.

124

Hall substantially reduces the exposed envelope area and, therefore, heat losses.

The innovative design and attention to envelope energy losses are not the only important factors affecting the building's energy performance. The church staff has been energy conscious and has impressed others with the need to save energy. For example, the air conditioning system has been switched on only once in the last two years. In addition, the staff holds short building operation seminars for classroom users and posts how-to instructions in the building.

Occupancy is light during most of the year. Although large groups occasionally meet in the addition, only 10 to 25 people a day typically use the classrooms. Thus, the building temperature is allowed to float up during the day and down at night. As a result, auxiliary heat is needed only for morning warm-up during the winter. Occupancy is even lighter and more intermittent during the summer, and internal loads are quite low. The extensive thermal mass is usually effective in maintaining comfortable temperatures except on the hottest summer days.

MODEST CONSTRUCTION COSTS

The one-story masonry structure cost \$47/ft^2. According to R. S. Means construction data, the median average 1981 price for a similar religious/educational building was about \$40/ft^2. As shown in Figure 3-3n, half the buildings similar to the church

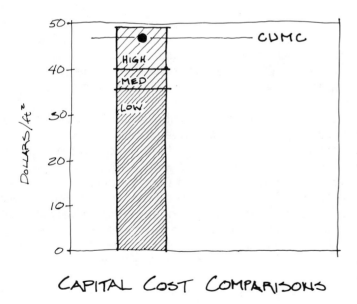

CAPITAL COST COMPARISONS

Figure 3-3n. Capital cost comparisons. Construction of the church addition costs more than half the construction of similar religious/educational buildings built in 1981, but less than one-third of the most expensive ones. (Low: 25% of buildings cost \$36/ft^2 or less to build; Medium: 50% cost \$40/ft^2 or less; High: 25% cost \$49/ft^2 or more.)

addition cost less than $40/ft^2, and one-fourth cost more than $49/ft^2. At $47/ft^2, the church classroom addition was slightly lower in cost than the high average cost for a similar building.

According to the architect, the cost might have been lower if construction were not complicated by the clerestories, which were chosen to facilitate solar access from the north side of an existing building. The church regards the $260,000 total price tag as modest, considering the anticipated energy savings. The owners note that parishioners were more willing to purchase church bonds to finance the building than for past construction projects because of the solar features.

Systems integration was accomplished with simple strategies for effective year-round operation. The energy savings were due in large part to effective integration of the heating, cooling, and lighting systems. The building performs well year-round, with most of the passive and conservation features contributing to both summer and winter occupant comfort.

LOW ENERGY CONSUMPTION

The relatively large aperture area (14% glazing-to-floor-area ratio) in the three clerestories allows large solar gains with low conductive losses. Together with the building's substantial thermal mass to absorb the solar gain, the apertures contribute most of the winter heating needs. The solar gain is sufficient for heating even on days with marginal insolation, as long as the furnace is used for morning warm-up.

A typical gas consumption pattern for winter is illustrated for a cloudy period in Figure 3-3o. A time clock is used to start the furnace at about 7:30 a.m. The furnace runs steadily for about two hours to raise the air temperature to the daytime thermostat setting (steady-state gas consumption is about 135,000 Btu/hr). On/off cycling of the furnace begins in order to keep the interior temperature within the comfort range.

During the morning warm-up, the furnace increases the air temperature to the comfort range, offsets conductive and infiltration heat losses, and heats the thermal mass of the masonry walls and concrete floor, which drops in temperature during the night setback period. Over the cloudy days shown in Figure 3-3o, the addition used less than 4 Btw/ft^2 per Farenheit-degree day. This rate of energy use is very low despite the absence of a solar energy contribution to heating. The building's conservation features are primarily responsible for the low energy consumption during cloudy periods.

Additional detailed analyses found that the solar gains from the large clerestories are sufficient to meet the heating load even on cloudy days, provided the furnace is used for warm-up. In addition, the relative stability of indoor temperature fluctuations indicated that conservation measures and the ther-

126

mal mass are sufficient to carry the building through a cold night with the indoor temperature above 60° F. Moreover, by allowing the building temperature to float up during the day and down at night, auxiliary heating is necessary only for morning warm-up.

The research also showed that under cold, sunny conditions, the solar gain stored in the mass each day is not carried over to the next day when the ambient temperature is too low (10° F or below). The threshold over which some overheating may occur, and under which all the heat stored during the day in the thermal mass is dissipated during the night setback period was identified as 15° F outside ambient temperature.

RARE DAYTIME USE OF ELECTRIC LIGHTS

The large clerestory apertures provide adequate natural light under almost all daytime conditions, and occupants responded well to the lighting strategy. According to most users, daylighting quality and levels were generally excellent.

Although lights are manually controlled by "untrained" occupants, they are rarely used when daylight is sufficient. One reason appears to be that most of the activities in the space are not visually demanding. As a result, lower lighting levels seem to be acceptable to occupants, and are more consistently observed than is typical for similar buildings. Moreover, much of the activity in the space is social in nature, involving more

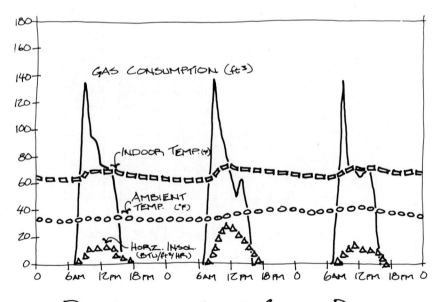

Figure 3-3o. Energy consumption during cloudy, winter days. Conservation features help keep energy consumption low.

discussion than paperwork. Occupants appear to feel no need to light the space even to minimum levels (i.e., minimum relative to U.S. standards of 50 foot-candles to 70 foot-candles).

A manual control strategy provides greater flexibility than either continuous dimming or on/off automatic controls because the automatic strategies are designed to provide a constant minimum light level set for the most visually demanding task expected during all occupied hours. Although a manual control strategy's flexibility may be far less important in a building where occupancy schedules are heavier and typical tasks are more demanding, the energy savings from a manual control strategy are greater than those achieved by automatic controls. The savings are shown in Figure 3-3p, which is based on computer simulation results.

A second reason for the success of the lighting system may be that the clerestories provide extended periods of sufficient light during which electric lighting is unnecessary. The size of the apertures in the addition is an important factor in the success of the lighting strategy. In studies of roof apertures with sensitive automatic dimming controls (Place 1983; Arasteh 1984), optimum energy use was achieved with a 2%-to-10% aperture ratio (roof aperture area/floor area). The aperture ratio for the classroom addition is almost 15%.

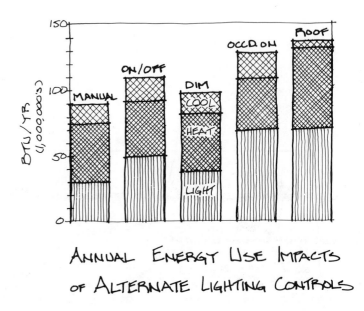

Figure 3-3p. Alternative lighting controls. Manual lighting controls significantly reduce energy use relative to automatic controls for a 30-foot-candle minimum illumination level. (Manual: measured data over a three-month period; On/off: automatic on/off controls; Dim: automatic continuous dimming; Occd.On: lights full on during all hours of occupancy; Roof: same as Occd.On, but without the roof apertures.)

The relatively low optimum glazing areas noted in the prior studies were possible because the automatic controls were able to adjust electric lighting levels constantly. Smaller apertures require a degree of "attentiveness," which is inappropriate to manual control. Large aperture areas, however, result in extended periods during which control is unnecessary. Once off, lights can usually remain off until dusk. Because sufficient natural illumination is provided during most daylight hours, occupants become used to the quality, dynamics, and levels of daylighting, and may be more likely to accept marginal daylight situations.

The amount of sunshine available for daylighting inside the building and the occupant response to natural light levels may provide a clue to the success of a manual lighting strategy that is coupled with large apertures. The relationship between insolation levels and electric light usage is shown in Figure 3-3q. The line running through the data shows increasing electricity for lights with decreasing horizontal insolation. The Y-intercept indicates an average load of 4 kW over the four-hour period at zero horizontal insolation, or what would be expected at night. This is equivalent to less than 1 W/ft^2 during the periods of heaviest occupancy. The data recorded during night occupancy indicate a similar load for the same rooms. Electrical energy consumption for lighting over a four-hour period on Sunday mornings (the most consistent occupancy period) suggests a strong correlation between lighting energy use and available sunshine.

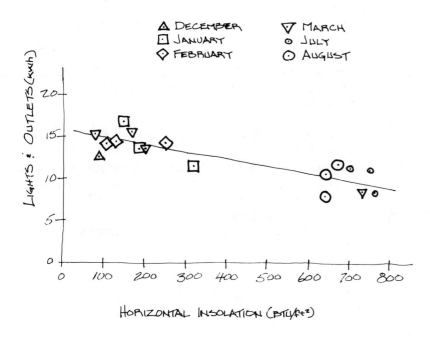

Figure 3-3q. Lighting (and outlet) use as a function of horizontal insolation available between 8:00 a.m. and noon on Sundays over a six-month period.

Figure 3-3q also suggests that summer sunlight is up to five times brighter than winter sunlight and that electric lighting tends to be used more often during the winter. The difference in electrical consumption, however, is minor, averaging roughly 0.5 W/ft^2 in the summer compared to about 0.7 W/ft^2 in the winter. This is approximately two to three times less lighting energy than is typical for a conventional energy-conserving building.

The daylight design and manual control strategy have substantial lighting energy cost benefits. The results of simulations to ascertain the annual energy cost impacts of alternative lighting control systems are shown in Figure 3-3r. These data show that energy costs incurred with manual controls are similar to, or lower than, energy costs incurred with automatic lighting control systems. The clerestory roof apertures, however, show a much greater potential to reduce lighting energy costs than heating costs. In fact, as shown in Figure 3-3r, neither heating nor cooling energy consumption is significantly affected by different lighting control strategies.

NIGHT VENTILATION OF THERMAL MASS

Mechanical cooling with the central air conditioning system is rarely used for several reasons:

- The summer shading of the clerestory apertures is effective, limiting the amount of direct-beam, admitted radiation to the space.
- Generally, light occupancy reduces internal loads of all kinds.
- The building is seldom used during the hottest part of the day, and the indoor temperature is allowed to exceed the comfort range.
- Night ventilation of thermal mass and the thermal capacity of the building provide effective cooling, given occupancy conditions.

The thermal capacitance of the building limits the average interior temperature to a range of 80° F to 84° F during the hottest summer days. A 10,000-CFM exhaust fan typically provides 5° F of cooling (at an average ambient temperature of 65° F) with the fan operating from three to six hours per night. The fan provides a complete air change every six minutes at about one-third the power requirement of the mechanical refrigeration system.

The significance of the night ventilation strategy is illustrated by one of the responses to an unusually high occupancy situation. In preparation for Sunday use of the building, the exhaust fan was switched on at 8:00 p.m. on a Saturday night in late August and remained on for 12 hours (researchers now believe that 12 hours was probably longer than necessary). With a minimum outside temperature of 60° F, the inside temperature dropped to 67° F, or about 8° F to 10° F below the normal minimum temperature with the building closed. The indoor temperature rose to 70° F the following morning at 9:00 a.m. Between 9:30 a.m. and 10:30 a.m. more than 100 people met in the classroom wing, and the temperature rose to 74° F. The indoor temperature slowly peaked at 78° F as the ambient temperature rose to a maximum of 88° F. The night ventilation effectively kept radiant temperatures reasonably comfortable despite heavy occupancy, high afternoon air temperatures, and solar effects.

Researchers have analyzed the effect of keeping indoor temperatures within the comfort range for about 40 hours per week during somewhat heavy occupancy (which would reflect a situation more typical of a normal office building). Simulation of night ventilation whenever effective showed that cooling loads would be about the same magnitude as winter heating loads, with both still very low. When the effect of the overhead fans is accounted for by allowing the temperature to float 2° F higher, those cooling loads are reduced but not eliminated. The analysis suggests that if this building had a more typical occupancy pattern and standard comfort requirements, mechanical refrigeration for cooling would be necessary, although the cooling loads would be very low.

During the first year of operation, users complained of feeling cold on early spring and winter mornings. They also complained about the amount of noise in the building. These early thermal comfort and acoustic problems have been easily solved.

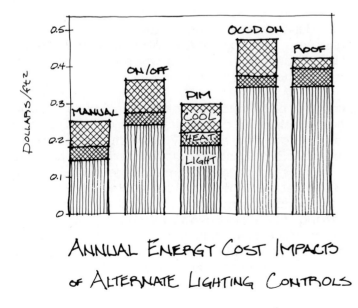

ANNUAL ENERGY COST IMPACTS
of ALTERNATE LIGHTING CONTROLS

Figure 3-3r. Cost impacts of alternative light controls. Based on three months of data, the energy cost benefits of manual controls, particularly with respect to lighting, are significant.

PROGRAMMABLE THERMOSTAT

In 1981, with two months of winter energy data, researchers noted that energy use in the new addition was too low to provide adequate comfort conditions. Apparently, a well-intentioned maintenance man simply thought the new solar building would heat itself and had turned the thermostat much lower than planned. Compounding the problem created by this frugality was the thermal lag of the building's extra mass. Once the thermostat was turned back to 50° F at night, the building mass often cooled to 60° F or less by morning. When the thermostat was turned up an hour before scheduled occupancy in the morning, the heating system had neither the time nor the capacity to heat the building to the comfort range. Naturally, occupants complained of the cold.

To overcome the problem associated with the thermal lag of the building mass, a 24-hour programmable thermostat was installed. Since the installation of the programmable thermostat, there have been few complaints of spring or winter morning discomfort. The daytime setpoint is 65° F; the nighttime setpoint, 55° F. The thermostat turns on the gas heat at 4:30 a.m. and turns off the heat around 4:30 p.m. In this manner, the heating system recharges the building mass, raising the radiant and air temperature into the comfort range by the time the first occupants arrive. By late afternoon (i.e., 3:00 p.m. to 4:30 p.m.), the thermal lag of the now "fully charged" building is sufficient to keep indoor temperatures within the comfort range for a typical 7:00 p.m. meeting.

Researchers now recognize it may be appropriate to move up the morning startup time by an hour or more during the swing months of fall and spring. By delaying morning heating system operation during these months, the church could take advantage of warmer nights and save a little more energy. In addition, it is less likely that overheating, which wastes energy and causes discomfort, would occur.

Although this night setback system works quite well, researchers question the cost-effectiveness of the strategy in view of the light and relatively unstructured occupancy schedule. Several researchers note that before the programmable thermostat was installed, morning occupants simply met in the older buildings. (The older structures lack the extra mass of the addition and warm up quickly in the morning.) Although the argument for using other church areas for winter morning activities rather than preheating a massive building may be technically and economically sound, the absolute amount of heating energy saved would be small.

ACOUSTIC TREATMENT

The major user complaint about the classroom addition is noise, which is caused by normal sources such as voices and footsteps. Noise levels are fairly high, making it difficult to concentrate, according to the full-time staff. The problem is caused in part by the hard surfaces of the exposed thermal mass. The noise problem is exacerbated by intense use of the facility by children. Most of the surfaces in the addition are hard, including the ceiling, south wall, north wall, and floor so there is very little material to absorb unwanted sounds.

Researchers suggest two solutions: (1) add acoustic tile to the ceiling and south wall, leaving the thermal mass surfaces alone (i.e., the floor and north walls), or (2) add acoustic treatment to one of those surfaces and carpet the floors. Computer simulations suggest that the first solution would have a minimal effect on the light-reflecting qualities of the treated surfaces, and would dramatically increase sound absorption. This solution would probably solve most of the noise problem.

The second option would create a similar acoustic effect and reduce the noise caused by walking. The carpeting, however, also would reduce significantly the effectiveness of the floor's thermal mass. The floor contains 70% of the building's thermal mass. Simulations indicate that the no-carpet solution does not affect heating, while carpeting increases the heating load by 10%. The heating load increase from the carpeting would be substantially greater without the thermal mass contained in the north walls.

Despite slightly increasing the heating load, the carpet has some advantages beyond acoustic performance. Advantages include reduced heating peaks, more rapid building response to morning warm-up, and the amenities that carpeting typically offers. Church officials, who are sensitive to the noise problem, have proposed that acoustic tile be installed.

Since the first occupancy in 1981, building users have taken responsibility for systems operation. Apparently users have enough pride in their building that they have learned to operate it effectively. In addition, the user orientation program and the responsiveness of church staff have resulted in fine-tuning the building and the building/occupancy relationship.

OPERATING BUILDING SYSTEMS

According to researchers, 85% of the occupants state that they enjoy being able to control their environment. This responsibility includes operating fans, lights, and windows in a purposeful manner intended to save energy. For example, occupants appear to approach cooling strategies in a variety of ways, depending on the season. In the spring, users first turn on ceiling fans. This action may be followed by opening windows and turning off lights. In the summer, occupants turn on the paddle fans. Sometimes the exhaust fan is used if open windows do not enhance comfort. Air conditioning is considered to be a last resort. In the early fall, users first open the windows and only occasionally use the ceiling fans or central exhaust fans.

The responsibility for summer night ventilation is assigned to one person. The task, which includes opening all windows and doors and turning on the exhaust fan, has been carried out faithfully and effectively.

EFFECTIVE COMMUNICATIONS

Although occupant sensitivity to building operation needs is important, the architect or other responsible design team member is responsible for systematically orienting occupants to correct procedures. For this project, the design team provided church staff with how-to instructions for each season. The staff elaborated on the instructions and held seminars to acquaint building users with proper building operation. Examples of the step-by-step instructions posted in the building for winter operation follow:

- *Room too hot?*
  - Try the ceiling fans first because moving air usually feels cooler.
  - Second, open two windows for cross-ventilation, but only in the room you are using.
  - Close the windows when you leave.
- *Room too cold?*
  - Try the fans first to bring down warm air that may be trapped near the ceiling.
  - If this does not work, turn up the thermostat in the hall, closing all doors on the corridor except yours.
  - Turn heat back to the 60° setpoint on the thermostat when you leave.

Similar instructions for the cooling season and general lighting operation were also posted. The operation of the passive systems and associated benefits are carefully explained in the instructions.

SUMMARY

The classroom addition to the Community United Methodist Church is performing well by all accounts. The church is happy with the building, occupants enjoy operating the building systems, and energy use is extremely low. Heating, cooling, and lighting systems are balanced between passive solar, conservation, and conventional mechanical systems; the balance allows for year-round integrated systems performance. Experience indicates that passive solar gains provide adequate occupant comfort during the heating season, with little overheating. The daylighting system clearly offsets the need for electric lights. Manual lighting control strategies are effective, although overall lighting needs are small. Fan-assisted night ventilation is adequate to cool the building through most of the summer at significantly less power consumption than mechanical air conditioning. The success of this cooling strategy, however, depends to some extent on allowing the building temperature to drift above the comfort range during the hottest part of the day. The thermal lag and acoustic problems appear to have been resolved satisfactorily and serve as valuable lessons for future designs.

BIBLIOGRAPHY

Andersson, B. et al. 1984. "Effects of Daylighting Options on the Energy Performance of Two Existing Passive Commercial Buildings," LBL Report No. LBL-18069, November 1984.

Miller, W. 1984. "Final Report: Solar Classroom Building," DOE Contract No. DE-FC02-80CS30334, Spring 1984.

Min Kantrowitz & Associates. 1984. "Analysis of Occupant Effects Interaction and Satisfaction: Community United Methodist Church," February 1984.

Yager, A., and D. Frey. 1984. "An Analysis of the Thermal Performance of the Passive Solar Classroom Addition at the Community United Methodist Church, in Columbia, Missouri," Architectural Energy Corporation Final Report, November 1984.

PROJECT SUMMARY
COMMUNITY UNITED METHODIST CHURCH

Building type: School classrooms and multipurpose rooms

Floor area: 5,500 ft^2

Location: Columbia, MO

Owner: Community United Methodist Church

Design completed: August 1980

Construction completed: August 1981

Occupancy: 10-25 people per day (highly variable); 8 hours per day; 11 months per year (excluding August)

Construction costs: $260,000 ($47/ft^2)

Annual energy use: 20,200 Btu/ft^2/yr

Climate:
5,081 heating degree days
1,296 cooling degree days

Insolation: 1,327 Btu/ft^2/day (annual average horizontal solar radiation)

Energy costs:
Natural gas, $43.67/MMBtu
Electricity, $22.20/MMBtu ($0.08/kWh)

Solar design elements:
Direct-gain sunspace
Mass walls
Mass floors
Natural ventilation
Operable windows
Mass thermal storage
Clerestories
Light shelves
White (reflective) roof

Other energy elements:
Ceiling fans (heat destratification)
Natural gas furnace (back-up)
Forced ventilation/night flushing
Ceiling fans (sensible cooling)
Air conditioning (back-up)
High insulation levels (R-38 ceiling, R-19 walls, R-9 triple glazing with Llumar shades, and Insulation under slab)
Roof overhang for shading

Architect: Peckham & Wright Architects, Inc.; Columbia, MO

Solar designer: Peckham & Wright Architects, Inc.; Columbia, MO

Monitoring period: November 1981-October 1983

Data collected:
Horizontal solar radiation
Outside air temperature
Indoor air temperature
Energy consumption (heating, cooling, lighting, fans, and DHW)

Data acquisition system: From November 1981 to December 1983, energy use was monitored on a weekly basis by sub-meters. The sub-metering included gas meter, watt-hour meters, and hour timers. Microprocessor-controlled system for continuous measured energy use was installed December 1983. Data was stored as hourly averages or totals.

136

SECURITY STATE BANK

The new Security State Bank of Wells, Minnesota, is a dramatic departure from former surroundings for Bob Hart, one of three owners. "In the old building," Hart recalls, "the only window was a single pane of glass in the door. Here, it's like standing under a tree." The dazzling daylight and snug winter warmth of Hart's passive solar bank not only inspires imagery, it also attracts new customers. (See Figures 3-4a and 3-4b.)

During the first three months of the new Security State Bank building's opening, the owners saw their utility bills drop 60% to 70% and their business grow by 25%. The energy savings are easily explained by the energy-conserving construction, economical HVAC systems, and passive solar features. "Winter was severe, but it cost less to heat this bank than it did most houses around here," Hart says. Although the daylit interiors of passive solar banks have contributed directly to business upturns elsewhere (see sidebar), other factors helped ensure new prosperity at the Security State Bank. "After all," Hart continues "it is a new and bigger building with better facilities in a more desirable location. But," he concedes, "the growth is pretty substantial. It's certainly beyond our expectations. . . . People have reacted very favorably to the pleasant atmosphere. . . . The new building has definitely drawn customers away from the competition." The competition Hart refers to involves his bank, a second bank, and an S&L that are after a small market in a town of 2,800 about 100 miles south of Minneapolis.

Figure 3-4a. Security State Bank.

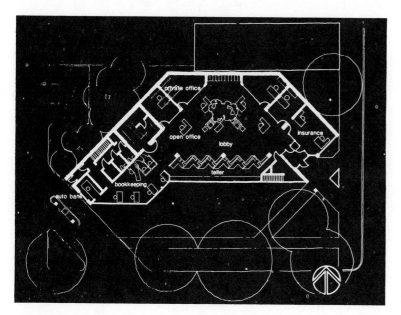

Figure 3-4b. Building plan. The building is located on a flat, 140-by-80-ft. corner lot, which allows landscaping for amenity and screening. Future solar access to the south is guaranteed by the building setback. In addition, the bank purchased the lot across the street to the south for parking.

Wooing Potential Customers With Solar Design Has Worked Before

Unlike the owners of the Security State Bank, the owners of the Friendship Federal Savings & Loan near Pittsburgh had an opportunity to gradually introduce solar strategies to several branch offices. The owners first built a highly insulated conventional building and retrofitted another with active solar systems. The active retrofit worked so well that they built a third branch with passive daylighting and active heating systems. The performance of the daylight system impressed the owners, and the fourth branch was an all-passive design with an emphasis on daylighting.

To their delight, the Friendship owners determined that the surge in new business was a direct result of the passive daylighting systems. Management attributes a staggering 400% increase in new depositors at the passive solar branch to the visibility of its design. Friendship president Richard Knapp claims, "We virtually recovered the cost of solar construction in the free publicity." System costs were recovered in less than a year.

SOLAR DESIGN MOTIVATIONS

Despite the amenities and energy savings the Security State Bank design provided through the winter of 1981-1982, the primary motivation to invest in solar design was economic. "Up here," Hart emphasizes, "the heating bills can kill you." Not even the fact that utility bills are tax deductible as operating expenses deterred Hart, his brother, Pat, and the bank's president, Frank Clarke, from their commitment to a solar building. "There's no way you're better off having higher expenses for anything," Hart says. "Besides, the building is cheaper to maintain than our old one even though it's four times the size."

In May 1979, the Hart brothers approached architect Jon Thorstenson with the idea of building a solar bank. The Hart brothers have had a personal interest in passive solar design for some time. In fact, Bob Hart had built passive features into his own new home, which included heavy insulation and large areas of south-facing glass.

In the fall of 1980, after a year and a half of design work, construction on the new 11,012-ft² bank began. After a few months of operation Hart proclaimed: "We are all pleased. The new building works real well."

TIGHT CONSTRUCTION DAYLIGHT CONTROL

Essentially, the new building functions like a thermos bottle, retaining heat in the winter and rejecting it in the summer. Heavy insulation and tight construction account for most of the year-round energy savings for heating and cooling. But the big difference between the Security State Bank and its conventional rivals is the daylighting system. The new building is designed to use less than one-tenth of the energy needed to light a comparable building in Minnesota.

The daylight system is also the most visible element of the passive solar design. The extensive glass area, hooded by bright orange awnings and framed by sleek aluminum paneling, makes the Security State Bank a stand-out building in Wells. The oversized clerestory windows that occupy most of the south wall achieve a sensitive connection with the outside. The amount and quality of light admitted by the clerestory are a constant source of wonder to customers, passersby, and employees. On clear days, from 300 foot-candles to 500 foot-candles of glare-free natural light are provided by the clerestory windows. From the outside, the building interior glows, even in bright sunlight. Inside, sunbeams are intercepted and scattered by pale surfaces and an overhead baffle system. The rich, warm colors of the furnishings enhance the airy and pleasant effect.

The clerestory windows are intended to provide most of the task and ambient lighting. To achieve this objective, high-quality, diffuse daylight is required to prevent glare at workstations on the main floor. Model studies (Figure 3-4c) indicated that light-colored ceiling and wall surfaces and a system of overhead baffles provided the most even and glare-free distribution of daylight throughout the main floor. Direct-beam illumination is confined to a small portion of the lobby area.

The baffle system consists of two 3-by-5-ft. box beams that span the length of the building. (See Figure 3-4d.) The baffles house the HVAC ducts and the back-up fluorescent lighting system. The dual function made the baffles cost-effective. A smaller, lightweight baffle grid is suspended between the two larger baffles to increase the diffuseness of the natural light.

Figure 3-4d. View of baffles at lobby level.

Figure 3-4c. Identical views of the model interior and the real thing. Solar designer John Weidt used scale models and a light meter to study the quality and intensity of light in various daylighting schemes under clear and overcast conditions. The distribution of direct-beam illumination was simulated by mounting the model on a heliodon.

139

COMBINED DAYLIGHTING, PASSIVE HEATING SYSTEMS

Gas is used for heating in Minnesota. It is a relatively inexpensive fuel in Wells ($4.10/MMBtu) and, therefore, there was little justification for a separate passive heating system. Moreover, the variety of separate heating and lighting systems studied complicated the design and significantly increased the building cost. Because solar gain would be used only to reduce the load on the gas-fired boiler system, the designers wanted to combine passive heating and daylighting. They reasoned that if the lighting system offset part of the heating load, particularly in the morning, the combined system would be economical despite gas prices.

Once the decision to combine passive heating and lighting was made, the designers determined that the clerestory windows would have to be oversized. Although a relatively modest aperture area would provide adequate background illumination, the same window area would not provide enough solar gain in the winter to make it a significant, secondary heat source. The designers responded to the problem by letting in more daylight and, therefore, more heat.

Concern existed, however, about controlling daylight from a southern exposure, particularly during the summer. The possible overheating problem was solved by the use of exterior, operable canvas awnings extended for shading during the summer. The awnings are operated by a solar cell with wind and manual overrides. The operational flexibility that retractable awnings add to the daylight/heating system made them cost-effective relative to fixed overhangs.

THERMOS-BOTTLE EFFECT

In earlier design schemes, the designers were concerned about building sufficient thermal storage mass into the structure to capture and retain the direct solar radiation coming through the clerestory. But their analysis revealed that massive storage capacity was not only unnecessary, it was undesirable. This finding contradicted rules-of-thumb used for residential passive systems, which emphasize the value of mass to flatten out the daily interior temperature curve.

Excess mass for heat storage was unnecessary principally because of the efficiency of the thermos-bottle construction, which very effectively moderates heat gains and losses. Analysis showed that greater mass than that already contained in the building would provide diminishing returns on energy savings. Moreover, the thermos-bottle effect and the direct irradiation of lighter-weight materials could be used to advantage on cold winter mornings. Since lighter-weight materials give up heat from solar gain more quickly than heavier materials, a less massive structure would respond more quickly to the sun coming through the south-facing clerestories on cold winter mornings. The rapid response to the morning sun allows the building temperature to be set back to 50° F at night. Although large amounts of mass would store the incoming solar gain during the day, the heat would be released at night during unoccupied periods and, therefore, be of little help in meeting daytime comfort needs.

The efficiency of the daylight distribution was critical to directing sunshine to the lighter mass in as many areas of the building as possible. Because the lighter mass gives up its heat more rapidly than heavier materials, it can use the lower intensity to diffuse solar gain to better advantage.

The Security State Bank, however, is not a low-mass building relative to conventional construction. It is low mass only in relation to the amount of mass directly irradiated by the sun. Most of the considerable mass (e.g., the basement area, the vault, and the floor) is secondary. The nonirradiated mass together with the tight construction, however, contribute to the temperature stability of the bank. The building temperature has never fallen below 50° F even during periods of subzero nighttime temperatures. In fact, Bob Hart notes that "All our tropical plants made it through the final construction stages even though the gas heating system wasn't hooked up yet."

COOLING SYSTEM EFFECTIVENESS

Although the cooling system is not passive, it provides maximum control and economy of operation. (See Figure 3-4e.)

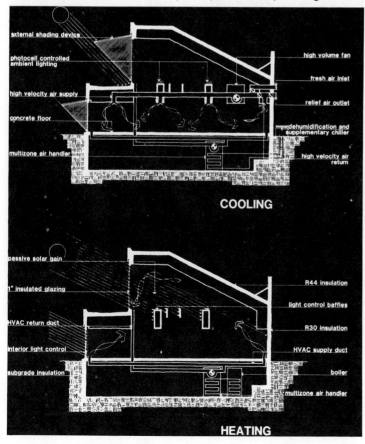

Figure 3-4e. HVAC system sequence. The system operates at constant volume during occupied hours. It is designed for about 45 hours-per-week occupancy. A time clock sets hours of operation and unoccupied period cycling conditions. A night thermostat allows for temperature setback or setup, as appropriate. The large-volume ventilation fan is designed to be manually operated and may be switched on or off at will. The cooling system is controlled by inside/outside thermostats, which provide the required mix of outside air ventilation and refrigeration to provide for comfort conditions.

141

Again, the thermos-bottle effect coupled with the reduction in undesirable solar gain by the awnings allows the use of 100% outside air to meet cooling needs rather than mechanical refrigeration, far into the normal cooling season.

In a typical building, mechanical refrigeration begins to be required when the outside air temperature rises above 50° F to 55° F. For the Security State Bank, however, the designers wanted a system that could provide adequate cooling using only outside air up to 65° F. Since electricity was expensive in Minnesota ($0.06/kWh), such an outside air economizer system would reduce cooling costs substantially. Conventional air conditioning and air-handling systems, however, could not provide a large enough volume of outside air to offset the amount of heat gain from the daylighting system effectively. Thus, a high-volume, high-velocity economizer system was installed.

This additional economizer fan and high-velocity duct system is "piggybacked" onto a conventional direct-exchange air conditioning unit and standard-volume multizone air handler. Together, the high-volume economizer fan system and conventional air handler can provide 26,400 cfm (18.5 air changes/hr) when operating in the full outside air mode.

The two air-handling systems, however, can operate independently. The only interface between the systems is the refrigerant coil, used to remove moisture from the air when the systems are operating in the mechanical cooling mode. In this mode, the high-volume system acts as a recirculating device to augment the conventional air handler. Returns located near the ceiling collect and discharge hot air at the clerestory windows before it can reach the cooling coil.

REDUCED ENERGY USE, UTILITY BILLS

Energy consumption in the bank is slightly less than three-quarters of that of a base case — a similar building in the same climate without solar energy features or special conservation measures. As shown in Figure 3-4f, the actual building uses less energy than the base case, and 16% more energy than a relatively energy-efficient BEPS building.

Space heating accounts for nearly two-thirds of total annual energy use, as shown in Figure 3-4g. The building uses 10% less space heating energy than the base case. Fans and other energy uses represent the second largest use of energy, accounting for about one-fifth of annual energy consumption. The principal fans are in the VAV system, which is used to circulate both heated and cooled air year-round.

The data presented in this case study have been synthesized to represent a full year of operation. They are based on performance monitoring results for the months of January, February, April, June, July, and August of 1982 and January through July of 1983. The heating fuel is natural gas, and fuel bills have been recorded for December 1981, January through September of 1982, and January through June of 1983. Electric bills (available for January through August and November and December of 1982; and January through June of 1983) were also used in developing the operational data.

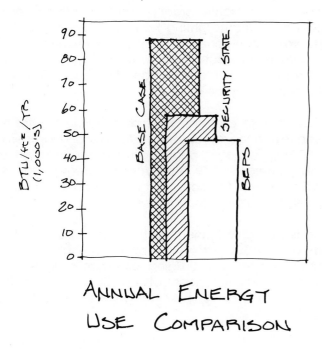

ANNUAL ENERGY
USE COMPARISON

Figure 3-4f.

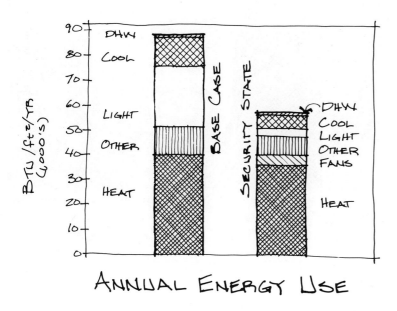

ANNUAL ENERGY USE

Figure 3-4g.

143

The most substantial savings over the base case are for lighting and cooling. The lighting load is very low, representing one-twentieth of total annual energy use. The actual lighting load amounts to only 12% of the base case lighting load. The principal reasons for the savings are the effectiveness of the clerestory and south-facing windows and an energy-efficient electric lighting/automated control system.

Cooling energy is a slightly larger proportion of total energy (representing 8%) than is lighting. However, the energy use for cooling represents only one-third of that required by the base case. The factors contributing to this low cooling requirement include the thermos-bottle effect and the reduction in undesirable solar gain by the awnings.

Monthly energy-use patterns are shown in Figure 3-4h. Although space heating represents two-thirds of annual energy use, or 5.12 Btu/ft^2/heating degree day, the building requires little cooling energy — 3.49 Btu/ft^2/cooling degree day. As shown in Figure 3-4h, fan operation and miscellaneous uses are relatively stable throughout the year.

Energy costs are slightly higher than those of the BEPS building ($0.50/ft^2/yr versus $0.35/ft^2/yr) and about one-half those of a comparable conventional building, as shown in Figure 3-4i. Annual energy cost differences between the base case and Security State Bank building are shown in Figure 3-4j. The

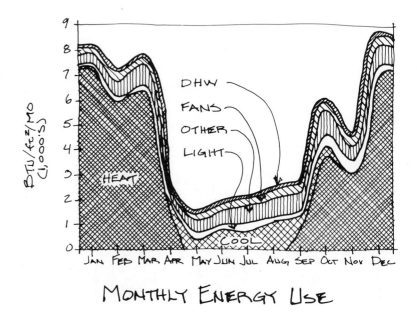

Figure 3-4h.

144

largest cost savings over the base case are in lighting and cooling — reflecting the low levels of energy use discussed above. At $0.06/kWh and $5.63/MMBtu for gas, the annual average savings are $0.50/ft^2 ($5,500/yr).

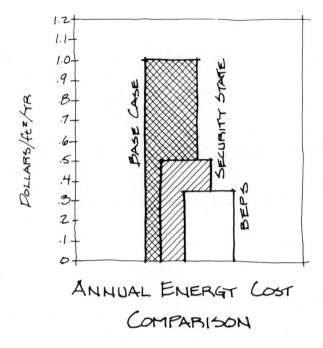

ANNUAL ENERGY COST
COMPARISON

Figure 3-4i.

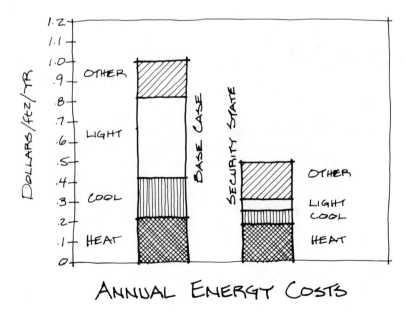

ANNUAL ENERGY COSTS

Figure 3-4j.

145

INCREASED ENERGY EFFICIENCY

Overall building costs per ft² ($62/ft²) fall well within the reasonable cost range for a comparable building in this region of the country. The solar portion of the building accounted for approximately 16% ($10/ft²) of total costs. The nonsolar building costs were within 4% of the original budget, reflecting the project team's cost-consciousness.

Analysis of the electrical-lighting-use profiles for representative winter months indicates that more artificial light is replaced by sunlight in the teller/bookkeeping area than in the lobby when the sun is at low altitude angles near midday. It appears that the beam and forward scattered diffuse radiation transmitted directly into the teller/bookkeeping area is better utilized for daylighting than the natural lighting that enters the occupied zone indirectly through the clerestory. Correspondingly, lobby lights were used for approximately 50% more hours than lights in the teller/bookkeeping area. Also, the percent of the total installed ambient lighting use is inversely related to the percent of sunshine available.

HEATING SEASON PERFORMANCE

The natural gas boiler supplies the energy required to maintain the thermostatic setpoint temperature. As discussed above, actual heating energy use was less than the amount predicted for the base case. The south-facing windows and clerestory provide the building with direct solar heat gain during the winter. However, solar gains do not always effectively meet occupant needs.

When the sun is at low angles during the heating season, most of the solar gain is reflected and diffused within the building. At these times, the heat is transferred more quickly to the air, leading to overheating in some cases. The solar gain is only absorbed by the thermal mass after convection and radiation within the space.

The peak heat input coincides with the peak solar gain, during certain days monitored in November. The indoor temperature in the teller area rises above the thermostatic setpoint in the late afternoon due to solar and internal electrical heat gain. This occurs after the boiler has turned off. The decay rate of the indoor temperature indicates that only a small amount of the solar contribution was absorbed by the building mass.

It is apparent that the space heating contribution due to solar transmittance through the clerestory does not effectively reach the occupied zone because of stratification. The distribution of temperatures on the main floor shown in Figures 3-4k and 3-4l for the sunniest and cloudiest days during the period illustrates this point. On November 6, the sunniest day, the clerestory temperatures were measured above 100° F due to the transmitted solar radiation. Nevertheless, gas was consumed despite significant solar transmittance. The clerestory temperatures on a very cloudy November 9 only reached levels similar to the teller and bookkeeping area temperatures. No temperature stratification was observed on this cloudy day. This appears to be due to adequate air movement by the supply fan.

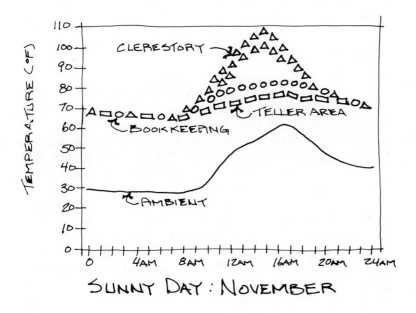

Figure 3-4k. Distribution of temperatures on a sunny day.

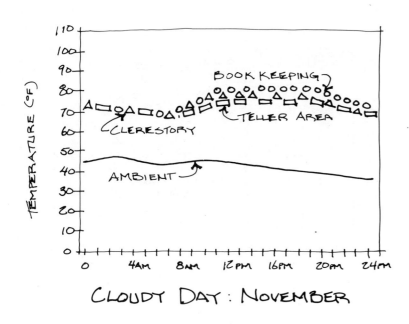

Figure 3-4l. Distribution of temperatures on a cloudy day.

At times, overheating was observed during the winter in the occupied space. Indoor temperature distribution is well matched to global radiation profiles. The peak clerestory temperatures are higher on the sunnier days. Temperature increases above the thermostatic setpoint in the occupied zone appear to be due to solar gains through the lower-level glazing. It is unclear whether some of the excess heat in the clerestory area contributes to overheating of the occupied zone.

OPERATIONAL PROBLEMS

Interior temperatures were often above the thermostatic setpoint on sunny summer days. This situation is illustrated in Figure 3-4m by tracking the performance of the chiller and indoor temperatures for a typical sunny summer day. The chiller operation begins at 7:00 a.m. because the indoor temperatures in the occupied zone are above the daytime setpoint of 74° F. The indoor temperature in the teller area is reduced to the setpoint by 9:00 a.m. and then rises to a peak of 78° F during the occupied period while the chiller is operating at full capacity. The measured temperature in the bookkeeping area was always about 4° F higher during the daytime hours. The average daytime ambient temperature was about 83° F, which is approximately the 5% summer design, dry-bulb temperature for this area of Minnesota. The indoor temperature profiles indicate that the chiller is slightly undersized to maintain the thermostatic setpoint with the 5% design value on a sunny summer day.

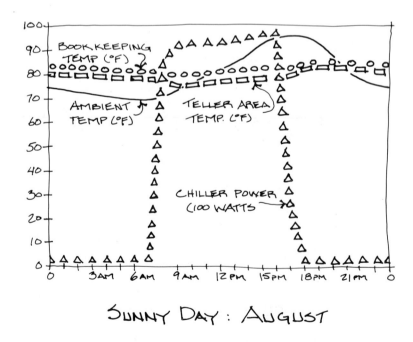

Figure 3-4m. Chiller performance and indoor temperatures on a sunny day.

The chiller operating at full capacity (for a cloudy day in August) is sufficient to maintain the temperature in the teller area near the comfort range while the ambient temperature is around 75° F. As illustrated in Figure 3-4n, the temperature in the bookkeeping area was maintained around 80° F during the same period. Also of significance on these sunny days is that the early morning indoor temperatures are on the order of 10° F above the ambient temperature. The use of outdoor air for "free cooling" appears to be appropriate for this building. Although a large fan was installed for this purpose, it was infrequently used because of noise.

Examination of horizontal solar radiation and chiller power use data indicates that the energy required for cooling is relatively constant and independent of solar gains during this August period. This suggests that the solar gains did not contribute much to the cooling load.

The cooling load apparently does not depend upon whether the ambient lighting is from an artificial or natural source. The difference in total electrical energy use between sunny and cloudy days is due to the energy required to provide only the artificial lighting.

OCCASIONAL THERMAL, VISUAL DISCOMFORT

The building was, by and large, a very satisfactory environment in which to work relative to a conventional office building. The overwhelming general satisfaction was associated

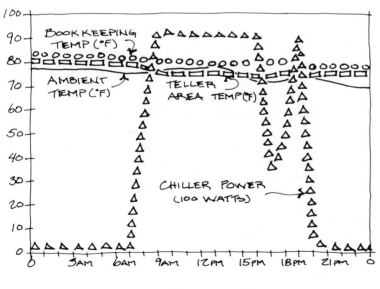

CLOUDY DAY: AUGUST

Figure 3-4n. Chiller performance and indoor temperatures on a cloudy day.

with the building's aesthetic and functional orientation. The natural daylighting created a warm, bright open space providing a pleasant and comfortable atmosphere for occupants.

Some complaints, however, provide insight into operational improvements that could enhance both thermal and visual comfort, and substantially reduce building energy use.

OVERHEATING

Occasional or frequent discomfort due to overheating was reported for the September-through-December period by approximately two-thirds of building occupants. Overheating occurs most often in the lobby/teller area in the afternoon. During the first six months of occupancy the problem was undoubtedly due in part to the malfunctioning of the outside air intake. Also, window blinds behind the tellers were installed only after complaints were made about glare and overheating.

Although overheating was due to unmoderated solar gain, illumination seems to have been adequately handled. Overhead baffles diffused sunlight as intended and too-bright lighting was reported by only 21% and glare by 47% of building occupants.

Although, generally, interior baffles and exterior awnings adequately modulated daylighting, certain conditions caused problems. Daylighting controls were employed erratically. Automatic solar-sensitive switching was often manually overridden. For example, on a sunny day with gusty winds, awnings retracted automatically causing tellers to lower the blinds. When the awnings re-extended, the blinds were not raised, which reduced illumination.

Sometimes gusty winds affected only the upper blinds, and the lobby was flooded with light. This created a problem for workers because of a strong contrast between high general illumination and lower levels on their work surfaces. Sensing the difference, workers used overhead and task lighting in an effort to achieve a balance, even when sufficient illumination was available.

COOLING SYSTEM

The cooling system was used more often than predicted even though the ventilation system would have kept temperatures in the comfort range. Evidently, this resulted from problems with high air velocity and annoying noise levels associated with the fan, which was designed to bring outdoor air into the occupied space. In addition, thermostat temperatures were set lower than the original design specified.

Complaints of too-cool temperatures were reported more often during the transition seasons than during the winter. Occasional or frequent discomfort occurred 39% of the time. Discomfort may be associated with draftiness, which was reported by 31%. High-velocity ventilation coupled with vents that were placed too close to some workers might have caused this discomfort.

SUMMARY

Passive solar strategies for space heating, daylighting, and cooling are used successfully in the Security State Bank in Wells, Minnesota. The building's energy efficiency and pleasing environment help both employees and management enjoy the building.

The daylighting contribution of the passive systems is substantial. Analysis of the heating season's thermal performance indicates that passive solar gains contribute to meeting heating needs. Heat gains during the cooling season are reduced by high thermal insulation levels and window overhangs that block direct solar gain.

Occupant satisfaction has been very high despite occasional individual complaints of glare and/or dimness and thermal discomfort. Complaints do not differ substantially from those encountered in conventional office buildings. Occasional reports of thermal discomfort are attributable to malfunctions in the mechanical as well as the passive solar systems.

Building type: Bank

Floor area: 11,000 ft^2

Location: Wells, MN

Owner: Security State Bank of Wells

Construction completed: December 1981

Occupancy: 30 people; 57.5 hrs/week

Construction costs: $64/ft^2

Annual energy use: 55,867 Btu/ft^2
89,177 Btu/ft^2 (base case)

Climate: 8,158 heating degree days; 585 cooling degree days

Insolation: 1,170 Btu/ft^2/day (annual average)

Energy costs: Natural gas — $5.63/MMBtu; Electricity — $0.06/kWh

Solar design elements: Building in the overall shape of a "V," with point and slope to the north to minimize exposure to northerly winds. The windowless north wall adjoins another building, and the northwest wall is heavily planted and bermed. Siting is toward the north edge.
Increased south glass in public areas
Clerestory in confidential zone
• Direct-gain walls and floor enhanced daylight distribution
• Baffles
• Adjustable blinds
• Light interior colors
Insulation
• R-38 walls and R-46 roof
• Concept of a low-mass, tight and highly insulated "thermal bottle"
• Automated solar shades and glazing insulation
Night ventilation to flush daytime heat gain

Other energy elements:
Earth berming
Photocell controls artificial ambient lighting with a time-clock delay to prevent cycling on cloudy days
Discretionary task and ambient lighting in the offices
High velocity air delivery with a multizone air handler
HVAC system with time clock with automatic setbacks and setups
Cooling system (direct exchange unit) with inside and outside thermostats for a proper mix of induced ventilation and chilling

Architect: Joe Thornstenson
Gene E. Hickey and Associates, Inc. Edina, MN

Solar designer and instrumentation:
John Weidt Associates, Inc. Chaska, MN

Monitoring period: October 1982-September 1983

Data collected:
Energy consumption by fans, electric lights, hot water, natural gas, and miscellaneous circuits
Horizontal insulation
Wind speed
Indoor temperatures
Ambient temperatures

Data acquisition system: In December 1983, an Aeolian Kinetics PDL-24 data acquisition system was installed in the building to collect hourly data. The results of detailed energy performance analyses presented in this report were determined using the hourly data collected on the PDL-24 system during the period of January through August 1984.

SHELLY RIDGE GIRL SCOUT CENTER

Energy education was one of the primary objectives of the building task force that began planning for the Shelly Ridge Program Center in 1978. Task force members felt that the new Girl Scout center should make a clear statement about energy efficiency. They agreed that a solar design would be consistent with the traditional scouting mission of training children to be sensitive to nature and the environment. They also believed that a solar building would help Girl Scouts become adults who knew how to live with expensive energy.

MULTIPLE FUNCTIONAL REQUIREMENTS

Although energy efficiency was a primary objective of the task force, it was by no means the only one. In fact, some of the other building objectives would make it difficult to design a solar showpiece.

For one thing, the new center had to be "conventional" enough to provide a comfortable environment for inner-city children who rarely, if ever, leave the city. The task force wanted the girls to find an environment that would not be totally unfamiliar. One of the advantages of the Shelly Ridge site was that, despite its rural appearance and white-tail deer, it is accessible by local bus from Philadelphia. The convenient bus line meant that urban children without access to private transportation would be able to use the center and, perhaps for the first time, experience an unspoiled natural setting.

Despite its small size (about 5,700 ft^2), the program center would also have to be flexible enough to accommodate a variety of user groups who have different seasonal and daily-use requirements. Occupancy in the building could range from 350 Scout parents on a weekend to two or three staff preparing for an outing. But the main purpose of the building would be to provide indoor space for Scout troop activities during the school year. For nine months of the year, the center would be used primarily for after-school activities in the late afternoon and early evenings. Less frequently, the building would be used for morning and afternoon school programs and occasional Scout troop overnight trips. In the summer, the Shelly Ridge site would be used for a day camp. The program center would then serve mainly as an activity staging area, because the campers would spend most of their time outside during good weather. Limited indoor activity during the summer meant the center's cooling energy needs would be minimal. But the center's relatively low average occupancy would not help the building's main energy problem — wintertime space heating.

The program center was expected to be energy efficient and to make a visible solar design statement without appearing unconventional. It would have to serve important educational and ceremonial functions and be flexible enough to meet the varied needs of different users at different times. The center would have to address those objectives while relating to existing buildings and the utility network already on the site. Clearly, the complex set of objectives and constraints would present a great challenge for any design team.

HYBRID INDIRECT-GAIN PASSIVE DESIGN

The project architect, Frank Grauman, felt that some type of passive solar design would be the best way to meet the diverse design objectives established by the task force. It would provide a clear statement about energy and be a good way to help teach children about natural energy flows. Passive solar design would allow them to be aware of, and participate in, the building's energy system. The design team believed an active solar space heating system would offer the Girl Scouts less opportunity for participation and learning and would probably be more expensive.

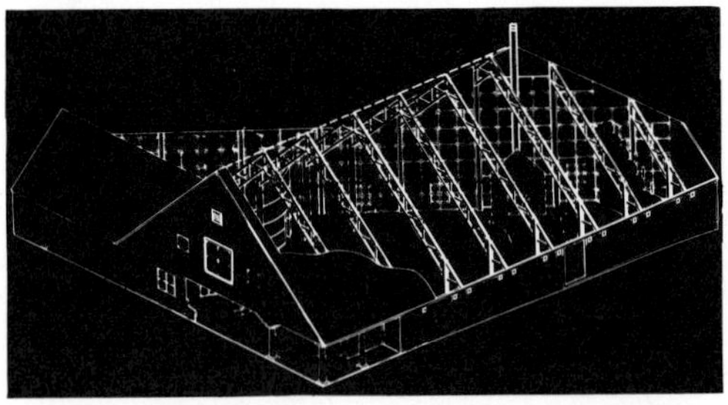

A hybrid system, mixing some direct-gain features with an indirect-gain mass wall, was chosen for the center (see Figure

Figure 3-5a. The cut-away isometric drawing showing an inside view of the south-facing solar wall.

Solar Building Saves Hard-Earned Cookie Money . . .

If the Shelly Ridge Program Center's solar design performs as anticipated, it should save the Girl Scouts the equivalent of 60,000 cookies per year. A similar structure without the same solar and conservation features would cost about $2,000 more to heat and light each year. Operating savings like that are especially important to nonprofit organizations that can't deduct energy expenses and have trouble raising the money to cover them. While the Girl Scout Council has found that foundations and corporations are often interested in supporting new construction projects, they are generally less willing to contribute money to cover the less glamorous operating expenses. Energy expenses for the Shelly Ridge Program Center must, therefore, be paid out of a tight operating budget that relies heavily on the proceeds of Girl Scout cookie sales.

The solar design of the program center had another unexpected financial benefit. Initially, the solar energy design features appeared economically unattractive for two reasons. First, the Girl Scouts would not be able to lower the building's capital costs because they would not be eligible for an investment tax credit. Second, it was feared that the solar design would make it more difficult to raise building funds from conservative foundations and corporations. Nan Mulford, the project fundraising director, recalled that in 1978 an independent fundraising consultant explicitly advised the task force to downplay the Center's solar features. The consultant believed that most foundation decision makers would avoid the project because they would see passive solar as an untested technology that was not likely to be cost-effective. Ms. Mulford discovered that in 1980, when the actual fundraising began, attitudes had changed. The fundraisers were surprised to learn that solar aspects of the building design were positive selling points. About 85% of the project's funding came from corporations and foundations, most of which were very much impressed by the center's passive solar design.

3-5a). A pure, direct-solar-gain passive system would provide a strong visual link with the wooded scenery outside the program center and be a good educational tool for allowing the Scouts to experience the changing energy flows of a passive solar system. But it would also present problems. A direct-gain design would make it difficult to darken rooms for audio-visual functions, temperature fluctuations could be uncomfortable, and glare might be a real problem. On the other hand, an indirect system would fit the expected occupancy pattern. With peak energy use expected during evenings, it would be important to establish a short thermal energy lag of several hours.

A FEW SUBTLE TWISTS

The basic configuration and orientation of the program center was determined early in the design process. The building would need to open up to the south to capture the sun and the expansive view best. A two-story solar aperture on the south side of the building would be large enough to provide heat and light without skylights or an extensive air distribution system. The northwest and northeast sides of the building would be shorter and lower so they would shed winter winds coming from those directions. These factors, plus the need to relate to the access road, utility network, and other buildings in the master plan, led to development of the triangular shape illustrated in the site plan (see Figure 3-5b).

The solar wall, the dominant energy feature of the center, received a great deal of analytical attention and underwent quite a few design revisions. The first variation on the basic concept, illustrated in Figure 3-5c(A), was made because of a desire to integrate the building entrance with the passive design. The logical entrance to the building would be from the northeast or northwest, but a visitor entering from that direction would not be exposed to or involved with the solar wall. The design solution, shown in Figure 3-5c(B), involved breaking

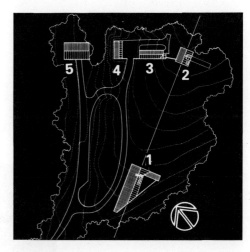

Figure 3-5b. Site Plan. The Girl Scout Program Center is one of several buildings, including the caretaker's residence, maintenance building, garage, and barn.

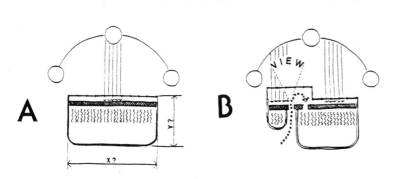
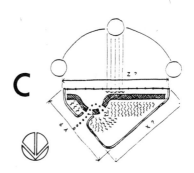

Figure 3-5c. Analytical design process.

155

the solar wall to establish an entrance sequence that brings the visitor through the solar space. The entrance sequence helps the visitor experience and understand the solar design as well as enjoy the southern scenic views. Refining the concept (see Figure 3-5c(C)) produced a meandering solar wall that maintained the building's compact external surface area, and brought the heating element closer to the north walls for better heat distribution.

The evolving passive solar design and the basic architectural program produced the floor plan displayed in Figure 3-5d. The main central space, rising two stories high, is open to accommodate large groups and allow for even ventilation and heat distribution. It is surrounded by smaller support areas: office, kitchen, storage areas, bathrooms, and so on. A multipurpose sleeping loft was added above the support areas.

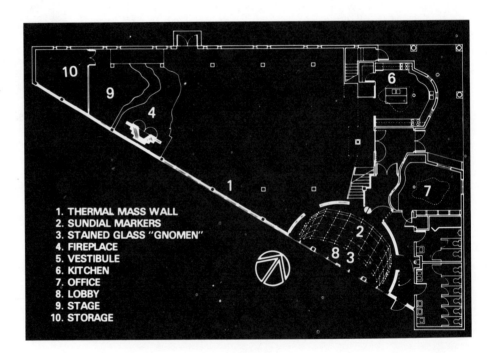

1. THERMAL MASS WALL
2. SUNDIAL MARKERS
3. STAINED GLASS "GNOMEN"
4. FIREPLACE
5. VESTIBULE
6. KITCHEN
7. OFFICE
8. LOBBY
9. STAGE
10. STORAGE

Figure 3-5d. Most of the Girl Scout Program Center's floor plan.

Although the basic passive strategy was established relatively early in the design process, a number of detail decisions remained to be made on specific design elements. The solar thermal wall underwent exhaustive analysis and was redesigned several times. Analysis showed that the original 24-in. absorbing wall would be too thick. It would impede the transmission of thermal energy, and create too long a time lag in energy delivery. A 10-in. wall, about the size of a standard residential thermal wall ("Trombe") system was proposed, but proved to be too thick. Trombe wall thickness studies using an energy simulation computer model indicated that an 8-in. wall would be the optimal size for thermal performance, but the studies also identified some trade-offs between solar performance and construction costs. Ultimately, a 4-in. wall was chosen because it would be less expensive to build and only 2% less efficient than the 8-in. wall. The shorter heat lag associated with the thinner wall also would better serve the building's heating needs. The final design called for a structural timber grid with 4-ft^2 brick panels. The 3-by-8-ft. timber system would visually and structurally integrate the solar wall with the rest of the building.

The building's daylighting plan also underwent a number of revisions as a result of architectural model testing. Originally, several small windows set low in the solar wall were proposed. But daylighting models showed that they alone would not adequately distribute natural light in the main meeting space. A suggestion was made to supplement the windows with glass set into the top part of the wall. Glazing set high in the wall would bring in more light without excessive glare, and actually improve the solar wall's thermal performance.

The computer model was used to test various combinations of thermal mass and glazing. The optimal plan, which was implemented, called for 860 ft^2 of thermal-wall brick panels with 960 ft^2 of clear glazing set in and above the wall. The glazing above the wall is double thickness and equipped with insulating shades to control heat loss and darken the room for audiovisual functions. The smaller windows, set lower in the solar wall for light and view, are triple-pane glass. The outside of the brick panels is glazed with Kalwall fiberglass panels. A system of crank-out awnings was designed to shade the solar wall. An analysis of the awning system showed it to be more efficient and less expensive than rigid overhang alternatives.

"PEOPLE-SIZE" SUNDIAL

The large solar sundial pictured in Figure 3-5e serves as the building's entrance and lobby. The sundial lobby concept fits well with the meandering solar wall and serves several functions. It symbolizes the solar nature of the building and helps Scouts learn about solar phenomena. It also complements the solar wall by bringing visitors through it, an unusual arrangement for a solar collecting wall. The lobby, with its fully glazed facade offering excellent views of the wooded areas, is an excellent indoor-outdoor transition space. As a direct-gain sunspace, the sundial lobby experiences a wider range of temperatures than normal, but the temperature fluctuations perform an educational function. In addition, because the lobby is separate from the main space and generally unoccupied, the temperature swings do not impair the building's general comfort and performance.

Figure 3-5e. The Girl Scout Program Center's life-sized sundial entrance. Visitors learn about solar energy while the sundial adds charm to the building.

ARCHITECTURAL EXCELLENCE, ENERGY EFFICIENCY

Two prestigious design awards attest to the architect's success in meeting the multifaceted design challenge of the Shelly Ridge Program Center. The International Solar Energy Society, in the first passive solar design competition, presented an award to the firm of Bohlin, Powell, Larkin and Cywinski. The firm also earned from the AIA's Philadelphia Chapter the Silver Medal—the AIA's highest design award for a building-in-progress.

Although measured energy-use data are available for just eight months (March through October), the trends established over that period suggest that the building's energy use is low and very close to the expected performance of 35,000 Btu/ft². As shown in Figure 3-5f, the Girl Scout center consumes about one-third less energy than a similar nonsolar building and about 10% less than a relatively energy-efficient BEPS building.

IMPRESSIVE ENERGY PERFORMANCE

An estimated two-thirds of the total annual energy budget is used during November through February. Space heating (electric resistance) is the largest end use, accounting for al-

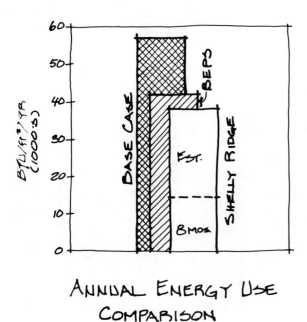

ANNUAL ENERGY USE COMPARISON

Figure 3-5f. Annual energy use comparison. The all-electric Girl Scout Program Center is one-third more efficient than a similar nonsolar building and has a 10% better performance than an energy-efficient BEPS building.

most two-thirds of total annual energy consumption, as shown in Figure 3-5g. (Eight months' measured data are also shown.) Lighting and miscellaneous end uses each account for less than one-fifth of yearly energy use. Heating energy is one-third less than that of the similar nonsolar building, while lighting energy consumption is almost two-thirds less.

The two end-use categories in which energy use is somewhat larger than expected are space "heat" and "other." Independently controlled electric-resistance heaters consumed excess heating energy. The heaters were used as a freeze-prevention measure for pipes located in unconditioned spaces. Due to the large building volume and low nighttime internal gains, the units ran in the summer, causing heating energy use to be recorded even during July and August, as shown in Figure 3-5h. This problem has been corrected. Energy consumption in the "other" category is skewed because the solar water heater uses significantly more energy than expected.

The Girl Scout center caretaker has full responsibility for controlling the building's energy systems and energy savings depend on the constant adjustment of the system thermostat. The caretaker, who resides on-site in a nearby house, has been conscientious about setting the seven-day time clock to accommodate the variation in occupancy patterns.

Despite the fact that occupancy varies in intensity and duration, and on a daily and weekly basis, the overall energy-use

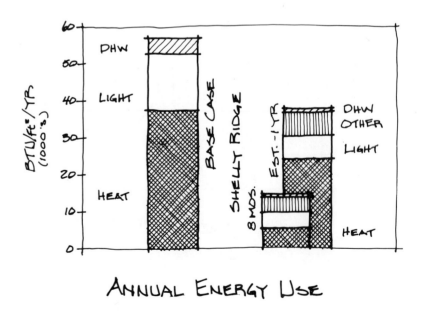

Figure 3-5g. Annual energy use. The Center consumes about one-third less space-heating energy and nearly two-thirds less lighting energy than a similar nonsolar building.

pattern is regular and close to the anticipated yearly patterns. This may occur because energy consumption is influenced more by solar gain and ambient temperatures than by internal gains. The building's large internal volume provides a large surface area that readily absorbs internal gains. The low-wattage, high-efficiency lighting is off during most daytime-use periods, reducing the typically large lighting impacts caused by irregular occupancy in commercial buildings. Solar gains also help regularize the diurnal energy pattern. The south aperture and Trombe wall are relatively large (each is about one-fifth of the center's floor area) allowing daily solar gain to contribute to a regular pattern of energy use over the course of a year.

OVERALL PERFORMANCE

Building users say they find the building architecturally beautiful. They also report the Girl Scout Program Center meets all its programmatic objectives and has generated unexpected operating income. The community knows the building so well and finds it so attractive that the Girl Scouts of Greater Philadelphia is able to rent the building during most of each summer at a modest fee without actively seeking rentals. Minor problems with summer ventilation, periodic winter overheating, and cool-morning chilliness have been corrected as the caretaker has become more familiar with the HVAC system operation and the optimum weekly thermostat setpoints. However, the building's hard surfaces create a noise problem during heavy occupancy.

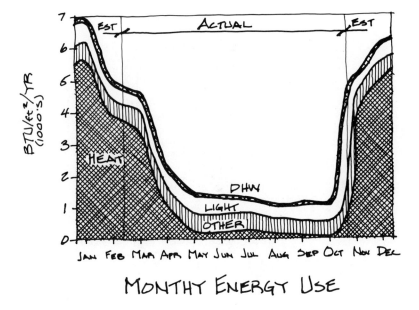

MONTHY ENERGY USE

Figure 3-5h. Monthly energy use. Nearly three-fourths of the annual heating energy budget is used from November through February, the height of school year activities at the Girl Scout center.

161

REDUCED UTILITY BILLS

Estimated energy costs are $0.83/ft^2$ for a total annual average energy cost savings of about one-third ($0.42/ft^2$) over the similar nonsolar building. (See Figure 3-5i, which also shows actual energy costs for eight months.) The Girl Scout center costs about 10% less to operate than the BEPS building. Heating energy costs are almost two-thirds of the total annual energy cost, as shown in Figure 3-5j.

The total construction cost was $85/ft^2 in 1983 dollars, as shown in Figure 3-5k. Compared to community centers of the same size and with the same construction characteristics, the Girl Scout center was fairly expensive. The center cost almost one-fifth more than the average for high-quality community centers. One reason is that many of the building's features are hand-crafted, which required skilled contractors and unusual workmanship. Examples include the hundreds of individually painted ceramic tiles around the fireplace and the treatment of the sundial gnomon in the entry space.

In addition, first costs are a relatively minor concern to the Girl Scouts because, as a nonprofit organization, raising construction funds is easier than raising operating funds. In fact, more construction funds were raised than were expected. Many contributors were impressed with the design's passive solar features as well as its architectural merits.

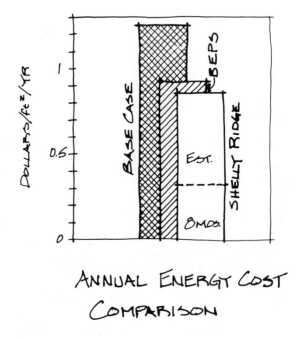

Figure 3-5i. Annual energy cost comparison. Energy costs track energy use closely in the all-electric building, with the Girl Scout center costing one-third and 10% less to operate than the similar nonsolar buildings, respectively.

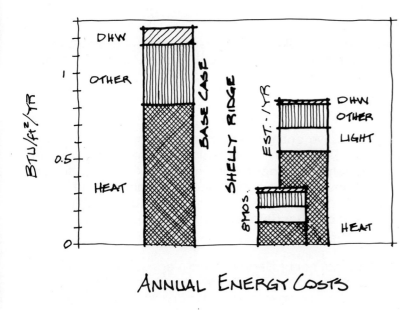

Figure 3-5j. Annual energy costs. Space heat costs companies nearly two-thirds of the average annual energy costs at the Girl Scout center.

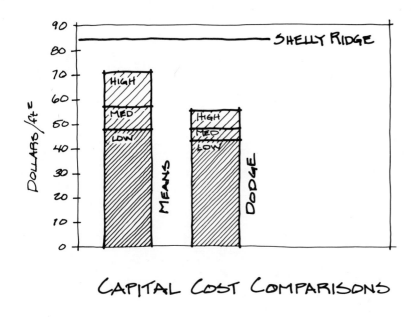

Figure 3-5k. Capital cost comparisons. At $85/ft², the Girl Scout center was 20% more expensive to build than the 1983 highest-average-cost, similar building.

163

SUMMARY

The Shelly Ridge Girl Scout Center is a very successful project. Its design process offers a textbook example of proper energy-efficient design. Analysis accompanied intuition throughout design development and resulted in a building that is both artistically and technically adept.

The impressive energy performance is largely the result of computer simulation, which helped arrive at the thin, un-vented Trombe wall approach. The cost of the computer runs and related analyses contributed significantly to the design costs. The deceptively simple and understated architectural design emphasizes detail and workmanship, which make the center a delight to use.

The fact that nonprofit groups find it easier to raise construction funds than operating funds suggests that innovative, energy-efficient architecture may be an excellent long-term investment for nonprofit organizations such as the Girl Scouts.

PROJECT SUMMARY
SHELLY RIDGE GIRL SCOUT CENTER

Building type: Two-story recreation and public assembly facility

Floor area: 5,700 ft^2

Location: Philadelphia, PA

Owner: Girl Scouts of Greater Philadelphia

Design completed: July 1981

Construction started: August 1981

Occupancy: Summer: mid-day peak, 125 people; morning peak, about 25; evening peak, almost 70; school year: dominated by early evening programs with 5:00 p.m. peak of 150; about 25 maximum during other times.

Construction costs: $85/ft^2

Annual energy use: 38,000 Btu/ft^2 (estimated); 57,000 Btu/ft^2 (base case)

Climate:
4,864 heating degree days/yr
1,103 cooling degree days/yr

Insolation: 1169 Btu/ft^2/day (annual average)

Energy cost: Electricity — $22/MMBtu

Solar design elements:
861-ft^2 thermal wall for indirect heating (4-in. thick brick panels)
410-ft^2 double glazing above the thermal wall for daylighting
558-ft^2 direct-gain sun space (triple glazing, no insulation)
Movable awnings for thermal wall shading
4-in. slab concrete floor for thermal storage
Minimal north-side wall and window area
Active solar system for hot water

Other energy elements:
No A/C system
General fluorescent lighting (1.72 W/ft^2)
Back-up electric resistance heating
10,000-cfm ventilation fan with infiltration shutters
R-27 walls (5.5-in. of batt insulation)
R-30 ceiling (9-in. of rigid insulation)

Architect: Bohlin, Powell, Larkin, Cywinski; Wilkes-Barre, PA

Solar designer: Burt, Hill, Kosar and Rittlemann Associates; Butler, PA

Monitoring period:
March 1984-October 1984 (November-February energy use estimated)

Data collected:
Energy consumption by blowers, electric lights, hot water, and miscellaneous circuits
Horizontal insolation
Wind speed
Indoor temperatures
Ambient temperatures

RPI VISITOR CENTER

The visitor center at the Rensselaer Polytechnic Institute (RPI) is a "front door" to the university, a secure headquarters for the "campus cops," and a laboratory of energy-conscious design (see Figure 3-6a).

As a front door, the building site was carefully chosen at the intersection of a main campus walkway and the main highway to the university (see Figure 3-6b). As a home for the campus police, the building must operate 24 hours a day with controlled access at all times—just about the opposite of an open front door. As a laboratory for students of energy-conscious design, the building must illustrate methods of saving energy whether the front door is open or not.

The integration of these three distinctly different — and at times contradictory — functions was the principal goal of the design team. At present, the building has accomplished at

Figure 3-6a. South-facing glass on the RPI Visitor Center, Rensselaer Polytechnic Institute.

Figure 3-6b. Visitor Center site at intersection of New York Route 7 and campus pedestrian bridge.

least two of its goals — it is operating comfortably as both a visitor center and a home for the campus police. It will be some time, however, before enough performance information is available to know if both have been accomplished in the context of reduced energy use.

HEATING PROBLEM, PASSIVE SOLUTION

In spite of some commercial uses (conference rooms, reception area, offices, employee locker rooms), the modest size and low occupancy of this building (5,200 ft²) causes it to be climate- or "skin"-dominated rather than internal-load-dominated. Also, the climate of Troy, New York (6,900 heating degree days and 600 cooling degree days), causes the building to have primarily a heating problem. There are enough warm days, however, to demand that cooling not be ignored.

Because the building requires more heating than cooling, the design team decided to choose between two passive solar heating systems — a direct-gain approach and an indirect-gain approach. The direct-gain approach eventually lost out for two reasons. First, the team believed that a direct-gain system would result in temperature swings that would be unacceptable to office occupants. Second, the team believed that the ultraviolet rays of the sun would cause costly damage to office furnishings.

The indirect-gain approach eventually settled on by the design team was a passive solar sunspace (see Figure 3-6c). This solution is clearly the most striking solar feature of the building with 680 ft² of glass extending the full length of the building's

Figure 3-6c. Sunspace/multipurpose room. South glass at right and windows onto offices at left.

south face. Sunshine strikes either a mass floor (6-in. slab-on-grade with quarry tile) or a mass wall (concrete block with brick veneer). The multipurpose reception area is approximately 900 ft^2 with a mass wall approximately the same area as the south glass.

At first glance, this sunspace is not what one might expect. For example, a high vertical wall section (like a clerestory) faces north instead of south (and is not glazed). Instead of opening to the sun like an amphitheater, the sunspace appears to be turning a cold metallic shoulder (the sunspace roof) to the sun. And finally, unlike what might be expected, there is almost no overhang extending over the south glazing. Although these features may seem odd, the theory behind each is reasonable.

First, the unusually shaped ceiling above the sunspace is both an area to store stratified heat and a plenum for circulating air through the sunspace. The upper portion of the north wall of the sunspace is not used for thermal storage (because it is never in direct sunlight) and thus does not need to be a mass wall. It is made of 2-by-6-in. frame construction with drywall interior finish as are most of the building's exterior walls.

Second, the long sloping roof over the sunspace is an overhang itself — protecting the mass wall and a portion of the mass floor from high summer sun. The roof is designed to allow sun rays from low winter sun to enter the sunspace. The building intends to turn a cold metallic shoulder to the sun, but only in the summer when solar heat gains are not wanted.

Finally, the entire sunspace has insulated curtains, which can be drawn at night to reduce heat losses through the glass or during the day to reduce solar heat gains. This curtain makes a large exterior overhang unnecessary.

The resulting sunspace is a multi-use space. From the occupants' point of view, it is a reception area, an overflow space for large meetings, and a pleasant room full of plants providing a lovely view of the campus. From a thermal point of view, the sunspace is a heat source for passive heating, a heat sink for passive cooling, and a buffer zone between interior and exterior temperatures. From a lighting point of view, the sunspace is a source of daylight to the interior offices located beyond the north wall of the sunspace.

PASSIVE FEATURES

Although the sunspace is the largest passive solar feature of the building, two other passive features have a striking impact on the final design. First, a tower over the main entrance serves as a source of daylight to the entry below, a so-called "chimney" to enhance natural ventilation, and an actual chimney for the entryway fireplace (see Figures 3-6d and 3-6e). In summer (the season during which these pictures were taken), vents opened from the sunspace into the "chimney" used for natural ventilation can be fan-assisted, as shown. In winter, the vents are closed, and the "real" smoke-pipe chimney is used to vent the fireplace below. The fireplace is installed with glass doors, a heat circulating insert, and an outside air supply to ensure maximum efficiency and to prevent uncontrolled loss of air from the space.

Figure 3-6d. Photos illustrating the combination of an architectural "chimney" for natural ventilation off the sunspace and a real chimney for venting a fireplace in the entryway.

Figure 3-6e. West entrance to the Visitor Center. Note the combined chimneys.

Figure 3-6f. Skylights over the central corridor. They are shaded in summer (as shown), and converted to reflectors to enhance solar gains in winter.

The other significant passive feature influencing design is a row of skylights located over the central corridor (see Figure 3-6f). These skylights provide daylight to the corridor and, in winter, some direct solar heat gain to rooms in the rear of the building. The skylights are equipped with movable reflector/shades, which are adjusted to increase the penetration of winter sun into the building (for heat) or to shade against summer sun to decrease unwanted solar gains. The shades are adjusted manually as needed depending on the time of year.

SOLAR FEATURES

Although the distinction between passive solar design and conservation is often difficult to make, this building has many energy-conserving features, which complement the basic passive design:

- Heavy insulation (R-23 to R-27 in the walls; R-30 to R-38 in the roof)
- Earth berming and reduced glazing on the north facade
- Occupied spaces in the core with buffer spaces on the perimeter (Figure 3-6g)
- Evergreens protecting the northern perimeter
- Double entry doors
- Fluorescent ambient lighting fixtures and task lighting
- Variable air volume HVAC system with enthalpy controls
- Automated energy-management system

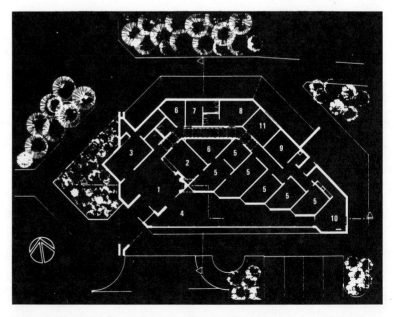

Figure 3-6g. Visitor Center site plan. The plan illustrates how occasionally occupied spaces buffer interior offices: (1) Lobby reception; (2) Central/reception; (3) Conference; (4) Sunspace; (5) Office; (6) Storage; (7) Women's Lockers; (8) Men's Lockers; (9) Mechanical room; (10) Lounge; (11) Workroom.

170

Although the list of passive solar and conservation features is long, the features have been integrated into a single building design that meets the objectives of the design team. For example, according to Dr. Walter Kroner, solar design consultant and RPI faculty member, "the appearance of masonry, metal roofing, and large expanses of glass sets the building apart from other campus buildings and supports the concept of pointing out this building as the 'front door' or entrance to the campus." The tower (illuminated at night) also serves as a strong visual focus for a visitor unfamiliar with the campus.

Once inside the building, the theme of "welcome" is continued by a combination of energy features and interior design. The visitor is met by sunlight (from the tower and sunspace), plants (in the sunspace), a fireplace, and the warm feeling of wood. This first impression is enhanced by a view of the surrounding campus.

ENERGY LABORATORY

This building, and the way in which it was designed, differs from typical practice because of the university context provided by RPI. For example, the entire design process was subject to public review. In fact, it was during this review process that the commitment was made to design an energy-efficient building.

Second, the entire design team, with the exception of a consulting engineering firm, was taken from the school's faculty. The project became an exercise in interdepartmental faculty cooperation and a learning experience for both faculty and students. For example, a simulation model was developed solely for the analysis of this building — a valuable learning experience not usually available to the general practitioner.

Another example of learning-in-progress is the wide variety of heating and cooling systems in the building:

- Indirect passive solar heating (sunspace)
- Direct passive solar heating (below skylights)
- Fan coil heating (main ducts)
- Individual radiant heating (in each office)
- Fireplace heat (entryway)
- Natural and fan-assisted ventilation (tower)
- Conventional (direct expansion) refrigeration (overall)
- 12 variable air volume (VAV) systems

It goes without saying that there must be some redundancy in all of this equipment. On the other hand, the building is, in itself, a learning experience for those who operate it and is part of a DOE program designed to encourage experimentation. There are many possible combinations of the various systems described above. At present, the building can be controlled in at least six significantly different operating modes. But it is precisely the combinations and configurations of these components that will demonstrate which system integration strategies work and which do not. It will be some time before performance data will be available to make this determination.

ENERGY PERFORMANCE SATISFACTORY

The RPI Visitor Center uses 39% less energy per ft^2 than a similar, nonsolar building (i.e., the base case) and about 8% more than a relatively energy-efficient BEPS building (Figure 3-6h). (The BEPS building simulation assumed an 8-hour-per-day occupancy, not the actual 24-hour-per-day schedule.) Heating, cooling, and lighting together account for about two-thirds of the annual energy use, as shown in Figure 3-6i. The "fans" and "other" end-use categories make up the remaining third. Heating energy use is slightly more than half that of the base case (a small police station). Cooling energy use is about 40% of that of the base case; lighting energy use, one-third less.

Most of the annual energy savings relative to the base case are attributable to reduced heating needs. The energy-use profiles shown in Figure 3-6j indicate that heating energy use is quite low considering the severity of the winters (6,900 heating degree days).

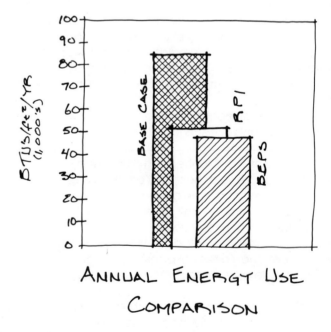

Figure 3-6h.

172

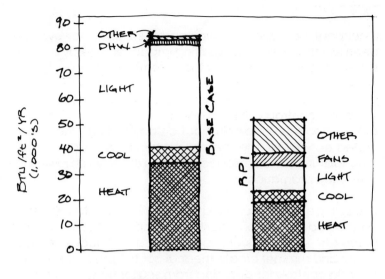

ANNUAL ENERGY USE

Figure 3-6i.

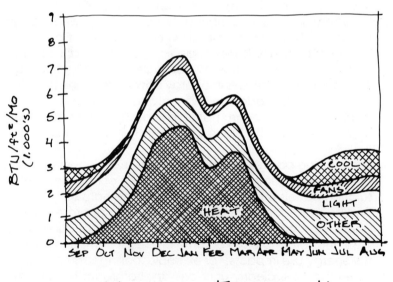

MONTHLY ENERGY USE

Figure 3-6j.

173

OCCUPANT IMPACT

Occupant operation of the energy systems, however, has been less than ideal; the resulting impact on energy use, substantial. Many users consider the systems too complex to keep track of, particularly because most of the systems serve multiple functions. For example, while the insulating shades in the sunspace control both heat gain and loss, the position of the shades also has a major impact on daylighting. Under automated conditions, the thermal curtain is lowered when the temperature in the sunspace exceeds 85° F, which lowers the light levels dramatically.

The split between manual and automatic control systems is considered inappropriate by many occupants. For example, automatic seasonal switching of operating modes between winter and summer create thermal control problems. The automatic controls for switching from season to season are unable to respond to unpredictable weather on a daily basis or during the swing seasons. As a result, complaints of discomfort are frequent.

Because of complaints, operating procedures were modified; key automated systems are now under manual control. The energy-consumption impacts of changing major energy systems from automatic to manual, however, have been substantial. Manual control of summer/winter operation allows effective passive systems to be bypassed. Placing insulating shades under manual control has resulted in decreased lighting loads but significant increases in energy consumption in other end-use categories. In addition, manual control of thermostats has increased energy consumption because the thermostat settings are consistently higher (or lower) than specified.

Some of the passive systems are unwieldy or inconvenient to operate. For example, manual operation of hallway night insulation panels is hampered because the hardware is faulty and because the panels are too heavy to operate easily. In addition, occupants simply forget proper procedures, leading to inappropriate use of some energy systems and substantial energy-use impacts. For example, ceiling lights are left on when they are clearly unnecessary. Bathroom exhaust fans are left on constantly. Movable insulation often is not used properly. Doors between conditioned and unconditioned zones are left open. When the fireplace is used, the glass doors are left open, which increases heat loss.

Several of the spaces in the visitor center were converted to functions not anticipated in the design program. These changes increase energy use and adversely affect occupant comfort. For example, the sunspace is often used as a classroom, which necessitates closing the insulating shades to prevent glare and overheating. Closing the shades, however, significantly reduces solar gain and daylight to the office spaces.

174

Several unconditioned areas intended as buffer zones were either converted to regular office uses or used more heavily than expected, and comfort conditions were difficult to achieve in these rooms. In addition, some usage patterns were unanticipated, particularly extended use of the front entrance (which tripled the infiltration rate) and heavy use of the locker rooms and lounge areas.

As a result of environmental control system difficulties, more than a third of the full-time occupants report being frequently uncomfortable. Complaints of discomfort have been particularly frequent in the winter. From 50% to 100% of the building users have reported being too cool, especially in the conference room and lobby and newly converted office spaces in several storage areas.

SAVINGS IN UTILITY BILLS

The energy costs shown in Figure 3-6k track energy use closely in the all-electric building. Visitor center energy costs are 10% less than those of the base case and about 10% more than those of the BEPS building. At electricity prices of $14.65/MMBtu, this amounts to a total annual average energy savings of about $500.

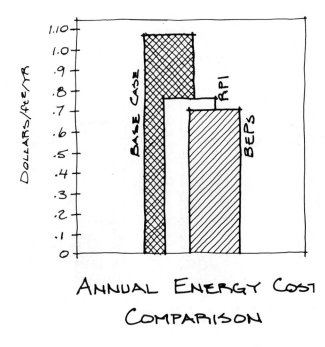

Figure 3-6k.

175

The energy cost breakdown is shown in Figure 3-6l. The savings achieved are due to reduced heating, lighting, and cooling energy use. Together these end uses account for more than 90% of the base case energy costs but only two-thirds of visitor center energy costs. The savings are somewhat offset by the combined energy costs in the "fans" and "other" categories. Total monthly electric costs are about $330.

The total cost of the RPI Visitor Center is $81/ft². As shown in Figure 3-6m, this is relatively high, compared to the industry average for small police stations constructed in 1981. The "medium" costs in Figure 3-6m indicate that half of the similar buildings built in 1981 cost more than $74/ft² to $75/ft², and half cost less. The RPI Visitor Center falls into the "high" category, which indicates that three-fourths of the comparable buildings were less expensive to build.

SUMMARY

The performance of this building suggests that occupants will actively seek their own level of comfort. People determine energy consumption more than building design and construction, regardless of established standards, rules, or procedures. Although comfort is taken for granted by occupants, it is one of the most important issues confronting designers of innovative, energy-efficient buildings.

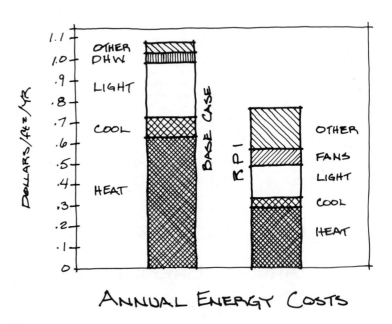

Figure 3-6l.

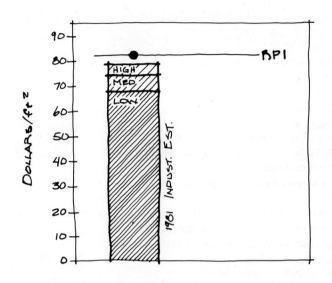

CAPITAL COST COMPARISONS

Figure 3-6m.

177

PROJECT SUMMARY
RPI VISITOR CENTER

Building type: Multipurpose visitor center with office space

Floor area: 5,200 ft²

Location: Troy, NY

Owner: Rensselaer Polytechnic Institute

Occupancy: Winter 1981
General visitors: 8 to 5, seven days/week
Campus police: 24 hours per day, seven days/week

Construction costs: $81/ft²

Annual energy use: 28,500 Btu/ft²/yr (projected); 85,000 Btu/ft²/yr (base case)

Climate: 6,900 heating degree days/yr; 600 cooling degree days/yr

Insolation: 1,129 Btu/ft²/day annual average

Energy costs: Electricity — $14.65/MMBtu ($0.05/kWh)

Solar design elements:
Sunspace (indirect gain)
680 ft² of south glass
900-ft² mass floor (6-in. slab on-grade and quarry tile)
700-ft² mass wall (concrete block with brick veneer)
Earth berming on building's north side
Fan-assisted natural ventilation with night refreshing of building
Solar shading
Skylights with movable shades
Clerestories on north wall
2-by-6-in. frame construction with R-23 to R-27 walls

Other design elements: Low occupancy "buffer" spaces on building perimeter
Double entry doors
Variable air volume HVAC
Heat-circulating fireplace
Heating: back-up 360 MBtuh (output) gas-fired boiler, 75% efficient
Cooling: back-up 240 MBtuh direct exchange unit (2.5 COP), 18,400 cfm outside air fan system with 50 fpm supply
Distribution: 7-zone air system, 8,000 cfm constant volume air handled with 100% economizer capability
Controls: night thermostat for setback/startup, time clock on HVAC, inside/outside thermostats (cooling), manual switch for large-volume fan system

Architect: William Winslow, Troy, NY

Project coordinator/solar design consultant: Walter M. Kroner, Troy, NY

Monitoring period: January 1982–August 1984

Data collected: Energy consumption by heating, electric lights, cooling, and fans
Horizontal insolation
Wind speed
Indoor temperatures
Ambient temperatures

PHILADELPHIA MUNICIPAL AUTO SHOP

The design of an effective energy retrofit scheme was a matter of survival for Philadelphia's huge automobile maintenance facility, one of the most energy-inefficient municipal buildings in the city. An energy audit performed as part of a citywide program showed that the building was consuming a whopping 230,000 Btu/ft^2/yr — more than double the average of 96,000 Btu/ft^2/yr for facilities of the same type. The building's poor performance was not surprising. Many of the single-glazed steel casement windows were broken or inoperable, and the aging, oil-fired boilers were obsolete and needed to be replaced. Abandoning the building would have meant job losses for the neighborhood, but with the yearly energy bill running over $100,000, the city had little other choice unless cost-effective, energy retrofit measures could be found.

The most pressing need was to reduce space heating costs, which made up 80% of the annual energy budget. One opportunity the design team hoped to exploit was the solar heating potential offered by the enormous windows on the south and southeast walls (see Figure 3-7a). The 1,000 ft^2 of glazing on the southeast wall represented 70% of the southeast facade, and an additional 600 ft^2 was available on the south wall. Solar access to the windows was unimpeded, and, given the low-rise residential and light commercial character of the neighborhood, construction that would reduce solar access was not likely to occur on the empty lots adjacent to

Figure 3-7a. Philadelphia Municipal Auto Shop prior to retrofit.

the building. Since the building was rarely used at night, the primary heating needs occurred during the day and the southeastern exposure was ideal for providing rapid morning heat gain.

While passive solar strategies would help displace conventional fuels, it was clear that improved insulation levels would be needed to reduce the total heating load. Obviously, the broken windows needed to be replaced. High conductive losses at the windows also suggested that increasing window insulation value would be cost-effective, particularly in view of the substantial square footage. Major conductive losses also occurred at the roof, which was uninsulated, and overhead garage doors were a significant source of heat loss.

SOLAR WINDOW HEATER

Initial design efforts focused on window retrofit techniques, because a good window treatment strategy would simultaneously address many of the building's needs. Not only would it take advantage of solar heating and lighting opportunities, it would reduce conductive losses and infiltration.

At first it appeared that a window with integral thermal storage capabilities would be required because the building's industrial wood flooring, which has a low storage capability, made a direct-gain system infeasible. Several possible configurations involving phase change rods (filled with calcium chloride or other hydrated salts) and water walls were devised and analyzed. After an initial design review, it became clear that thermal storage would not be necessary or desirable because the building was not used at night.

Other than space and water heating, the only energy area that seemed ripe for efficiency improvements was lighting. Measures to enhance the performance of large clerestories, which ran the length of the top floor, looked promising. Improved window treatment and rehanging existing lighting fixtures could also help cut conventional lighting costs. Cooling did not offer any potential savings, because the building already relied on natural ventilation. The prevailing winds in summer were generally from the west-southwest, providing air flow through the southeast garage doors. Elevator shafts and stairwells on the northern and western sides of the building induced air flow through the doors as well, and workers in the building had no complaints about summer comfort levels.

One special requirement was that the retrofit equipment be vandalproof. The broken windows were a testament to problems in the neighborhood, and the city wanted to avoid the time and expense of making repeated repairs. The city sought a system that would require minimal maintenance, and it preferred passive over active solar techniques.

The selected window retrofit unit makes use of a metal radiant panel designed to transfer solar heat to the workplace (see Figure 3-7b). The choice of a unit that is primarily radiant rather than connective was dictated largely by the inability of existing design tools to model energy flows in the building. The huge volume and odd shapes of the interior spaces made air flow and stratification very significant factors, but they could not be simulated accurately. Analyses of alternative window designs using the Lawrence Berkeley Lab's BLAST computer code had shown that window units that transfer heat primarily by convection are consistently more efficient; however, trying to heat a large volume of air that might be subject to stratification was not considered realistic. Radiant units would control heat distribution more effectively by warming nearby objects and workers rather than the air. The radiant units also provided insulation at the outside surface that would reduce heat loss.

Essentially, the final design consists of a standard Kalwall insulating window modified to include the radiant panel, a damper, and a light shelf. The damper vents the space between the Kalwall and the metal panel during the summer, thereby inducing air flow to cool the radiant panels. Opening the vent in the spring and closing it in the fall are the only maintenance activities required to operate the windows. The metal radiant panel is perforated to allow light to penetrate, which cuts the glare from the window above.

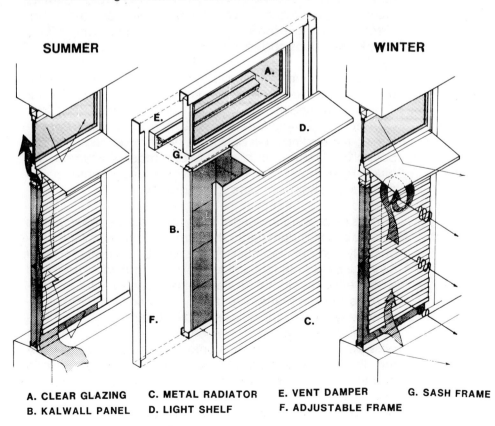

SUMMER WINTER

A. CLEAR GLAZING   C. METAL RADIATOR   E. VENT DAMPER   G. SASH FRAME
B. KALWALL PANEL   D. LIGHT SHELF   F. ADJUSTABLE FRAME

Figure 3-7b. Solar window retrofit unit.

Although the panel does not collect more solar thermal energy (in absolute terms) than that which enters a normal window, it more usefully distributes available energy and provides a warmer enclosing surface.

During cold weather a window is normally a radiant drain because it presents a colder surface to the space and its occupants than surrounding walls. By providing a warm radiant surface, the absorber panel converts the window from a source of discomfort and conductive loss to a source of warmth. Because radiant heat can provide satisfactory comfort conditions at lower air temperatures with more efficient and direct thermal distribution, the thermal benefits gained by adding the absorber plate to the window are considerable. The "window furnace" is 60% efficient at ambient temperatures of 10° F to 20° F, with the radiator panel often reaching temperatures of over 100° F on cold, sunny winter days.

Figure 3-7b shows the light shelf and fixed sash, which are located above the radiator. The light shelf consists of a brushed aluminum plate angled 9° below horizontal, which helps project natural light to the building's interior. Window units on the upper floors have operable sashes, but fixed sashes are used as an economy measure on the lower floors where workers have more access to the outside and are not as likely to experience a closed-in feeling. Fixed sashes also avoid potential maintenance problems with the window-opening mechanisms. To help make the windows more vandal resistant, a ⅛-in. acrylic shield was added to the design.

In addition to the light shelves and glare-reducing perforations, a reflective styrofoam-and-concrete roof covering was designed to enhance the lighting capabilities of the third-floor clerestories and improve the roof's thermal integrity. Repositioning the existing lights beside, rather than across, the repair bays allowed a reduction in the total number of fixtures. In addition, a fresh coat of white paint on the building's interior was expected to help distribute light more evenly.

Various steps were investigated to help reduce air incursions into the building. Here again, the inability to model air flows accurately complicated the design process. The designers and client decided not to consider a system that was costly and whose effect could not be determined, and to consider inexpensive systems that seemed likely to work. One of the inexpensive systems to be included was the automatic, weather-tightened overhead doors which would ensure the shortest possible exposure when cars entered or exited. Another system to be included was PVC-strip doors installed between heated and unheated spaces. Air exchangers, wing walls at doorways, air curtains, and several other options were deemed too expensive and were rejected.

Predicting the combined impacts of all the energy-saving measures was not an easy task, but even allowing for a substantial margin of uncertainty, the effect seemed likely to be dramatic. The designer's estimates indicated a drop in energy consumption from 230,000 Btu/ft^2/yr to 69,000 Btu/ft^2/yr with first-year cost savings of $85,000. Given the total project cost of $398,000, the simple payback period would be less than five years. The city decided, even before the auto shop retrofit had been completed, to investigate passive solar and energy-conserving designs for other municipal buildings.

Actual performance monitoring shows that the retrofit measures, including the metal absorber/radiator panels mounted behind the insulated portion of the new windows, reduce energy use by over 135,000 Btu/ft^2/yr. The garage requires about 60% less total energy per ft^2 than the original pre-retrofit garage, as shown in Figure 3-7a. By today's standards, however, the garage is still quite inefficient, using more than two and one-half times the energy of a BEPS building (see Figure 3-7c). Heating and miscellaneous electric end uses account for more than 90% of the annual energy use, as shown in Figure 3-7d. Heating energy use is about two and one-half times less than the original pre-retrofit garage, which was drafty and

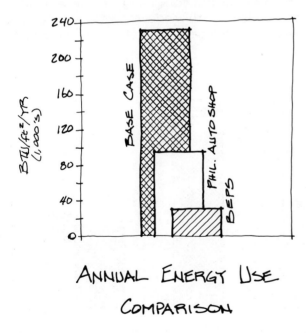

ANNUAL ENERGY USE

COMPARISON

Figure 3-7c. Annual energy use comparison. The magnitude of improvements in performance over the pre-retrofit building is credited mainly to conservation.

uninsulated. Although heating energy use is the greatest source of energy savings, lighting loads are very low in both buildings (see Figure 3-7d) because of infrequent night occupancy, large windows, and the building's southeastern orientation. Both the daytime-only use and the orientation enhance the value of daylight admitted to the building.

Energy-use patterns for the 12 months of August 1983 through July 1984 are shown in Figure 3-7e. Although the energy retrofit considerably reduces conductive losses, the large monthly heating needs may be traced to envelope and infiltration losses in the old (c. 1914) masonry structure. Auxiliary heating energy use is high even though operation of a standard oil-fired heating system was cut by more than a third. This indicates the persistence of sizable envelope losses. Figure 3-7e, for example, shows that 90% of total annual energy use occurs during the six months of November through April, and heating accounts for over 90% of that energy use. By comparison, energy consumption for other end uses shown in Figure 3-7e is very small and stable.

RADIANT WINDOWS, RADIANT HEATING SYSTEM

Generally, the occupants appreciate the changes to the garage, especially the new windows and reflective white paint used to enhance natural lighting. Pinhole perforations in the absorber plate of each window furnace reduce the contrast between the clear glazing and the surrounding walls by

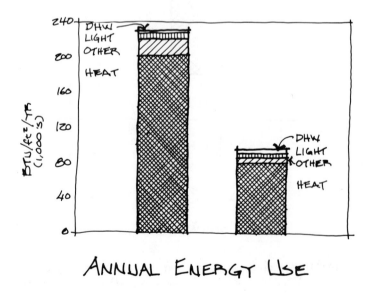

Figure 3-7d. Annual energy use. Reduced space heating loads account for most of the energy savings.

producing a diffused glow over the panel. Although extremely effective in reducing glare on bright days, the permanent window panel assembly diminishes the amount of natural sky light admitted to the interior on overcast days. If the panel were adjustable, the garage interior could receive more daylight on cloudy days.

The principal complaint about the energy retrofit relates to the gas-fired radiant heating system in each work space. The systems interact with petrochemicals in the air and cause air pollution, a condition exacerbated by the tighter envelope. The pollution problem, however, is being mitigated by a recirculating, air-cleaning system that removes odors and particulates.

The radiant heating strategy also causes some discomfort because large areas of the garage remain cool. Like a room with a fireplace, the side nearest the radiant source receives all the heat, while the side away from the source remains cold.

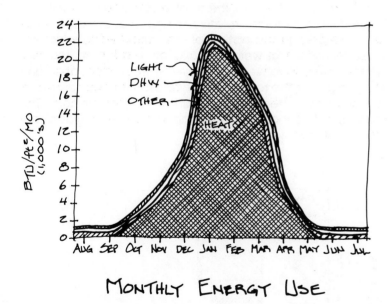

MONTHLY ENERGY USE

Figure 3-7e. Monthly energy use. Compared to the volume-driven space heating load, other end uses are almost insignificant.

LOW UTILITY BILLS

As shown in Figure 3-7f, energy costs are about 60% less than the bills for the original garage. Heating costs make up more than half the yearly energy bill, but are still two and one-half times less than the space heating costs of the old garage. "Other" end uses (e.g., blowers and various appliances) account for one-fourth of the total annual costs, but are also two and one-half times less than the original, pre-retrofit garage. Together, the "heat" and "other" end-use categories yield the largest cost savings. Lighting costs are slightly more than half of the original garage's lighting costs, but less than one-fifth of the post-retrofit energy bill. Water heating costs (electric for DHW, gas for industrial uses) are twice the pre-retrofit hot water costs at $0.04, but are still a small proportion of the total annual energy bill at less than 5%.

The estimated capital costs of the energy retrofit package are shown in Figure 3-7g. At $4.11/ft², the conservation features account for about half the total reconstruction costs of $8.26/ft². The window furnaces were the big ticket items at slightly over $2/ft², about half of the total retrofit energy package. Part of the reason for the relatively high replacement window costs is related to the nature of renovation work, which requires demolition as well as installation. In addition, the new windows are innovative and required custom fabrication and fitting. Together the roof insulation and radiant window panel assembly accounted for three-fourths of the retrofit costs. The white paint to enhance daylighting of the interior was about one-fifth of the total cost.

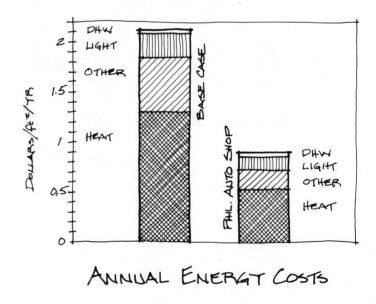

ANNUAL ENERGY COSTS

Figure 3-7f. Annual energy costs. Reduced energy use for space heating and miscellaneous electric loads lead to the largest operating cost savings.

186

Total annual average savings of almost $70,000 ($1.23/ft^2/yr.) makes the energy retrofit an attractive investment for the city. The simple payback of the energy investment alone is less than three and one-half years, with the total construction payback less than seven years. For an institutional client, the retrofit is an exceptional investment. Given the cost of new construction to replace the old garage, the project is an even more impressive investment.

SUMMARY

The success of this retrofit project suggests that choosing an energy solution may be strongly affected by the size of the conditioned space. The envelope-based solutions for Philadelphia's municipal garage provide comfort and reduce utility bills. The overhead door and the plastic strip doors help compartmentalize the large volume, thereby reducing infiltration losses and enhancing the effectiveness of the radiant heat sources. The project demonstrates that conservation is a cost-effective and essential approach to a successful retrofit project. Correctly defining the building's energy problems and opportunities at the outset led to the development of an appropriate and clever solution that achieved the project's main objectives.

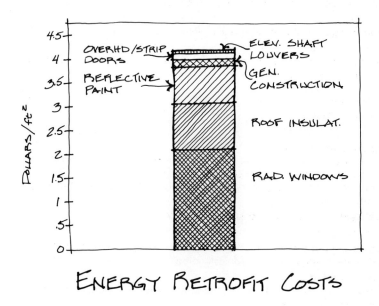

ENERGY RETROFIT COSTS

Figure 3-7g. Energy retrofit costs. The energy-related retrofit costs were half the total rehabilitation costs.

187

PROJECT SUMMARY
PHILADELPHIA MUNICIPAL AUTO SHOP

Building type: Automobile maintenance facility

Floor area: 57,000 ft^2

Location: Philadelphia, PA

Owner: City of Philadelphia

Design completed: August 1981

Construction started: October 1982

Occupancy: Daytime only

Construction costs: $8.25/ft^2 total

Annual energy use: 69 MMBtu/ft^2/yr (projected);
230 MMBtu/ft^2 (base case)

Climate:
4,864 heating degree days
1,103 cooling degree days

Insolation: 1,169 Btu/ft^2/day (annual average)

Solar design elements:
Retrofit solar window unit to provide radiant space heating, daylighting, and ventilation and glare control
Styrofoam and concrete roof covering to increase reflectance of daylighting and provide thermal insulation

Other energy elements:
Motion-sensitive, automatic, and weather-tightened overhead doors
PVC-strip doors between heated and unheated spaces
Aluminum louvers to permit summer venting through elevator shaft
Gas-fired radiant heating units for back-up heating

Architect: Charles Burnette & Associates;
Philadelphia, PA

Solar designer: Charles Burnette & Associates;
Philadelphia, PA

Monitoring period: August 1983-July 1984

Data collected:
Energy consumption by blowers, electric lights, hot water, natural gas/oil, and miscellaneous circuits
Horizontal insolation
Electric lights
Indoor temperatures
Ambient temperatures

Other energy elements:
Three-zone, gas-fired hydronic heating system with wall-fin radiation (forced air assist in assembly room for destratification)
Central A/C (office wing, entry lounge); incremental, wall-mounted heat pumps (crafts wing)

Architect: The Paul Partnership; New York, NY

Solar designer: The Paul Partnership; New York, NY

Monitoring period: January 1984-September 1984 (October-through-December energy use has been estimated)

Data collected:
Energy consumption by fans, electric lights, hot water, natural gas, and miscellaneous circuits
Horizontal insolation
Wind speed
Indoor temperatures
Ambient temperatures

ESSEX-DORSEY SENIOR CENTER

Standard architectural practice doesn't often require designers to consider the physical and psychological comfort needs of older people. In designing the Essex-Dorsey Senior Center, however, The Paul Partnership had to be particularly sensitive to the needs of the elderly. The facility, completed in February 1983, was designed exclusively for senior citizens and was expected to meet most of the residents' comfort needs with passive solar techniques. (See Figure 3-8a.)

The architectural objective was to preserve two 3,000-ft^2 Victorian schoolhouses located on the site and to incorporate the schoolhouses into one 13,000-ft^2 unified structure by adding another 7,000 ft^2. The original concept was to expand and upgrade the facility, using the old schoolhouses as the centerpiece of the design. The schoolhouses were identical woodframe buildings constructed around 1900 and were considered to be of historic value. Since many of the senior citizens had attended school in them, sentiment for the old buildings was strong and it was decided to maintain the integrity of the facades.

The energy design objective was to reduce energy use by about 50% over the base case, which was designated as a typical nonsolar community center in Washington, D.C. This would mean using 86,000 Btu/ft^2/yr in nonrenewable energy. The energy priorities were cooling, lighting, and, to a lesser extent, heating. The basic energy design concept involved developing a structure that could be opened to summer breezes and closed tightly in the winter, providing natural lighting year-round. The existing schoolhouses, which were 30 ft. apart, provided the basic ingredients for achieving good ventilation and natural lighting. The ceilings were 11 ft. high; the windows, 6 ft.

Figure 3-8a. View of the center from the southeast.

189

The initial design stages were intuitive, rather than analytical. The designers were concerned that if they used analytical design methods at the outset, the set of alternative design solutions would be limited and, possibly, predetermined. Energy computations were used only to verify intuitive design decisions during the schematic phase of the project. After the schematic designs were developed, the design team calculated heating loads according to the heating-degree-day method and cooling loads according to the bin method.

Design concepts were explored by researching historical analogies. The purpose of the research, however, was to understand concepts, not to transplant architectural forms. The design team looked at climate adaptation in the vernacular architecture of two very old cultures — those of Sweden and Japan. Over the centuries, these two countries had adopted simple, straightforward approaches to designing with climate, and these approaches could be adapted to the Essex-Dorsey Senior Center.

The design team selected Sweden and Japan because the two countries developed culturally along strikingly similar lines despite the fact that they were once isolated from one another and the rest of the world. (The similarity is largely due to the cultural emphasis on nature rather than theology.) The design team felt the most important similarity between the two cultures was the simple, intuitively conceived designs that used "appropriate" indigenous techniques. Those techniques stressed the quality of relationships between buildings and their environments.

The design team was especially impressed with Japanese traditional architecture, and Oriental influences are apparent in the final design. The design team selected several major Swedish and Japanese design elements to be adapted to the center. They include the following:

- The sensitive, but different, uses of unadorned wood (Swedish and Japanese)
- Use of recessed entries to keep out drafts (Swedish)
- The "engawa" (veranda) used to provide shelter from the elements while allowing proximity to nature (Japanese)
- Emphasis on spatial continuity between interior and exterior and between public and private areas (Japanese)
- Methods for diffusing sunlight with wooden shades and paper "shoji" screens (Japanese)
- Courtyards that divide large buildings into wings and facilitate natural ventilation (Japanese)

NATURAL LIGHT, LANDSCAPING

A series of clear spatial relationships, beginning at the main entrance, provides a comfortable sense of timing to the center's patrons. By joining the two existing schoolhouses, the final design creates a new recessed entry that presents a continuous and symmetrical facade to the street. The new wing is located behind the schoolhouses and is L-shaped. (See Figure 3-8b.)

The new assembly room is separated from one of the existing buildings by an enclosed, landscaped courtyard. The courtyard is critical to the cross-flow ventilation scheme during the cooling season, and also serves as a light well for the office wing, social area, and assembly room. For summer ventilation, air is drawn under the two storage areas on the courtyard's southwest side and pulled through sliding glass doors in the new wing. For nighttime ventilation, the windows and doors facing the courtyard can be opened and the center's outside entries secured.

As a light well, the courtyard allowed the design team to achieve the full 40-ft. depth required in the assembly room and retain the existing schoolhouse windows' daylighting value to light the office wing. Awnings and built-in plant shelves controlled the glare from the large windows in the existing buildings. (See Figure 3-8c.)

The clerestory windows in the final design provide heat, natural light, and ventilation. The shed roofs of the entry/lounge

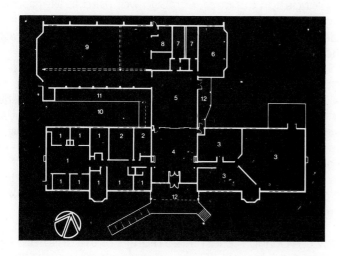

Figure 3-8b. Floor plan: (1) Offices; (2) Meeting rooms; (3) Crafts areas; (4) Reception/lounge; (5) Social area; (6) Game room; (7) Rest rooms; (8) Kitchen; (9) Assembly/dining; (10) Courtyard/garden; (11) Wood deck; (12) Porch.

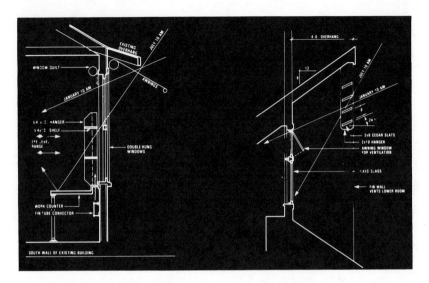

Figure 3-8c. Plant shelf detail.

area and assembly rooms are fitted with operable awning-type clerestory windows that allow exhaust of stratified air. Sunscreens and overhangs are designed to control glare at the new addition's clerestories. The southeast-facing clerestory, which runs the entire length of the new addition, is also intended to provide direct-gain heating in winter, as is the southwest-facing greenhouse attached to the assembly area.

Landscaping was considered integral to the design. All existing, mature deciduous trees were retained as part of the passive solar design concept. Bamboo was used to filter sunlight along the southwestern corner. The courtyard and Japanese garden provide summer cooling, winter sunlight, and a year-round area for quiet contemplation.

Measured whole-building energy performance data are available for only nine months. However, the trends established over that period suggest that the center's year-round energy performance is marginally better than that of the nonsolar base case. Including estimates of total energy use for the last three months of 1984, the annual total is less than that of the base case, but 90% more (or almost twice the energy) than that of a relatively energy-efficient BEPS building, as shown in Figure 3-8d.

Energy use during the last three months of the calendar year increases total annual energy consumption by over 50%, indicating excessive heating energy use. Heating energy consumption rises from two-thirds of the total energy budget at nine months to three-fourths of estimated total annual consumption at 12 months, as shown in Figure 3-8e. The energy-use profiles in Figure 3-8f show that about one-third of the total annual energy budget is consumed during October, November, and December. Space heating is almost four-fifths of the total energy use for those three months. Three-fourths of the center's total annual energy use is consumed during the heating season (six months); four-fifths of this amount is for space heating. Although space heating needs may have been underestimated for a 4,700-degree-day climate, system operation also may have caused excessive space heating energy use.

Energy use in categories other than heating, however, is very low in absolute terms. Nonheating energy use is virtually the same proportion of the total energy consumption at both 9 and 12 months. While space heating consumption is almost one-fifth higher than that of the base case, lighting and cool-

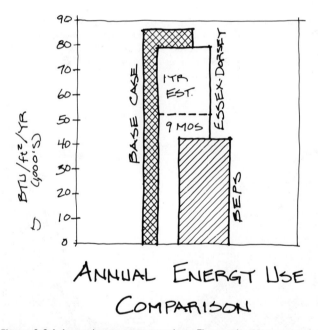

Figure 3-8d. Annual energy comparison. The center consumes about 10% less energy than a comparable conventional building, but almost twice the energy of an energy-efficient conventional building.

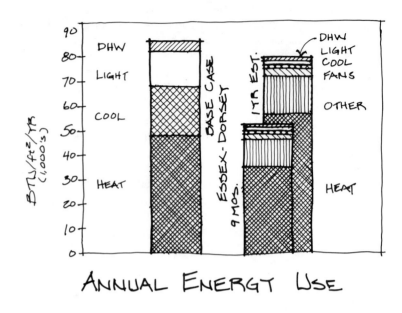

Figure 3-8e. Annual energy use. Although heating energy use is significantly greater than the base case, cooling and lighting loads are dramatically lower. (*Note:* "9 MOS DATA" indicates the actual end-use breakdown for January through September, 1984. "1 YR EST" is an estimate of total annual energy use based on the Technical Monitor's estimates.)

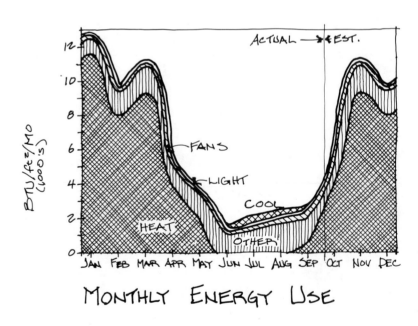

Figure 3-8f. Monthly energy use. Most energy consumption occurs during the heating season, and space heating is the largest end use.

ing energy use are reduced by almost 90% over the base case. The substantial miscellaneous energy use in the "other" category includes DHW, air conditioning, kitchen appliances, and several large kilns. The kilns in the craft rooms are the largest energy users in the "other" category.

EXCESSIVE SPACE HEATING ENERGY CONSUMPTION

System losses may be the principal reasons for excessive space heating energy use. For example, the boiler is located in an unconditioned ventilated crawl space. Although the piping for the hydronic system is covered with at least 1 in. of insulation, it also is located in the crawl space. Temperatures in the crawl space are typically higher than those in the occupied space above, indicating substantial distribution system losses in spite of the insulation. Since system efficiency is greatly affected by system losses, the anticipated 72% heating system design efficiency may actually be closer to 50%.

Heating energy use is very sensitive to ambient temperatures in this relatively nonmassive building. As late as mid-April, occupants complained of cold, damp mornings. Rather than change the setback time, occupants turned up thermostats to 75° F, which led to higher-than-expected heating energy consumption.

Lighting energy use also was low enough to reduce internal gains by as much as 1,000 Btu/ft^2/month. Over the course of a year, the contribution of lights to the heating load would reduce space heating energy use by about 20%. Total annual energy use would drop by up to 16%.

OVERHEATING

Overheating occurred in both the crafts wing and the assembly/dining room. Two large kilns in the crafts area created considerable radiant and convective heat, causing discomfort during both summer and winter. The radiant heat was so strong that power ventilation could not maintain comfortable temperatures even during the coldest weather. A power-ventilated, fully insulated enclosure around the kilns, however, has corrected the problem.

Summer overheating in the assembly/dining room led the center's director to comment that "90° F is just too warm for some of the seniors." Natural ventilation is not sufficient, mainly because key apertures are not sized to allow free air circulation. As a result, the intended stack effect for inducing ventilation in the assembly/dining area, for example, does not work well.

Unplanned latent and sensible cooling loads, such as the kitchen and heavy midday occupancy, also contribute to summertime discomfort. Because the night flushing strategy was eliminated for security reasons, the overheating situation during summer days is exacerbated.

REDUCED UTILITY BILLS

Estimated energy costs for 1984 are $0.85/ft^2 for a total annual savings of about 20% ($0.20/ft^2) over the base case, as shown in Figure 3-8g. (Actual energy costs for nine months are also shown.) The BEPS building, however, costs almost 50% less to operate than the center.

Heating costs are about 20% higher than the base case, while cooling costs are less than 10% of base case energy costs for space cooling, as shown in Figure 3-8h. Lighting energy costs are also only about 10% of base case building costs. Although energy costs in the "other" category (i.e., kilns, kitchen, some A/C, and power ventilation) may offset lighting and cooling savings, comparable base case data are not available to evaluate the extent to which the savings are offset.

The total construction cost was $65/ft^2 in 1982 dollars, as shown in Figure 3-8i. It suggests that the center was fairly costly when compared to industry-wide estimates for a new building of the same size and type and with similar construction characteristics. However, because this project is a renovation/rehabilitation project and a "new" addition, $65/ft^2 is reasonable for the Baltimore-Washington, D.C. corridor.

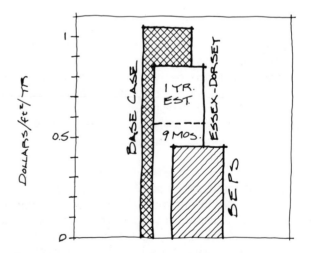

ANNUAL ENERGY COST COMPARISON

Figure 3-8g. Annual energy cost comparison. The BEPS building designed by the U.S. DOE as a cost-effective energy-efficient building, is considerably less expensive to operate than either of the other buildings shown.

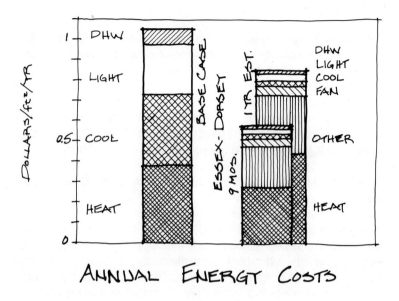

Figure 3-8h. Annual energy costs. Energy costs reflect the annual energy-use profile. Senior center heating costs are high despite the fact that natural gas prices were less than half of electricity costs in 1982.

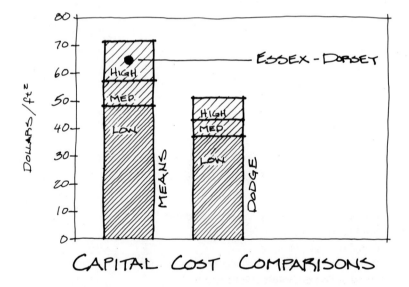

Figure 3-8i. Capital cost comparisons. The difference between the center's construction costs and Dodge and Means average new construction cost data may be misleading because the center is also a renovation/rehabilitation project.

SUMMARY

The Essex-Dorsey Senior Center is functionally successful. The design of the spaces and addition of new facilities fill a community need, while preserving two historic structures. Moreover, the center achieved energy conservation by applying vernacular architectural concepts and using very little energy in end-use categories targeted for reduction, particularly lighting and cooling. Energy conservation, however, is achieved largely at the expense of occupant comfort.

Greater use of analytical techniques early in the design process might have enhanced the ability to identify energy and comfort problems. Heating needs, for example, were probably underestimated for the 4,700-degree-day climate. In addition, heating system losses led the occupants to respond adversely, which ultimately resulted in excessive energy consumption during the winter season. Cooling by natural ventilation was less than effective. Comfort was achieved only by adding mechanical air conditioning in key areas, using portable fans, and making substantial modifications in the crafts rooms to prevent overheating from the kilns. In general, considerable adjustments are likely to be necessary for some time.

PROJECT SUMMARY
ESSEX/DORSEY SENIOR CENTER

Building type: One-story community center
Floor area: 13,000 ft² (6,000 ft² existing)
Location: Essex, MD
Owner: Baltimore County Aging Program and Services
Construction completed: February 1983
Occupancy: 55-60 hr./wk.; 25-40 occupants, average; 100-200, peak
Construction costs: $65/ft²
Annual energy use: 78,600 Btu/ft²/yr (estimated);
86,000 Btu/ft²/yr (base case)
Climate:
4,729 heating degree days/yr
1,108 cooling degree days/yr
Energy costs: Electricity, $17.58/MMBtu; Gas, $7.92/MMBtu
Solar design elements:
Space heating (sun tempering, direct gain, movable insulation)
Daylighting (atrium with glass perimeter, light shelves, clerestories)
Space cooling (natural ventilation, forced ventilation-winter, building load management (operating schedule, awnings, and sunscreens))

4 KEY DESIGN ISSUES

Two levels of performance evaluation were conducted for the Department of Energy (DOE) Nonresidential Experimental Buildings Program. The basic level of evaluation, intended to determine how well the buildings work from both energy and functional points of view, was carried out for all 20 buildings (Gordon 1984). This level used submetered energy data and occupant response to questionnaires regarding perception of the building's comfort and functionality. An advanced level of evaluation was carried out on some buildings to examine cause-and-effect relationships between various features, and between features and occupants' actions. These more detailed evaluations have utilized the building energy analysis computer program BLAST (Building Loads Analysis and System Thermodynamics) and, in some cases, have required additional monitored data and on-site observations to examine relationships between energy performance and passive strategy. The full scope of these extended analyses and the motivations for them are described in Andersson (1983), the studies reported here are part of that work.

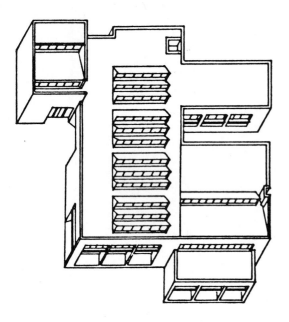

Figure 4-1. Lighting/heating apertures, Mt. Airy Public Library.

DAYLIGHTING OPTIONS

Several observations contributed to defining the scope and direction of this project. First, roof monitors play a major role in 80% of the buildings in the DOE program, contributing to both heating and lighting. Typically, the monitors face south, and are either vertical or have a modest tilt. Second, in most of these buildings, the electrical lighting system is manually controlled by the occupants in response to their own perceptions of illumination requirements, rather than by automatic control systems that typically respond at a predetermined illumination level. Third, the roof aperture area in most of the buildings is substantially larger than suggested by more recent research (Place 1983) which assumed automatic, continuous dimming of the electric lights. Fourth, the basic level of performance evaluation conducted on these buildings indicated that the daylighting systems were extremely effective in reducing lighting requirements, surpassing the designers' expectations. Given that roof monitors are of considerable interest to designers, two issues were suggested for examination in the advanced evaluation:

- The extent to which the manual electric lighting control strategy contributed to, or detracted from, the performance of the entire lighting system
- The extent to which the "larger than necessary" roof monitor area contributed to the effectiveness of the daylighting system and/or enhanced or detracted from the heating and cooling performance of the building

The first issue was addressed by comparing the simulated performance of the building as designed and used to the simulated performance of architecturally and functionally identical buildings using alternative lighting control strategies. The second issue was examined by comparing the simulated performance of the actual building to that of a functionally identical building whose architecture was modified by removing the roof monitors and incorporating scheduled lighting.

BUILDING DESCRIPTIONS

Two buildings were used in this study: Mt. Airy Library in Mt. Airy, North Carolina, and Community United Methodist Church (CUMC) of Columbia, Missouri (DOE 1983). They provided an opportunity to study one situation with regularly scheduled use and centralized responsibility for lighting control (Mt. Airy) and another with very irregular use and lighting controlled by the immediate occupants of each room (CUMC).

The Mt. Airy Library is a 1,200-m² (13,000 ft²) public library (Figures 4-1, 4-2, and 4-3) serving a rural community of 7,000. The winters are generally mild, with about 2200°C heating degree days (4000°F), and summers are warm and humid. The library is typically open to the public from 8:30 a.m. to 8:00 p.m. (shorter hours on weekends), with a staff of three or four on duty most of that time. There are usually two to eight visitors in the building. Studies of architectural integration (Adegran et al., *Qualitative Study,* 1984), energy-use patterns (Swisher and Frey 1984), and total building impacts of passive systems (Adegran et al., *Building Impacts,* 1984) have been performed. The library was designed by J. N. Pease of Charlotte, North Carolina and Ed Mazria of Albuquerque, New Mexico.

There is a variety of daylighting techniques used (Figure 4-1), but this analysis concentrated on the dominant technique, the roof apertures (Figure 4-3) illuminating the "core" area, consisting of about 520 m² (5,500 ft²). This section of the library contains the circulation desk, card catalog, reading areas, and work tables. Sunlight enters through vertical glazing on the south of the aperture, which has an area of more than 20% of the floor area. It is then reflected by the ceiling and by a set of baffles spaced to ensure that no sunlight directly enters the space, thereby preventing glare and damage to library materials. In this section of the library there are no interior partitions, permitting evenly distributed sunlight across the entire area. A tile-covered concrete floor slab and massive walls provide thermal energy storage to absorb the solar radiation scattered downward from the ceiling and baffles.

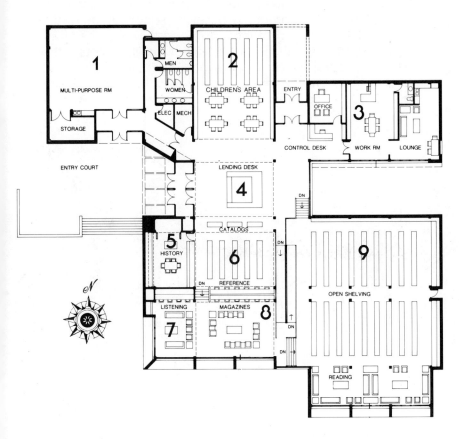

Figure 4-2. Plan, Mt. Airy Library

The library staff controls the electric lighting for the core of the library from the circulation desk. The staff has been instructed that the goal of the design is to save energy and that lights should be turned off if they are not necessary. Control is based on the staff's judgment of what lighting is necessary.

The Community United Methodist Church (CUMC) added a 420-m² (4,500 ft²) classroom, meeting, and nursery wing as part of the DOE program (Figures 4-4 and 4-5). The church is located in a small university city with cold winters of about 3000°C heating degree days (5500°F) and warm, often humid summers. The wing is used heavily on Sunday mornings for church school and the nursery, but only one or two other times are regularly scheduled. At irregularly scheduled times during the week, some rooms may be occupied by various church and community groups. Studies of energy-use patterns associated with the passive systems (Yager and Frey 1984) and occupant education, effects, and response (Kantrowitz 1984) have been performed. The addition was designed by Peckham and Wright of Columbia, Missouri.

The large, tilted aperture (over 18% of the floor area, Figure 4-5) and extensive use of thermal mass were designed to maximize the effect of solar heating. Much sunlight is reflected, especially in the summer, off the roof south of the apertures and off the light shelf just inside the windows. It is spread over the ceiling to distribute the light throughout the space. In the winter, for thermal storage purposes, the angle of the light is such that it directly strikes the massive north wall. In the classrooms, internal partitions further reflect the light around the room. In general, the daylight is evenly distributed, though not as effectively as in the library. Compared to the Mt. Airy Library, the CUMC roof aperture design puts more emphasis on direct-

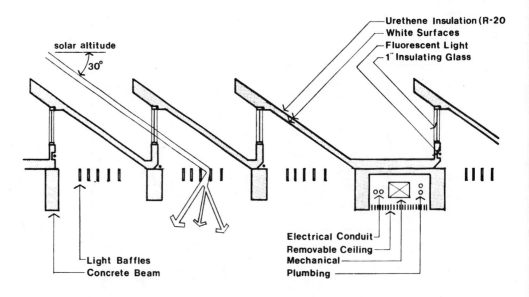

Figure 4-3. Section through roof apertures, Mt. Airy Public Library

gain heating relative to daylighting. Less obstructive over-hangs, tilted glazing, and direct transmission of beam solar radiation into the space (no baffles) allow higher solar gains but lower light quality (i.e., higher potential for glare associated with unobstructed beam light).

Control of the lighting is much different in this case. Each of the six classrooms, the two nursery rooms, and the corridor have separate switches, which are available to the users of those spaces. An orientation seminar was held when the wing was opened. In addition, instructions on how to use the various solar systems are posted in the wing, but the church staff does not exercise direct control of the lighting. Various users are able to control the lights in each space to their satisfaction. Occupant education, effects, and response have been reported (Kantrowitz 1984).

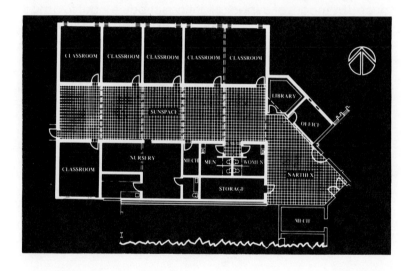

Figure 4-4. Plan, CUMC

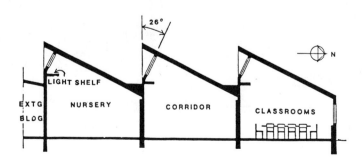

Figure 4-5. Section, CUMC

ENERGY REQUIREMENTS COMPARISONS

In this study, comparisons were made of the annual energy requirements of the building assuming actual lighting control by occupants and alternative automatic control strategies. In both cases, energy requirements were obtained by computer simulation. For the actual building, performance of the electric lighting system and controls was measured and used as an input to the simulation in order to ensure that the simulation properly represented reality. The actual measurements were short term and extrapolated to the full year in order to allow annual simulations, as explained below. Existing building energy analysis computer programs are limited in their ability to model lighting effects of unusual glazing configurations and properly treat thermal and visual comfort. For this reason, a combination of physical and computer modeling was used to study these buildings. A procedure was developed by which analysis of the lighting use could be performed external to the building energy analysis program, BLAST, and the results introduced by means of a special lighting schedule input to a modified BLAST version. The only differences in the BLAST simulations were the lighting schedule and the way in which each lighting schedule was generated.

Figure 4-6 illustrates the method for analyzing lighting control strategies at the two sites. Four steps were necessary to complete the comparisons:

1. Illumination levels due to daylighting at the work plane throughout the space were determined using solar energy data from a standard weather tape from the site in conjunction with time-dependent functions relating external solar energy to interior illumination; the functions were based on data from physical models of the buildings. The illumination levels were calculated hourly for a year.

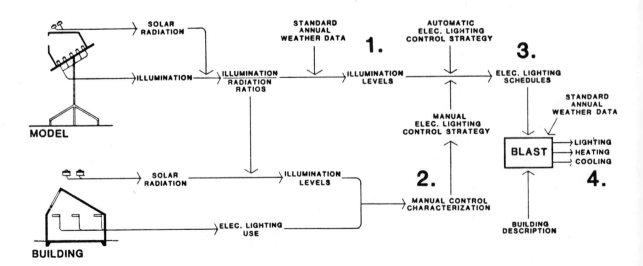

Figure 4-6. Methodology

204

2. The electric lighting requirements, as affected by the manual lighting control at the building, were measured over a test period of three to five months. The patterns of lighting control were characterized to define a control strategy reflecting experience at the site.
3. The actual illumination levels (from step 1) and the characterization of the control strategies (from step 2) were compared in order to generate an hourly lighting schedule (8,760 hours), which would result from the control strategy in question.
4. A special BLAST version, which will accept hourly lighting schedules, was used to calculate the lighting, heating, and cooling performance throughout the standard year, and performance of alternative strategies was compared and evaluated.

A detailed discussion of these steps follows.

ILLUMINATION LEVEL CALCULATION

For each building, a physical model was built to simulate the daylight illuminance distribution in the building. About 30 photometers were placed in the model at the work plane in a grid to measure illuminance values throughout the space. The entire apparatus was placed outdoors and a heliodon was used to achieve various relationships between the model and the sun.

As a first step, the research team prepared a "map," which shows the interior illumination resulting from each of a variety of sky conditions. Measurements were taken for both overcast sky conditions and a grid of nearly 200 sun positions for clear skies. For each of these conditions, both direct normal beam irradiance and diffuse irradiance on a horizontal were recorded simultaneously with the interior illuminance measurements. Further processing of this information produced a series of tables (illumination/radiation tables), which stored the ratio of illumination at a certain point in the building (corresponding to a sensor) to beam irradiance and to diffuse irradiance for a given sky condition (clear or cloudy and sun position).

The illumination/radiation ratio tables were used together with solar radiation data contained in a standard annual weather tape to produce a set of illumination data. A typical meteorological year (TMY) (National Climatic Center 1981) weather tape for Columbia, Missouri was used to represent the weather at the church. TMY data for Greensboro, North Carolina was used for Mt. Airy, which is near Greensboro and has a similar latitude and altitude. For each hour, the tapes contain the altitude and azimuth angles of the sun and the beam and diffuse irradiances. Multiplying the appropriate illumination/radiation ratios times the beam and diffuse irradiances produces the illuminances for each hour of the typical meteorological year at each location within the building. These illuminance distributions were stored for further processing.

To establish patterns of manual electric lighting control, instrumentation was added to each of the buildings. The additional instrumentation was used at Mt. Airy from November 1983 to early April 1984, and at CUMC from late December 1983 until the planned completion in December 1984. Only the first three months of data at the church were available for this analysis. The additional instrumentation consisted of (1) two solar measurements in order to separate the resource into beam and diffuse components and (2) sensors to indicate which electric lights were being used in the areas of interest.

By using the illumination/radiation tables (in much the same way as the standard weather tape was used), the hourly solar radiation measurements from the building could be used to determine the illumination levels that actually occurred throughout the building during that hour. This information could then be compared to the use of electric lights during that period to develop a relationship between the daylight illumination levels in the space and the response of the occupants in using electric lighting.

At the Mt. Airy Public Library, characterization of the electric lighting control was made easier by the regular schedule of the building and the relatively long, uninterrupted data collection period. Electricity usage on each of the six lighting circuits serving the core area was matched against the work-plane illumination in that area resulting from daylighting. First, it was assumed that the lights were controlled based on the average illumination in the area serviced by a given lighting circuit. However, distribution of daylight in the space is good but not perfect, and some areas are likely to be darker than others, especially when much of the daylighting is provided by beam sunlight. Therefore, a second lighting control characterization was made based on the *minimum* work-plane illumination due to daylighting.

In addition to this division, Architectural Energy Corp., in their analysis of the hourly building data at Mt. Airy (Swisher and Frey 1984), discovered a tendency for the lights, once turned on, to remain on for the rest of the day, regardless of the amount of available daylight. Also, lights in some areas would be turned off during periods of particularly low usage, even though the daylighting illuminance level was substantially below the standards for activities normally conducted in those areas. To account for these effects, each hour of the day was dealt with separately. A series of tables was developed, each with a ratio of "average lighting used / full lighting use" for each hour of the day, for each lighting circuit, and for each of a set of six "bins" representing different illumination levels. A sample of these tables, for 110 to 330 lux (10 to 30 foot-candles), based on average daylight illumination, is shown in Figure 4-7. Thus, when daylighting provided 110 to 330 lux between 2:00 p.m. and 3:00 p.m. (hour 15) there was a 36% probability that the lights on circuit L-1 would be on. This characterization allowed an average value of lighting use to be assigned given a distribution of illumination due to daylighting.

Hour of Day	9	10	11	12	13	14	15	16	17	18
Circuit										
L-1	.01	.13	.39	.57	.38	.40	.36	.13	.09	.25
L-3	.00	.01	.09	.24	.24	.18	.18	.12	.07	.26
L-6	.00	.01	.04	.15	.17	.10	.18	.13	.05	.14
L-7	.00	.01	.03	.03	.03	.06	.02	.07	.03	.00
L-9	.00	.05	.09	.03	.16	.10	.15	.06	.07	.40
L-12	.01	.07	.13	.21	.17	.12	.13	.12	.21	.31

Figure 4-7. Lighting energy use ratios based on average lighting illumination of 110 to 330 lux.

The solar wing of CUMC posed a different problem. The only regularly scheduled use during daylight hours was Sunday morning church school and the nursery and some meetings on Thursday mornings. During the test period, there were also about 12 additional periods of irregular occupancy. Although there were not enough hours to take statistical averages as with the Mt. Airy information, a very simple characterization developed upon observation. During the 28 periods of regularly scheduled occupancy, the lights were turned on when the minimum illumination dropped below 200 lux (~20 foot-candles). The occupants meeting irregularly were even more conservative in their use of lighting, leaving the lights off unless the minimum work-plane illumination level dropped below 100 lux (~10 foot-candles). At these levels, average illumination was about 50% higher than minimum illumination. In the 40 periods of the sample, only 3 failed to conform to these characterizations.

By examining building performance at these control levels, a range of manual control characteristics could be evaluated.

GENERATION OF LIGHTING SCHEDULES

Generation of the lighting schedules was relatively straightforward. Manual control of electric lights in response to daylighting was defined above. Automatic control of electric lights was based on sensor information about the illumination in the space and characteristics of the control hardware. Reference controls simply lit the space whenever it was occupied. Illuminance levels for every hour of the standard year were stored in the first step of this process. For each control strategy, a computer routine applied the control algorithm to the stored illuminance value for any hour to determine the amount of electric lighting to be provided as a supplement to the available daylight in order to satisfy the illumination requirement. It is important to note that the assumption regarding the illumination requirement may not always correspond to the functional demands for lighting at a specific time. Of course, choice of appropriate alternatives and illumination requirements is important to realistic performance evaluation.

In addition to evaluating annual performance of the buildings based on manual control of lighting, six alternative electric lighting control strategies were investigated at both buildings. Two reference cases were run: one with the lights on whenever the building was occupied ("OCCD.ON"), the other with the same lighting schedule, but with the roof aperture replaced by standard roof structure ("ROOF"). The basis for the second alternative is the argument that if no daylighting was being used, it might have been more effective to remove the roof glazing altogether. The "ROOF" run was the only one in which anything in the BLAST building description had been changed.

The daylighting system in the two buildings was also evaluated assuming two different automatic electric lighting control strategies: on/off switching and continuous dimming. In this study, both were assumed to respond to daylight on the work plane, and were intended to supplement daylight to maintain a specific level of illuminance on the work plane. The on/off control turned the lights on whenever the daylight illumination dropped below the required level. Dimming controls adjusted the power to the electric lights in response to the amount of daylighting in order to achieve *total* illumination at the required level. Based on common hardware limitations, the assumption was made that the fluorescent lights could not be dimmed below 20% of their capacity.

While there is debate as to the proper lighting standard in spaces where reading, writing, and paperwork are done, 50 foot-candles (550 lux) is widely used as a standard, and was used for *all* automatic controls in the Mt. Airy Library. Because the tasks and occupants change with time, the standard may not represent the optimum lighting level or the level the occupants would choose if they had access to the electric lighting controls.

At the Mt. Airy Library, considerations of lighting distribution led to characterization of the manually controlled lighting based first on response to average work-plane illumination (i.e., "MAN.AVE") and second on response to minimum work-plane illumination (i.e., "MAN.MIN"). For the same reasons, lighting schedules were generated based on both average and minimum illumination for both automatic on/off controls and for automatic dimming controls, yielding four more strategies for Mt. Airy: "O/O.AVE," "O/O.MIN," "DIM.AVE," and "DIM.MIN."

The library receives an even distribution of light and is occupied continuously, but at very low density. Most occupants have the ability to move away from a location of particularly poor lighting. These factors made lighting control based on average illumination a reasonable alternative to that based on the minimum. Occupancy at CUMC required a different treatment. Most use of the solar wing involved classes, meetings, or the nursery activities, generally within a relatively small room. If there was a less illuminated section of the room, someone was likely to be there. CUMC also tended to have more spatial variation in illumination levels than Mt. Airy. These factors led to a decision to base all of the control strategies at CUMC on the minimum work-plane illumination level from daylighting.

The two manual control strategies, based on the upper and lower estimates of the illumination level at which the church occupants responded, are designated by "MAN.HIGH" and "MAN.LOW." Two automatic control strategies, on/off and dimming controls, both using the ∽550 lux (50 foot-candles) standard, are designated by "O/O" and "DIM." Because of the very low illumination levels, which appeared to satisfy the occupants under most circumstances at CUMC, and because of the visually less demanding activities (classes and meetings rather than office work or continuous reading) that take place there, the performance of the daylighting system was examined assuming automatic controls with a lower illumination requirement, ∽330 lux (30 foot-candles). These are designated "O/O.LOW" and "DIM.LOW."

BLAST SIMULATIONS

The BLAST computer simulation models for Mt. Airy and CUMC were developed from a variety of sources. Working drawings were used for basic building information. Information on scheduling of activities and equipment use was obtained from owner projections submitted to DOE during early phases of the Nonresidential Experimental Buildings Program; from occupant analyses performed later in the program; from hourly and monthly data collected at the library and church; from contact with library, city, and church staffs; and from observation at the sites. HVAC system information was obtained from design drawings, manufacturers, and project staff. Initial results of BLAST runs were compared to monthly measurements of energy use at the buildings. Where discrepancies occurred, better information was sought and incorporated into the models (Andersson et al. 1984; Andersson 1984). There is confidence that the BLAST models are sufficiently representative of the existing building that sensitivities to building and operation parameters discovered by simulations would be found in the buildings.

The simulation models produced reasonable thermal representations of the library and church as they were operating at the time. To make it more representative of similar buildings for this study, the CUMC model was modified to reflect the higher and more regular occupancy the church will achieve in its new wing. Parametric annual simulations were made, changing only the lighting schedules to reflect the alternate manual and automatic electric lighting control strategies. Each simulation had the same building descriptions and annual weather information for each building. (The only exception was the "ROOF" run at each site, in which the roof was changed while the lighting schedule remained the same as in the "OCCD.ON" run.)

Some aspects of the simulation are limited and favor one control strategy or another. The weather tape and the BLAST simulation covered one hour, during which the solar resource might vary considerably, but only an average value was reported. This probably had little effect on the total performance of the dimming systems, as they responded to such variations. Because the manual control schedules were based on measured data, which undoubtedly included hours of solar variability, those schedules should accurately represent the response of the occupants in that situation. But the on/off controls, typically kept on during periods of rapid solar fluctuation, would show slightly better performance because of the simulation limitation. Furthermore, the automatic control strategies in this study assumed that the automatic systems were never overridden. They assumed that if the sensors indicated there was sufficient light, no more would be used. The occupants' pattern of control of the lights would lead one to suspect that such overriding is likely to be rare, but it is good to keep in mind that the automatic controls' results, both on/off and dimming, were a "best case" situation in that respect. In addition, occupant control of the lights was based on performance over a five-month period. Although it represented more than 3,000 hours of information at Mt. Airy, there was no guarantee that performance would remain constant. Change in library use, library staff, and season could easily change the amount of lighting used in a particular situation, for better or worse. The sample at CUMC was much smaller, and more likely to experience changes in control. Finally, the test period ran during the winter months. To the extent that additional lighting provides both thermal and psychological benefits during cold weather, and less lighting provides similar benefits during warm weather, lights may be turned on less frequently during the summer cooling season when occupants have control.

SIMULATION RESULTS

The results of the computer simulations are shown in Figures 4-8 and 4-9 and in Figures 4-10 and 4-11. The tables show building energy performance in terms of lighting, heating, cooling, and total energy at three levels. The first level is the space load, the amount of energy that must be supplied to the space to maintain the conditions specified by the heating, cooling, and lighting controls. The second is the system load, the amount of energy consumed in supplying the space load. For lighting, the two are the same. At the Mt. Airy Library (Figure 4-8), the system load for both heating and cooling is lower than the space load, because the heat pumps used to meet both loads have an average COP greater than one for both conditions. The same is true of the central air conditioning at CUMC. Heating at CUMC is provided by a gas furnace, which has an efficiency factor of less than 1. At the third level, energy usage is converted to annual cost in units of dollars per m², where the costs are based on local utility rates ($.075/kWh and $.076/kWh for Mt. Airy and CUMC, respectively) and fuel costs ($0.126/kWh = $3.67/MMBtu at CUMC). Electricity costs represent an average cost per kWh, accounting for both consumption and demand charges (DOE 1983).

The cost figures are also plotted in Figures 4-10 and 4-11. On each graph, a reference line is marked from the most repre-

Strategy	Space Load (1000 KWH)				System Load (1000 KWH)				Energy Cost ($/M²)			
	Ltg.	Htg.	Clg.	Total	Ltg.	Htg.	Clg.	Total	Ltg.	Htg.	Clg.	Total
MAN.HIGH	8.70	8.09	7.21	24.00	8.70	13.30	4.12	26.12	1.57	.40	.75	2.72
MAN.LOW	8.06	8.26	6.98	23.30	8.06	13.56	3.99	25.61	1.46	.41	.72	2.59
O/O	14.39	7.50	9.20	31.09	14.39	12.50	5.26	32.15	2.60	.38	.95	3.93
O/O.LOW	10.08	7.88	7.85	25.81	10.08	13.07	4.49	27.64	1.82	.39	.81	3.02
DIM	11.02	7.85	8.03	26.90	11.02	12.97	4.59	28.58	1.99	.39	.83	3.21
DIM.LOW	8.52	8.18	7.18	23.88	8.52	13.44	4.10	26.06	1.54	.40	.74	2.68
OCCD.ON	20.45	6.65	10.20	37.30	20.45	11.42	5.83	37.70	3.70	.34	1.05	5.09
ROOF	20.45	11.64	2.66	34.75	20.45	18.26	1.52	40.23	3.70	.55	.28	4.53

Figure 4-8. Mt. Airy core area energy use for alternative lighting controls.

Strategy	Space Load (1000 KWH)				System Load (1000 KWH)				Energy Cost ($/M²)			
	Ltg.	Htg.	Clg.	Total	Ltg.	Htg.	Clg.	Total	Ltg.	Htg.	Clg.	Total
MAN.AVE	4.84	24.30	22.13	51.27	4.84	13.50	15.42	33.76	.70	1.95	2.22	4.87
MAN.MIN	4.60	24.3	22.04	51.02	4.60	13.54	15.37	33.51	.66	1.95	2.22	4.83
O/O.AVE	9.79	22.54	23.36	55.69	9.79	12.52	15.79	38.10	1.41	1.81	2.28	5.50
O/O.MIN	14.77	21.78	25.29	61.84	14.77	12.10	16.43	43.30	2.13	1.75	2.37	6.25
DIM.AVE	7.50	23.24	22.66	53.40	7.50	12.91	15.57	35.98	1.08	1.86	2.25	5.19
DIM.MIN	10.64	22.57	23.77	56.98	10.64	12.54	15.94	39.12	1.53	1.81	2.30	5.64
OCCD.ON	27.67	18.76	29.57	76.00	27.67	10.42	17.65	55.74	3.99	1.50	2.55	8.04
ROOF	27.67	23.65	21.72	73.04	27.67	13.14	15.49	56.30	3.99	1.90	2.23	8.12

Figure 4-9. CUMC solar wing annual energy use for alternative lighting controls.

sentative manual control result so that alternatives can be easily compared.

Several observations could be made from the results:

- Energy cost with manually controlled lighting was similar to or lower than energy costs with alternative automatic controls and showed dramatic savings compared to the cases where electric lights were fully powered during all occupied hours.
- South-facing roof apertures showed much greater potential for reducing lighting energy costs than heating energy costs.
- Heating and cooling loads were not substantially affected by changes to the lighting control strategy.

Clearly, the most striking result is that the occupants in both buildings kept the lights off during the majority of the time that daylighting provided illumination above accepted standards and during much of the time that illumination dipped below — even substantially below — those standards.

The type of building being evaluated is important in interpreting these results. The buildings and the activities taking place in them strongly influenced the effectiveness of the daylighting and associated lighting control. In the Mt. Airy Library, the only permanent occupants were the few staff members, who tended to work in a few areas within the core area studied. Transient users of the library tended to accept the lighting. Since the light switches were located only within control of the staff, even marginal lighting was likely to be accepted by the temporary visitor. Occupant responses to questionnaires, however, indicated that library visitors were quite satisfied with the lighting. The question of the quality of light — in terms of visibility, visual comfort, distribution, and rendering — is critical to answering the question of why the occupants of this space seemed satisfied with illumination levels that would appear to be insufficient for the visually demanding tasks that take place in a library. Such an investigation has been made (Adegran et al., *Qualitative Study*, 1984).

In the church addition, acceptable illumination levels seemed to have been even lower and were adhered to more consistently. In part, this may be because much of the activity was social in nature, involving more discussion than paperwork, for example, meetings, nursery activities, and classes, which were not visually demanding. The occupants may have felt no need to light the space above a minimal level. The manual control benefited from its flexibility in contrast to the simple automatic control described, which had to provide light for the most visually demanding task expected in a space during

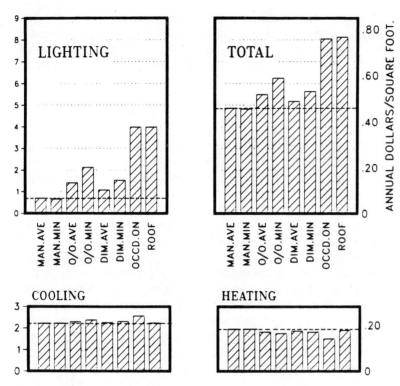

Figure 4-10. Mt. Airy Public Library core area, energy costs.

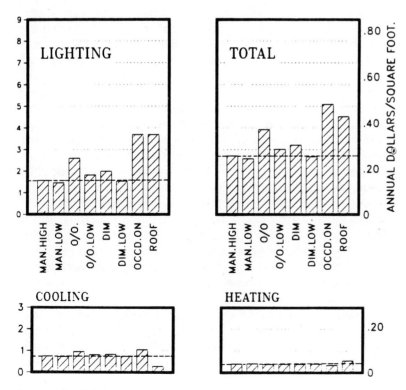

Figure 4-11. CUMC solar wing, energy costs.

all hours of occupancy. With manual control, occupants could adapt the lighting limits to the tasks being performed. This benefit may be far less significant in buildings where spaces are more heavily occupied and identified with particular tasks.

In both buildings, the size of the aperture was certainly an important factor. In studies of roof apertures with sensitive automatic dimming controls (Place 1983; Arasteh 1984) optimum energy use was achieved with 2% to 10% aperture ratio (roof aperture area/floor area). The aperture ratios for both the Mt. Airy Library and CUMC are around 20%. The relatively low optimum glazing areas noted in the studies were possible because the automatic controls were able to adjust electric lighting levels constantly. Smaller apertures require a degree of "attentiveness" inappropriate to manual control. Providing large aperture areas resulted in extended periods during which no control was necessary. Once off, lights could usually remain off until dusk. Since a large proportion of daylight hours provided sufficient natural illumination, occupants became used to the quality, dynamics, and light levels of daylighting, and may have been more likely to accept marginal daylighting situations.

Acceptance of daylighting might also have been improved by extended periods of high illumination because it was achieved without significant glare problems. Large apertures have ramifications beyond lighting, of course. In both of these buildings, placement of the glazing in the insulated roof ("ROOF" -> "OCCD.ON") caused reductions in heating loads and increases in cooling loads. The net difference was minor compared to the savings realized in lighting electricity when the comparison accounted for daylighting. However, a "non-solar orientation" might well have resulted in higher cooling *and* heating loads, and a much less advantageous overall thermal impact. The south vertical orientation of the roof apertures permitted the use of large areas without associated heating and cooling energy penalties. When the thermal effects of reduced electric lighting loads (associated with daylighting) were considered (compare "OCCD.ON" to the first column in Figures 4-10 and 4-11), the increase in cooling from the addition of roof apertures was reduced at CUMC and eliminated at Mt. Airy; the heating reduction was lost at Mt. Airy, but largely retained at CUMC.

It could be argued that there are methods for achieving lower lighting usage with more sophisticated automatic controls than those examined above. However, the level of electric light usage during daylight hours is already so low in these buildings that measures that entail any cost or maintenance are not likely to be cost-effective and would reduce the flexibility and satisfaction of occupant control.

In both buildings, the dimming systems showed superiority to the simpler on/off switching, as expected. The advantage was substantially greater when the lighting requirements were more difficult to meet (compare "O/O.MIN" to "DIM.MIN" at Mt. Airy, and "O/O" to "DIM" at CUMC), not a particularly surprising result, but one worth noting.

CONCLUSIONS ON DAYLIGHTING

While it is difficult to draw general conclusions from case studies such as these, several points should be made. First, in these buildings, manual control of the electric lighting in response to daylighting from roof apertures performed as well or better than simple automatic controls. Analysis indicated that contributing factors were:

- Frequent occupant satisfaction with daylighting levels well below current standards for electric lights (reflecting the flexibility of manual control to match the lighting level to the immediate task)
- Use of large apertures, allowing lights to remain off for extended periods
- Particular use patterns of these buildings

Second, in these buildings, which have a significant heating season, a relatively large aperture area with appropriate shading could be used without substantially aggravating cooling energy requirements, and enhancing the viability of manual control strategies. In addition, the potential for energy reduction from the use of roof apertures appeared far greater in the lighting component than in heating and cooling. Lastly, investigations into similar passive systems in larger buildings with more typical uses and schedules would be very valuable in confirming, contradicting, and/or extending these findings.

Consideration should be given to occupant lighting controls when the conditions of a daylighting system and building indicate its feasibility.

OTHER OCCUPANT ISSUES

The scope and direction of this project was defined in large part by the findings of Min Kantrowitz and Associates' occupant analysis studies of the buildings of the DOE Nonresidential Experimental Buildings Program. The findings indicated areas in which similar occupant effects occurred in several buildings. In some of these areas, thermal analysis was determined to be an effective method of measuring the sensitivity of energy performance of passive buildings or comfort of the occupants to modifications to the building's design or its occupants' activities.

The purpose of this analysis was to identify areas in which occupants and passive systems affect each other, and to determine the building's thermal sensitivity to variations in those building and occupant areas. The analytical process was divided into four steps, described below.

IDENTIFICATION OF OCCUPANT ISSUES

The primary source of comprehensive occupant information was Min Kantrowitz and Associates, the group responsible for gathering reports on occupancy evaluation for each building, ensuring the quality of data, identifying implications of the detailed data, and finding common threads of occupant satisfaction and effects across several projects. Results from this work have been published as project case studies (Kantrowitz 1984) and as part of broader performance analyses (Gordon et al. 1984; DOE 1985).

Those occupant issues expected to have direct effects on energy use and thermal comfort were identified, as well as occupant problems whose solutions were expected to have such effects. Both were then evaluated to determine those for which information could be gained using available energy analysis tools. The following issues were chosen for analysis:

- *Thermal mass amount and exposure.* What is the energy and comfort effect of changes to total volume of thermal mass and to exposed area of mass and its placement? Occupant descriptions of comfort and discomfort suggested that thermal mass played a significant role in perceptions of comfort.
- *Variation in setback strategies.* What are the energy and comfort effects of changes to thermostat setback strategies, and how is setback related to thermal mass? Comfort complaints during morning periods of recovery from night setback suggested degradation of comfort as the cost for energy savings resulting from setbacks.
- *Acoustic treatment.* How does acoustic treatment of interior surfaces used for reflection or absorption of sunlight affect energy use and thermal comfort? Acoustic problems, resulting from competition for surface areas

between acoustic treatments and passive systems were reported in many projects.

- *Shading of solar apertures.* What is the energy effect of operable shading devices on solar apertures and of their control by occupants? Lack of shading devices or improper use are thought to have contributed to energy and comfort problems in several cases.

DEVELOPMENT OF COMPUTER MODELS

The building energy analysis computer program, BLAST, has advantages over other analysis techniques for investigating passive building operation. These advantages and program verification have been documented elsewhere (Bauman et al. 1983). BLAST's use of an iterative thermal balance technique, and its detailed treatment of thermal mass, solar gains, ventilation, shading devices, and thermostatic control make it a preferred analysis technique when dealing with passive buildings and their complex energy flows. Its hourly calculation of surface temperatures allows radiant temperatures to be fully considered in comfort analyses. Because of these strengths, it was used for all simulations described below.

Because of the time and effort involved in preparing a representative and accurate description of an existing building, it was decided to use a limited number of buildings to analyze the four occupant issues identified above. Therefore, the building descriptions prepared for the Mt. Airy Library and the Community United Methodist Church's solar wing were used.

DEVELOPMENT AND EXECUTION OF PARAMETRIC PLANS

After identifying four significant occupant issues for analysis and developing computer models for two buildings, a general approach to parametric study was developed. In this case, because the issues were not simply energy use and because the buildings were only representative of a larger set of passive commercial buildings, understanding thermal *mechanisms* underlying the buildings' sensitivity to tested changes had to be emphasized. The importance of occupant interaction with passive systems made evaluating comfort just as crucial as evaluating energy use.

For these reasons, hourly energy and comfort information was deemed necessary to study these issues properly. However, annual information on an hourly basis is difficult to evaluate because of the quantity of data. On the other hand, design days may not give sufficient information to evaluate mechanisms of occupant/passive system interaction effectively. It was decided, therefore, to make each parametric run for a set of four 10-day periods, in January, April, July, and October. Most of the periods have both sunny and cloudy days, and warmer and cooler temperatures. The four periods covered winter, summer, and two swing seasons. Because April is typically sunnier but cooler than October, the information provided some insight into the relative importance of solar and temperature effects during the two swing seasons. A method for transferring to a graphic display system was developed, so that trends were easier to find and anomalies quickly identified.

For each issue, simulations were run for each building. The simulations analyzed changes that might have been made to the building design or occupant interaction in response to those issues. The energy and comfort impacts of such changes to the building could then be evaluated.

Each of the simulations produced seasonal energy-use results and graphic hourly presentations of temperatures and loads. The energy-use results helped determine whether changes being tested improved the energy situation or detracted from it. Graphs of hourly loads supplemented this information by indicating more precisely the pattern of energy-use changes in response to a building modification.

Hourly temperature graphs also provided information on comfort conditions in the space. Temperatures, of course, are not the only indicators of comfort, but an effective temperature derived from mean air and radiant temperatures indicates general comfort levels. This is especially true in the absence of rapid air movement or extreme humidity, as is generally the case in these buildings. Effective temperature (taken as a simple average of mean radiant and mean air temperature for these studies) is a better indicator of comfort than simple air temperature, because it accounts for radiant heat transfer between building surfaces and occupants. This is particularly important in very massive buildings, such as those studied, where radiant and air temperatures can be quite different for extended periods. It is also important in evaluating the effect of changes that are expected to impact surface temperatures more quickly and dramatically than air temperatures, such as solar gains. The hourly temperature graphs show either effective temperatures or both radiant and air temperatures. All hourly graphs show the full 10-day period simulated and a more detailed 5-day subperiod.

BUILDING DESCRIPTIONS

The two buildings used in the daylighting options work were used in this study: Mt. Airy Library in Mt. Airy, North Carolina (Figures 4-1, 4-2, and 4-3) and Community United Methodist Church (CUMC) of Columbia, Missouri (Figures 4-4 and 4-5).

Including a variety of south-facing solar apertures, on both roof and walls (Figures 4-1 and 4-3) provides daylighting and, in conjunction with thermally massive walls and floors, solar heating. The thermal mass and effective solar control contribute to low cooling requirements. The architectural plan is open, so that light and heat flow freely through most of the library. Auxiliary heating and cooling are provided by five heat pumps serving five thermal zones. Supplementary electric resistance heat is provided for particularly cold days.

The large, tilted roof apertures and extensive use of thermal mass were designed to maximize solar heating. In winter, for thermal storage purposes, light directly strikes the massive north walls. Passive cooling is provided by fixed shading of roof apertures, substantial night ventilation of thermal mass in the space, and ceiling fans. Auxiliary heating is provided by a gas furnace; cooling, by a standard rooftop air conditioning unit.

Although current scheduling is intermittent, for purposes of these studies, a heavier schedule of use more representative of anticipated use (about 50 hours per week, including day, evening, and weekend use) was assumed.

Daylighting is a major passive strategy in these buildings, as in most of the buildings in the DOE Nonresidential Experimental Buildings Program. Energy reductions resulting from daylighting are an important contributor to low energy use in the buildings. Because building modifications investigated during this study had little or no direct effect on daylighting or the buildings' responses to it, no lighting effects are presented in the results. However, daylighting's importance as a passive strategy influenced the choice of building modifications for analysis and the application of this study's results, as indicated in parts of the following discussion.

MASSIVE BUILDINGS

Mt. Airy and CUMC are very massive buildings in terms of both amount of mass and surface area of mass exposed. Both have concrete floors with conductive surface treatments and additional mass in the walls. Mt. Airy has a 5-in. concrete slab, topped with quarry tile, and exterior walls of 6-to-12-in. masonry with filled cores inside the insulation layer. There are few interior walls. Swisher (1984) estimates the building's time constant at five days. CUMC has a concrete floor with asphalt tile. The north walls have a layer of solid concrete blocks added to the standard construction. Other walls and the ceiling are faced with gypsum building board.

To compare these buildings better with each other, with modifications simulated as part of this study, and with other buildings, a method of characterizing thermal mass configurations was used. It consists of three indices, each the ratio of the surface area of a type of thermal mass to the floor area of the space or building. Surface area provides an estimate of both the quantity of thermal mass and its ability to interact with thermal forces in the building. The first index refers to heavy thermal mass directly exposed to the space, such as a concrete floor with a high conductivity surface treatment. The second is for similar mass, but with a thin insulating layer (e.g., carpet or acoustic tile) separating it from the space. The third index quantifies the area of thinner materials that nevertheless provide some thermal storage, such as gypsum board or plaster, which are exposed to the space.

These indices say nothing about the location of the mass, except that it is not separated from the space by a major insulating layer. Nor do they indicate specific material properties such as absorptivity or density. However, they provide a general description of the thermal mass environment. A typical house might have an index of 0.1/0.0/2.0. A partially carpeted office building might have 0.4/0.6/0.5. Both of the buildings in this study have substantially greater mass than is typically seen in such buildings. Mt. Airy has both massive walls and floor, while CUMC has large areas of light mass on walls and ceiling. There is a small amount of carpeted floor slab in each building. Mt. Airy's mass index is 1.9/0.1/0.8; CUMC's is 1.1/0.1/2.6.

This high thermal mass performs well in most circumstances. Both buildings have very modest heating and cooling loads for April despite low temperatures, swings of up to 20°C (36°F), and highly variable solar conditions at both buildings. The moderating effect of the thermal mass maintains the temperature within the setpoints with only modest auxiliary cooling. Low loads occurring under summer conditions reflect the effectiveness of thermal mass to store heat for dissipation during cooler parts of the day, often by ventilation at night. During winter days, when solar gains through very large south-facing apertures might be expected to drive temperatures up to uncomfortable levels, temperatures never rise more than 3°C to 5°C (5°F to 9°F) above the heating setpoint.

Occupant response from the sites indicated that temperatures were generally maintained at comfortable levels. The major exception to this at these buildings and other high-mass buildings in the program was a complaint that on cloudy winter mornings, it just never got warm enough. The cause of this problem can be seen easily by looking at a cloudy day (hours 24-48) at Mt. Airy in Figure 4-12. Although the air temperature was maintained by the heating system at the setpoint, the radiant temperature was nearly 3°C (5°F) lower, and did not increase through the entire day. Likewise, the second of two cloudy days at CUMC showed a similar pattern, although the radiant temperature seemed to recover somewhat as the day went on. There was an associated consequence at CUMC. Because of the difficulty in raising the radiant temperature of the space after several hours with the thermostat set back, much of the intermittent use that would naturally take place in the solar wing was assigned to other, less massive spaces in the church because they were quicker to heat up. Thus, even after two years of use, the solar wing was occupied less intensively than anticipated.

To test whether this problem could be solved by variation within a high-mass configuration, the building descriptions were modified to reduce the amount of thermal mass in one case, and the surface area of mass exposed to the space in another. For Mt. Airy, the thickness of the floor slab and wall mass was reduced by half for one simulation, resulting in the same mass index — 1.9/0.1/0.8. The heavy block walls were completely removed for the other, while retaining the full floor, for a mass index of 0.9/0.1/0.8. There was almost no change in temperature from the first modification, while removal of the mass walls caused greater temperature fluctuations on sunny days, but very little change on cloudy days. Figure 4-13 shows the heating and cooling loads resulting from these changes. Halving mass thickness produced minor increases in both heating and cooling, likely due to a slightly diminished capacity to store solar gains over extended periods. Removing the

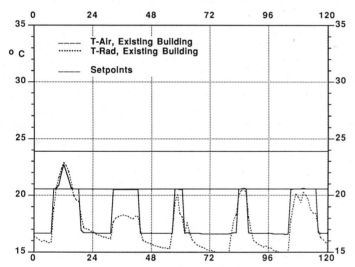

Figure 4-12. 120 hours, Mt. Airy, January, reference temperatures.

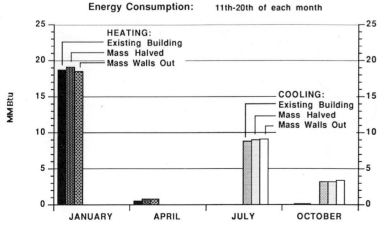

Figure 4-13. Mt. Airy mass options.

mass walls had a similar effect except in winter, when reduced mass exposure allowed quicker temperature reduction during thermostat setback periods. The more effective setback produced a small decrease in heating loads. However, reduction of mass, especially reduction in exposure, resulted in greater temperature excursions outside the comfort zone in April and October.

For CUMC, a similar approach was tried. Mass thickness was halved for the first simulation, retaining the 1.1/0.1/2.6 index. The second modification was to carpet the floor, greatly reducing exposure of the major mass, for an index of 0.2/1.0/2.6. As at Mt. Airy, halving the mass resulted in small heating load increases, but produced little change in cooling load (Figure 4-14). Carpeting resulted in essentially unchanged heating loads, presumably a balance between less heat storage and a more effective night thermostat setback from quicker nighttime temperature reduction. The effect on temperatures was much more pronounced than on loads, especially in the carpeted case. Figure 4-15 shows that sunny January days produced higher daytime temperatures, often reaching the cooling setpoint. Higher temperatures increased heat loss but also provided a welcome "extra" warmth to the occupants. At night, however, the temperature can drop much farther than with the original mass configuration, and on cloudy days (hours 72-120) it does not recover any better than the original configuration, so cloudy mornings are still cold. In addition, reduction of mass results in greater temperature swings during other seasons. In April and July, the effects are modest but add 0.5°C to 1°C (1°F to 2°F) to occasional discomfort situations. In October, however, when warm temperatures and large solar gains combine to create regular overheating problems, reduced thermal mass results in about 2°C (4°F) to 4°C (7°F) increases to already excessive temperatures.

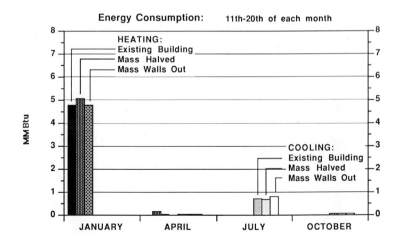

Figure 4-14. CUMC mass options.

Attempts to relieve the coldness of cloudy winter mornings by adjusting the amount and exposure of thermal mass in the simulations, while still retaining a generally high level of mass, failed. They tended to permit additional undesirable temperature fluctuations, due in part to large solar apertures. If one is committed to a high-mass, large-aperture solution, it may be wise to ensure sufficient mass to hold temperatures consistently within the desired comfort range.

THERMOSTAT SETBACK

An explanation for the difficulty in raising temperatures to the setpoint on cloudy days can be found by taking into account the long-term effects of thermostat settings on mass temperatures. If the time constant of the building is sufficiently long, the average mass temperature will not respond to temporary fluctuations in air temperature, but will tend to reflect the average air temperature over a longer period. This period may be several days in these buildings, longer at Mt. Airy than CUMC because of the former's larger amount of exposed heavy mass (1.9 versus 1.1). In winter, although the space temperature may sometimes rise in response to solar gains, it is typically at the heating setpoint while heating is provided, and well below it during setback periods. The relatively constant heavy mass temperature during this period is likely to be the average of those temperatures, that is, below the heating setpoint, and the mass is likely to resist any attempts to raise its temperature during a relatively short heating period, even a full day of occupancy.

A logical solution to this problem is to remove the setback so that the average air temperature is at or above the setpoint, and the mass temperature can be maintained at a level that will allow maintenance of comfort conditions in the space. To

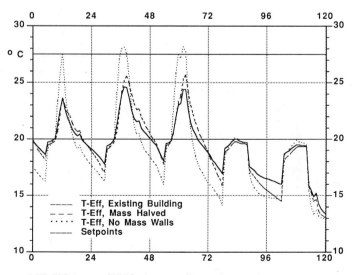

Figure 4-15. 120 hours, CUMC, January, thermal mass, temperatures.

test the effect of a thermostat adjustment on comfort and energy use, the setback was eliminated in both buildings.

At Mt. Airy, the winter heating load was increased about 10% (Figure 4-16), and the effective daytime temperature (Figure 4-17) in the space was raised to or above the setpoint on all but the cloudiest day (hours 24-48). Even on that day, the temperature was only about half as far below the setpoint as in the original case. At CUMC, the increase in heating load was greater (Figure 4-18), with effective daytime temperatures (Figure 4-19) raised to or above the setpoint, even on the cloudiest days (hours 72-120). But the heating energy use of both these buildings is very low in comparison to typical buildings, and the absolute magnitude of the energy-use increases is actually rather small. In July and October there is minimal effect, because neither building requires heating during these months. In April, when both heating and cooling are required in limited amounts, removal of the setback causes both higher heating loads and higher temperatures during periods of overheating. Therefore, setback, if restricted during winter, should be restored as soon as overheating periods begin to appear.

LOW-MASS BUILDINGS

The heating load increase due to eliminating the setback may seem small compared with the benefits usually associated with adopting it. This is because high-mass levels, which prevent deep temperature drops, limited the effectiveness of setback strategies by keeping the temperature from dropping quickly. Thus, the penalties for removing the setback were similarly limited. An alternative that might mitigate occupant discomfort on cold mornings and reclaim greater heating load benefits for setback thermostat strategies would be to reduce mass to more typical levels.

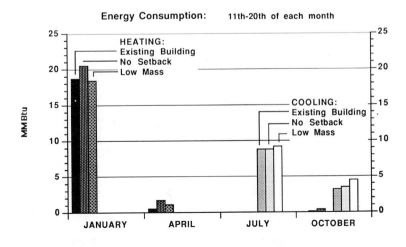

Figure 4-16. Mt. Airy setback and low mass options.

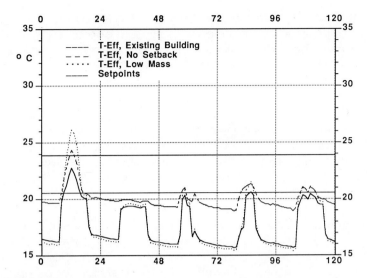

Figure 4-17. 120 hours, Mt. Airy, January, thermostat, temperatures.

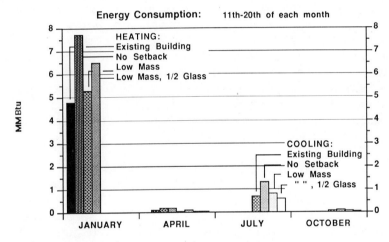

Figure 4-18. CUMC thermostat and low mass options.

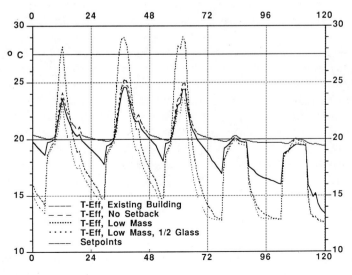

Figure 4-19. 120 hours, CUMC, January, thermostat, temperatures.

225

Both buildings were modified by carpeting the floor, changing all walls to stud construction with gypsum board facing, and providing acoustic ceilings. This produced a mass index of 0.1/1.0/1.8 for Mt. Airy and 0.2/1.0/1.6 for CUMC, only a minimal amount of exposed heavy mass in both cases. Although the modifications greatly reduced the amount of thermal mass, they are only "low mass" relative to the original configurations. They are not atypical of usual commercial construction. The results of these configurations, along with those of the no-setback, high-mass case were compared for energy and comfort impacts and for effectiveness of dealing with the cold morning problem.

At Mt. Airy, January daytime temperatures in the low-mass case with setback strategy were higher than in the constant thermostat configuration (Figure 4-17) only on totally sunny days, when the temperature became too high for comfort, although ventilation could control overheating at that time of year. On cloudy (hours 24-48) and partly cloudy days (48-120), the effective temperatures, while an improvement over the original configuration, did not reach the warmer levels achieved with high mass and no setback. April shows results similar to January. However, increased overheating is not always subject to ventilation in April because of high outside temperatures. In July there is little difference in temperatures. Unlike April, October shows only minor differences in daytime temperatures, due to much lower night temperatures in the low-mass case.

Cooling loads for the low-mass case are marginally higher than the no-setback case (Figure 4-16), but heating loads are lower, especially in January, when effective setback provides greatest benefits. The constant-thermostat case produces higher peak loads during the heating season (Figure 4-16), which can be costly in this case, because Mt. Airy uses electric (heat pump) heating. Cooling peaks are not greatly affected, although the low-mass configuration is more susceptible to increased peaks when associated with solar gains.

For CUMC, Figure 4-19 shows wider temperature swings in January than at Mt. Airy, but in the same pattern. Sunny days show significant overheating with low mass, while the setback is so deep that during the early part of the occupied period of cloudy days, temperatures were even lower than with the original configuration, and considerably short of the comfort conditions achieved by the constant thermostat option. Both heating and cooling loads are much lower than the no-setback case (Figure 4-18). Cooling load reduction resulted from restoring a cooling thermostat setup, which in the constant-thermostat case had caused cooling even during unoccupied periods. Extremely high, effective temperatures occur in the low-mass case in all seasons (Figure 4-20). It is presumed that this is caused by the very large solar apertures coupled with the inability of the limited mass to store large solar gains.

The previous study of daylighting at these two buildings suggested that the full effectiveness of daylighting at Mt. Airy requires the large apertures in the roof. However, the pattern of lighting control at CUMC suggested that the roof aperture area could be reduced without substantially affecting daylighting utility. Reducing the glazing area could prevent overheating, reduce heat losses through the glazing, and produce a more controllable environment. For CUMC, an additional simulation was run with the low-mass configuration and the roof glazing reduced by half.

Reducing the aperture area increases the January heating load by diminishing solar gains (although it is still less than the constant-thermostat case), but reduces cooling in all seasons (Figure 4-18). Most important, however, the consistent overheating so prevalent in the fully glazed case during April and October is considerably reduced, often with daytime temperatures at or below those of the existing configuration (Figure 4-20). Although neither of the low-mass configurations (with full or reduced glazing) satisfactorily solved the problem of heating on cloudy mornings, both showed rapid temperature increases from the deep setback, suggesting that setting the temperature up earlier might be effective in warming the building sufficiently for comfort.

THERMAL MASS SUMMARY

In summary, the existing configurations work quite well, with a very large reduction in energy use compared to typical buildings and generally good comfort conditions. They do, however, create a problem on cold, cloudy mornings, when the mass cannot be heated sufficiently to raise the radiant temperature to an acceptable level. Moderate reductions in mass

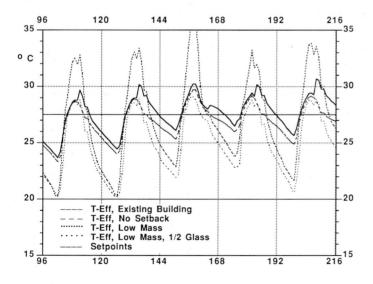

Figure 4-20. 120 hours, CUMC, October, thermostat, temperatures.

amount and exposure did not reduce that problem, and resulted in some decrement in energy and comfort performance. Elimination of thermostat setbacks has a distinct, but possibly acceptable, energy cost in winter and improves the comfort conditions on cloudy mornings. In other seasons, lack of a setback may cause overheating, so a setback should be reactivated when cooling loads may be significant. Lower (typical) mass configurations may result in warmer cloudy winter mornings and lower heating loads than other alternatives, but tend to exacerbate overheating and cooling loads. Adapting other elements of the building design such as apertures, thermostats, or HVAC may be necessary to fulfill the potential of low-mass options.

A decision must be made whether a high- or low-mass solution will be used. Once that decision is made, other decisions on glazing area, thermostat control strategy, ventilation, acoustics (discussed below), and other passive system and building elements must respond to that decision.

ACOUSTICS

Many of the buildings in the DOE Nonresidential Experimental Buildings Program have little acoustic treatment, resulting in acoustic problems, particularly high ambient noise levels and lack of acoustic privacy. Mt. Airy has modest acoustic treatment, while CUMC has virtually none, but both could have better acoustic environments within the same general building design. Improved acoustic environments were simulated to determine their effect on energy use, in particular the effect they would have on the use of thermal mass.

The open plan at Mt. Airy, which resulted in part from design constraints imposed by the daylighting system, together with hard surfaces on floors and walls to absorb solar radiation, led to potential acoustic problems. That the building is a library naturally imposes more stringent requirements on noise. Fortunately, three factors appear to contribute to a reasonable acoustic environment: the ceiling treatment is very effective in lowering the general noise level throughout the building, even though there is limited surface area to work with around the roof apertures; staff and visitors try to minimize noise because they are in a library; and occupancy is typically sparse.

Given this situation, the only acoustic problem comes at those times when noise is unavoidable in an otherwise hushed environment. Impact noise from walking in the library can distract others using the library. Carpeting of traffic areas would essentially eliminate this problem without changing the thermal mass index greatly (1.4/0.6/.08). Such a modification (carpeting half the floor, Figure 4-21) results in minor changes to energy consumption, slightly decreased heating, and increased cooling. Temperatures are barely affected, although cloudy winter mornings are slightly improved. This acoustic amenity could be incorporated with virtually no impact on total energy consumption or thermal comfort.

Acoustics are a significant problem at CUMC. There is no acoustic treatment in the solar wing beyond carpeting in the nursery. As a result, the general noise level is much too high. This causes annoyances within each room, between rooms, and between the solar wing and the rest of the church (there is a large open passageway between the solar wing and the main church lobby). The lack of acoustic treatment may have resulted from competition for surface area with reflective and absorptive surfaces required for passive heating, lighting, and cooling (ventilation) systems.

Two acoustic approaches were tested at CUMC to determine whether including such treatment would adversely affect energy use or thermal comfort. In the first modification, the ceiling was faced with acoustic tile, and the floor was carpeted to provide a second sound-absorbing surface and to minimize foot-traffic noise. The resulting mass index is 0.2/1.0/1.6. In the second modification, acoustic tile was applied to ceiling and south walls of each zone, to avoid covering passive solar gain surfaces (floor and north wall), giving a mass index of 1.1/ 0.1/1.2. In both cases, the effect on energy consumption was negligible (Figure 4-22). The small reductions in heating energy are likely due to the insulating effect of the ceiling treatment. When the floor is carpeted, rapid response of temperatures to solar gain (Figure 4-23) causes higher daytime temperatures and some loss of comfort, so the option using the south wall rather than the floor for acoustic treatment may be preferred, although this would have to be weighed against the cost, maintenance, and amenity of carpeting.

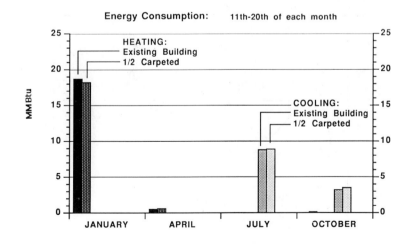

Figure 4-21. Mt. Airy acoustic options.

In high-mass buildings, comfortable acoustic environments can be achieved without severe impacts on energy consumption or comfort. As long as a significant portion of the heavy-mass surfaces is still exposed to the space, little difference will be seen in energy or comfort. However, if most of the heavy mass is covered (most often by full carpeting of a slab floor), short-term temperature swings are likely to reduce comfort, although energy use remains relatively constant.

SHADING CONTROL

Operable shading of apertures is generally used to control overheating or glare or both. Some of the questions that arose regarding control of shading were addressed using the two buildings in this study. Different situations were analyzed in the two buildings.

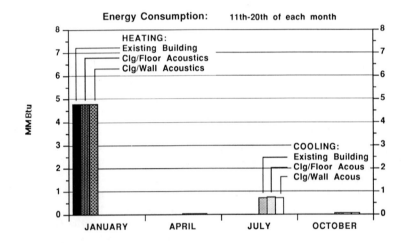

Figure 4-22. CUMC acoustic options.

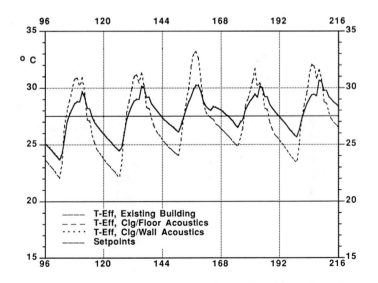

Figure 4-23. 120 hours, CUMC, October, acoustics, temperatures.

At Mt. Airy, there had been some confusion over the role of venetian blinds on view glazing on the south and west sides of the building. Perceptions of their thermal and visual effects led to a compromise on their positioning — always lowered, but tilted open — which does not effectively address either issue (Adegran et al., *Qualitative Study,* 1984). These apertures, although large, were considered by occupants to be view glazing, whose energy contributions were secondary, in contrast to roof glazing, whose primary purposes were energy related. Extreme cases were investigated to determine the sensitivity of the building's energy consumption to different shade control strategies. The initial run (the existing building) assumed that the blinds were always up. Two additional runs assumed the blinds were down, one with slats closed and one with slats open.

Figure 4-24 indicates that the effect on energy consumption when the blinds were down but open was negligible, as most of the sunlight passed through the shades or was absorbed by them after multiple reflections. Little passed back through the glass. The effect on energy consumption of having the blinds completely closed was still quite small, on the order of 2% (increase in heating, decrease in cooling). Temperatures were a little lower than the unshaded case, perhaps 1°C (2°F) with blinds completely closed, and half that with blinds tilted open. One reason for these small changes was that part of the solar gains was still absorbed by the blinds. Thus, light was obstructed but heat remained in the space. Perhaps a more important reason was that exterior shading rendered view windows insignificant as a source of solar gain in summer and, in winter, roof apertures provided sufficient solar gain, so that additional gains through view glazing had a very modest effect in comparison.

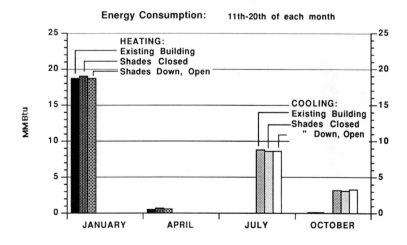

Figure 4-24. Mt. Airy shade options.

Both lighting and heating in the spaces affected by the shades were provided primarily from roof apertures. Those apertures required no shading because they had been carefully designed to avoid direct-gain radiation during most overheating periods, and the baffling system (Figure 4-3) effectively eliminated glare problems. It would seem that the best approach to the blinds in this building would be to encourage occupants to maximize their visual comfort and lighting quality, and ignore energy-consurnption impacts.

Because of the limited amount of view glazing at CUMC, most of it facing north, no serious problems from glare or overheating were encountered from that source. However, the large roof apertures have no baffling system to mitigate glare, nor do they have operable shading. A simulation was run with a shade on the roof apertures that was 70% reflective, allowing about one-third of the available light into the space. No insulating properties were given to the shade. It is expected that such a shade would be used primarily during periods of abundant daylighting, so that daylighting effects would be unchanged.

With the sun angles and external shading configurations at CUMC, the greatest glare would be expected in winter, with less in the swing seasons and relatively little in summer. However, in January, frequent use of the shade would result in heating load increases of about 40% (Figure 4-25). In swing seasons, the energy effect would be negligible. These results would suggest that during the heating season, occupants should use the shade *only* when there is serious visual discomfort caused by incoming solar radiation. This is most likely to occur during a sunny midday because inside temperatures

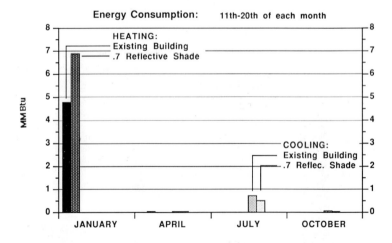

Figure 4-25. CUMC shade options.

232

are high and the shade will improve thermal comfort; sunlight is entering the space directly and the shade will improve visual comfort; and excess daylighting is entering and the shade may be drawn without requiring additional electric lighting. During other heating season situations, occupant control must be carefully applied to avoid unwanted heating and lighting energy consumption and reduction in thermal comfort. In any case, the shade will reduce solar gains and associated storage, resulting in increased heating energy consumption or degradation of thermal comfort at a later time. Alternatively, a method for eliminating glare and direct radiation on occupants, such as that at Mt. Airy, would reduce the need for shading and maintain the full thermal benefits of solar apertures.

The benefits of regularly using an operable shade to avoid overheating in April, July, and October are evident from the results. Shading further reduces the already small cooling load without introducing a heating requirement (Figure 4-25), and reduces the temperatures during those periods from 1°C to 3°C (2°F to 5°F). With operable shades in place, effective temperatures rarely rise above the cooling setpoint during swing seasons, whereas without them they reach above the setpoint several times in April and daily in October. Occupants should be encouraged to use shading liberally outside the heating season, but it is important that shading not be used when it reduces available sunlight so much that electric lighting must be used. In addition to the cost of additional lighting electricity, it is quite possible that electric lights would add more heat to the space than roof apertures would without shades.

When view glazing is not the primary aperture for solar gains or daylighting, as at Mt. Airy, shading operation on those windows can be left to the occupants to adjust as they see fit. When shading is applied to *primary* solar apertures, as at CUMC, its cooling season effect on energy consumption and comfort are usually beneficial, and use of shading should be encouraged. However, during the heating season, overuse of shading can seriously diminish the benefits of solar heating, and occupants should be discouraged from using it except to prevent significant visual or thermal problems. In all seasons, thermal effects must be weighed against the potential reduction of daylighting by using shading.

CONCLUSIONS

This study has led to conclusions about both passive systems in general, and about the specific issues investigated. Passive strategies affect the occupants' environment as well as the building's energy use. Passive systems must be evaluated with respect to *both* effects.

Interactions of solar apertures, thermal mass, climate, operating schedule, mechanical systems, and control strategies must be considered in designing passive buildings, especially where thermal storage plays an important role. Sophisticated analytical tools may be necessary to understand fully such interactions.

The following relate to specific issues:

- Early in a passive commercial design, a decision should be made whether to provide thermal storage mass for the long term (multiple days) or short term (smoothing effects during the occupied period of one day), based on the building function, operating schedule, and passive strategies applied. Mass amount and exposure should be allocated toward the chosen goal. Misunderstanding of the implications of this decision can lead to occupant discomfort and poor energy performance.
- If long-term thermal storage is used in a building, elimination or radical restriction of thermostat setback in winter should be considered and analyzed for mitigation of morning coldness problems.
- Appropriate acoustic solutions can be found that do not detract from passive system effectiveness. The thermal, acoustic, lighting, and aesthetic role of each surface of a space must be understood to achieve a proper combination of surface treatments.
- Occupants can be given wide latitude in deciding the preferred position of operable solar aperture shading during the cooling season if that aperture (with *fixed* shading) has been configured to limit summer solar gains. They should be strongly discouraged from overuse of shading on solar apertures during the heating season. This might be accomplished by configuring apertures to avoid glare and direct radiation on occupants and work surfaces, diminishing the desire for winter shading.

BIBLIOGRAPHY

Adegran, Mari et al. 1984. "Total Building Impacts of South-Facing Roof Apertures," Lawrence Berkeley Laboratory Report, LBL-17562 Berkeley, CA, August 1984; in *Proceedings*, "Windows in Building Design and Maintenance," 13-15 June 1984, Göteborg, Sweden, Swedish Council for Building Research.

Adegran, Mari et al. 1984. "Mt. Airy Library, a Qualitative Study of Daylighting in a Passive Solar Building," Lawrence Berkeley Laboratory Report LBL-18527, Berkeley, CA, December 1984.

Andersson, Brandt et al. 1983. "Thermal Effects Resulting from Occupant Behavior and Building Operation," Lawrence Berkeley Laboratory Report, LBL-16738, Berkeley, CA, September 1983; in *Proceedings*, "Passive and Hybrid Solar Energy Update," 26-28 September 1983, Washington, DC.

Andersson, Brandt. 1984. "C.U.M.C.: Baseline BLAST Model Analysis," Draft Technical Note, Lawrence Berkeley Laboratory, Berkeley, CA, January 1984.

Andersson, Brandt. 1984. "Mt. Airy: Baseline BLAST Model Analysis," Draft Technical Note, Lawrence Berkeley Laboratory, Berkeley, CA, February 1984.

Arasteh, D. et al. 1984. "Skylight Energy Performance and Design Optimization," Lawrence Berkeley Laboratory Report LBL-17476, Berkeley, CA, February 1984.

Bauman, Fred et al. 1983. "Verification of BLAST by Comparison with Measurements of a Solar-Dominated Test Cell and a Thermally Massive Building," *Journal of Solar Energy Engineering*, Vol. 105, May 1983.

Department of Energy. 1982. "Typical Electric Bills January 1, 1982" Report DOE/EIA-0040(82), Washington, DC.

Department of Energy. 1983. "Passive Solar Commercial Buildings Program, Case Studies," Report DOE/CE-0042, September 1983.

Gordon, Harry, and William Fisher. 1984. "The DOE Passive Solar Commercial Buildings Program: Performance Evaluation," in *Proceedings*, "Passive and Hybrid Solar Energy Update," Washington, DC, September 1984.

Gordon, Harry et al. 1984. "Performance Overview Report of the DOE Passive Commercial Buildings Program," submitted to the Department of Energy, December 1984.

Kantrowitz, Min. 1984. "Analysis of Occupant Effects, Interactions, and Satisfaction: Community United Methodist Church," submitted to the Department of Energy, February 1984.

National Climatic Center. 1981. "Typical Meteorological Year User's Manual: Hourly Solar Radiation—Surface Meteorological Observations." TD9734, April 1981.

Place, Wayne et al. 1980. "Human Comfort and Auxiliary Control Considerations in Passive Solar Structures," Lawrence Berkeley Laboratory Report LBL-10034; in *Proceedings,* AS/ISES Solar Jubilee, Phoenix, June 1980; in *Proceedings,* International Congress on Building Energy Management, Portugal, May 1980.

Place, Wayne et al. 1983. "The Predicted Impact of Linear Roof Apertures on the Energy Performance of Office Buildings," Lawrence Berkeley Laboratory Report LBL-16782, Berkeley, CA.

Swisher, Joel, and Don Frey. 1984. "Performance Analysis of the Mt. Airy Library Building," submitted to the Department of Energy, April 1984.

Yager, Andrew, and Don Frey. 1984. "Performance Analysis of the Community United Methodist Church Solar Addition," submitted to the Department of Energy, September 1984.

APPENDIX

APPENDIX A

ENERGY PERFORMANCE DATA
(Btu/ft^2/yr)

PROJECT NAME	BASE	BEPS	PREDICTED	ACTUAL	DATES MEASURED
Johnson Controls Branch Office	72,500	36,000	51,000	35,661	10/82-09/83
Two Rivers School	113,000	N/A	31,861	52,437	06/83-05/84
Essex-Dorsey Senior Center	86,000	42,000	40,300	N/A	
Abrams Primary School	54,000	35,000	22,180	N/A	
Mt. Airy Public Library	55,700	46,000	17,350	26,012	01/83-12/83
Philadelphia Municipal Auto Shop	230,000	28,000	69,000	92,255	08/83-07/84
Blake Avenue College Center	100,000	48,000	33,000	N/A	
Comal County Mental Health Center	72,000	33,000	31,000	33,222	09/82-08/83
Community United Methodist Church	112,400	43,000	16,000	20,164	11/82-10/83
Shelly Ridge Girl Scout Center	57,000	42,000	35,000	N/A	
Gunnison County Airport	86,400	63,000	66,700	70,589	09/81-08/82
Kieffer Store	62,000	59,000	23,000	47,315	05/82-05/83
Princeton School of Architecture	158,000	42,000	75,000	115,947	06/79-05/80
Princeton Professional Park	76,000	42,000	15,000	N/A	
RPI Visitor Center	85,000	48,000	28,500	51,953	09/83-08/84
Security State Bank	89,177	48,000	25,577	55,867	01/84-12/84
Touliatos Greenhouse	67,469	N/A	33,320	N/A	
Walker Field Terminal	87,500	72,000	42,000	N/A	
St. Mary's School Gymnasium	78,000	51,000	27,100	27,329	05/83-04/84

ACTUAL ENERGY CONSUMPTION (BTU/FT²) AND DEGREE DAYS

PROJECT	MONTH	HEAT	DHW	COOL	LIGHT	FANS	PASS	MISC	TOTAL	HDD	CDD
Community	1	4133	73	0	216	62	0	0	4506	1038	0
United	2	2931	73	0	146	55	0	0	3205	783	0
Methodist	3	2567	73	0	156	51	0	0	2847	697	0
Church	4	2276	73	0	178	42	0	0	2569	510	0
	5	182	73	0	146	5	0	0	406	180	25
11/82-10/83	6	0	73	0	109	15	0	9	206	15	225
	7	0	73	5	89	29	0	42	238	0	449
	8	0	73	71	80	29	0	27	280	0	511
	9	0	73	0	129	13	0	18	233	205	140
	10	0	73	0	167	7	0	2	249	266	3
	11	1802	73	0	146	36	0	0	2057	630	0
	12	2913	73	0	309	73	0	0	3368	775	0
	TOTAL	16804	876	76	1873	437	0	98	20164	5099	1353
Gunnison	1	9032	47	0	3457	0	0	0	12536	1674	0
County	2	6848	49	0	3457	0	0	0	10354	1528	0
Airport	3	3300	58	0	3833	0	0	0	7191	1103	0
	4	2249	53	0	3132	0	0	0	5434	780	0
09/81-08/82	5	543	52	0	3370	0	0	0	3965	615	0
	6	0	49	0	3070	0	0	0	3119	428	38
	7	0	48	0	2781	0	0	0	2829	254	130
	8	0	50	0	3216	0	0	0	3266	191	229
	9	301	44	0	3417	0	0	0	3762	349	49
	10	239	48	0	3377	0	0	0	3664	713	0
	11	1003	53	0	3517	0	0	0	4573	945	0
	12	6321	46	0	3529	0	0	0	9896	1348	0
	TOTAL	29836	597	0	40156	0	0	0	70589	9928	446
Kieffer	1	8538	169	0	573	0	76	158	9514	1413	0
Store	2	5612	152	0	526	0	37	154	6481	1160	0
	3	4336	158	0	508	0	33	156	5191	1011	0
06/82-05/83	4	2198	154	0	503	0	0	177	3032	730	0
	5	978	146	0	432	0	0	195	1751	459	0
	6	425	152	0	201	2	0	68	848	219	39
	7	364	175	0	259	0	0	82	880	24	210
	8	549	171	0	265	0	0	107	1092	83	115
	9	1158	173	0	302	0	0	82	1715	220	3
	10	1224	171	0	354	0	0	72	1821	527	0
	11	4887	142	0	395	0	8	164	5596	1000	0
	12	8352	150	0	561	0	107	224	9394	1224	0
	TOTAL	38621	1913	0	4879	2	261	1639	47315	8070	367

PROJECT	MONTH	HEAT	DHW	COOL	LIGHT	FANS	PASS	MISC	TOTAL	HDD	CDD
RPI	1	4562	0	21	1141	426	1	1223	7374	1302	0
Visitor	2	2927	0	20	997	312	1	1160	5417	934	0
Center	3	3520	0	16	883	327	1	1157	5904	1069	0
	4	1610	0	7	775	264	4	1055	3715	393	0
09/83-08/84	5	272	0	11	858	264	7	1159	2571	236	25
	6	42	0	654	627	554	59	998	2934	26	275
	7	16	0	966	659	649	69	1020	3379	5	343
	8	19	0	962	753	636	128	1064	3562	11	331
	9	21	0	472	988	480	45	937	2943	194	134
	10	658	0	55	1064	317	5	1003	3102	512	0
	11	1891	0	20	1052	290	1	1161	4415	825	0
	12	3995	0	20	1054	394	1	1173	6637	1194	0
	TOTAL	19533	0	3224	10851	4913	322	13110	51953	6701	1108
Johnson	1	3249	49	0	134	774	0	531	4737	925	0
Controls	2	3619	39	0	121	719	0	618	5114	742	0
Branch	3	2402	44	0	127	795	0	659	4027	632	0
Office	4	2352	41	0	102	755	0	120	3370	575	0
	5	2597	31	1	110	678	0	124	3541	293	7
10/82-09/83	6	0	31	45	99	917	0	120	1212	81	160
	7	0	35	91	94	780	0	124	1124	7	364
	8	0	28	170	117	1053	0	124	1492	0	398
	9	0	31	93	94	817	0	121	1156	79	163
	10	1129	39	14	106	704	0	557	2549	502	0
	11	2020	40	1	117	661	0	115	2954	807	0
	12	3004	37	0	129	702	0	513	4385	1088	0
	TOTAL	20372	445	415	1350	9355	0	3724	35661	5731	1092
Mt. Airy	1	3257	21	77	292	865	2	32	4546	876	0
Public	2	2405	13	9	273	691	4	26	3421	750	0
Library	3	1521	10	227	370	563	4	31	2726	504	0
	4	1075	9	0	300	454	4	29	1871	355	0
01/83-12/83	5	0	4	0	212	179	5	27	427	151	128
	6	0	1	539	131	343	6	30	1050	33	311
	7	0	0	1692	86	560	7	32	2377	0	481
	8	0	5	1807	157	578	6	31	2584	0	460
	9	0	1	401	26	132	1	7	568	0	405
	10	24	13	78	235	306	3	34	693	254	39
	11	700	17	104	307	394	2	32	1556	540	0
	12	3050	21	0	288	797	1	36	4193	1085	0
	TOTAL	12032	115	4934	2677	5862	45	347	26012	4548	1824

PROJECT	MONTH	HEAT	DHW	COOL	LIGHT	FANS	PASS	MISC	TOTAL	HDD	CDD
Comal	1	4021	259	0	544	143	0	280	5247	240	12
County	2	2936	248	2	601	118	0	286	4191	158	42
Mental	3	2315	225	0	777	95	0	306	3718	71	133
Health	4	729	175	10	683	28	0	298	1923	16	259
Center	5	64	109	90	565	0	0	284	1112	0	507
	6	0	88	666	543	0	0	340	1637	0	640
09/82-08/83	7	0	60	815	579	0	0	352	1806	0	750
	8	0	55	902	533	0	0	331	1821	0	837
	9	0	124	935	595	0	0	279	1933	0	435
	10	581	215	254	712	17	0	245	2024	0	318
	11	1864	222	23	627	64	0	234	3034	42	118
	12	3530	241	1	604	130	0	270	4776	156	44
	TOTAL	16040	2021	3698	7363	595	0	3505	33222	683	4095
Philadelphia	1	21500	53	0	456	0	0	860	22869	790	0
Municipal	2	18947	53	0	404	0	0	772	20176	580	0
Auto	3	14316	70	0	386	0	0	965	15737	666	0
Shop	4	4895	35	0	386	0	0	912	6228	435	0
	5	965	35	0	351	0	0	772	2123	173	18
08/83-07/84	6	0	35	0	351	0	0	894	1280	0	255
	7	0	35	0	351	0	0	894	1280	0	279
	8	0	35	0	263	0	0	1158	1456	0	341
	9	70	35	0	316	0	0	947	1368	16	181
	10	2175	53	0	351	0	0	860	3439	236	3
	11	4509	35	0	351	0	0	982	5877	510	0
	12	9123	53	0	421	0	0	825	10422	837	0
	TOTAL	76500	527	0	4387	0	0	10841	92255	4243	1077
Two Rivers	1	218	0	0	1206	143	0	88	1655	1690	0
School	2	245	0	0	1359	171	0	109	1884	1831	0
	3	116	0	0	1257	183	0	111	1667	1097	0
06/83-05/84	4	87	0	0	1215	177	0	107	1586	789	0
	5	38	0	0	1131	183	0	60	1412	169	45
	6	0	0	0	408	157	0	0	565	211	31
	7	0	0	0	422	133	0	0	555	146	223
	8	20	0	0	1039	190	0	19	1268	103	213
	9	446	0	0	1821	177	0	0	2444	597	0
	10	198	0	0	1182	63	0	102	1545	1193	0
	11	240	0	0	1748	185	0	32	2205	1247	0
	12	236	0	0	1011	147	0	32	1426	1427	0
	TOTAL	1844	0	0	13799	1909	0	660	18212	10500	512

A-4

PROJECT	MONTH	HEAT	DHW	COOL	LIGHT	FANS	PASS	MISC	TOTAL	HDD	CDD
Princeton	1	15940	0	0	2176	0	0	0	18116	995	0
School of	2	13670	0	0	2333	0	0	0	16003	1008	0
Architecture	3	7357	0	0	2201	0	0	0	9558	758	0
	4	5765	0	0	2252	0	0	0	8017	327	0
06/79-05/80	5	2061	0	0	2404	0	0	0	4465	89	93
	6	6105	0	0	0	0	0	0	6105	35	139
	7	5139	0	0	3845	0	0	0	8984	0	293
	8	6887	0	0	1340	0	0	0	8227	0	295
	9	5635	0	0	1645	0	0	0	7280	42	114
	10	3131	0	0	3036	0	0	0	6167	316	0
	11	5948	0	0	2302	0	0	0	8250	426	0
	12	12574	0	0	2201	0	0	0	14775	794	0
	TOTAL	90212	0	0	25735	0	0	0	115947	4790	934
Security	1	7227	48	80	131	217	0	456	8159	1668	0
State	2	6018	66	9	196	284	0	646	7219	1018	0
Bank	3	6527	75	9	190	296	0	744	7841	1175	0
	4	1789	53	54	135	187	0	448	2666	486	0
01/84-12/84	5	0	70	445	220	265	0	625	1625	109	220
	6	0	66	832	197	276	0	619	1990	28	169
	7	0	65	759	312	308	0	682	2126	16	239
	8	0	64	1156	158	337	0	789	2504	0	467
	9	782	65	570	203	253	0	715	2588	136	123
	10	3982	66	296	366	332	0	858	5900	296	0
	11	3200	66	33	308	306	0	727	4640	843	0
	12	6927	71	12	347	447	0	805	8609	1346	0
	TOTAL	36452	775	4255	2763	3508	0	8114	55867	7121	1218
St Mary's	1	4810	0	0	202	317	0	273	5602	1079	0
School	2	4208	0	0	239	249	0	256	4952	674	0
Gymnasium	3	3156	0	0	354	227	0	273	4010	781	0
	4	822	0	20	311	120	0	264	1537	365	0
05/83-04/84	5	0	0	37	421	137	41	273	909	128	63
	6	0	0	0	15	119	144	256	534	0	240
	7	0	0	0	153	113	202	273	741	0	439
	8	0	0	60	197	128	237	273	895	0	432
	9	0	0	8	389	111	211	256	975	24	192
	10	2	0	0	541	110	176	273	1102	210	7
	11	931	0	0	534	140	0	264	1869	501	0
	12	3352	0	0	298	280	0	273	4203	961	0
	TOTAL	17281	0	125	3654	2051	1011	3207	27329	4723	1373

APPENDIX B
ECONOMIC DATA

TABLE B-1
COMPARISON OF
PASSIVE SOLAR COMMERCIAL BUILDING
TO R. S. MEANS DATA BASE

PROJECT DESCRIPTION		MODIFIERS				DATA MODIFICATION					
						1/4		Median		3/4	
Name	Cost/ft²	Building Type	City Cost Mod.	Size Mod.	Year	Given	Mod.	Given	Mod.	Given	Mod.
Two Rivers	$149			— No comparable building type —							
Abrams	36	Elementary school	Birmingham	93.8	1.012	1981	39.85	37.83	49.05	46.56	59.30	56.29
CUMC	47	Religious classrooms	Springfield	99.7	1.012	1981	35.45	35.77	39.70	40.06	48.85	49.29
Blake Avenue	64	Student union	Pueblo	98.0	1.000	1981	53.80	52.72	70.20	68.80	87.00	85.26
Mt. Airy	88	Library	Raleigh	94.9	1.000	1982	54.00	51.25	67.00	63.58	85.00	80.67
St. Mary's	74	Gym	Washington, DC	100.4	1.015	1982	41.70	42.53	51.80	52.84	65.80	67.12
Johnson Controls	57	Office	Salt Lake	99.8	.977	1982	38.90	38.12	49.60	48.61	66.00	64.68
Princeton Park	46	Office	Trenton	102.6	.955	1982	38.90	38.12	49.60	48.61	66.00	64.68
Security State	59	Bank	Minneapolis	98.6	.950	1981	58.00	54.33	72.80	68.19	96.50	90.39
Essex-Dorsey	65	Commercial center	Baltimore	100.8	.988	1982	48.30	48.30	57.50	57.50	71.50	71.50
Shelly Ridge	85	Commercial center	Philadelphia	97.7	1.012	1982	48.30	47.82	57.50	56.93	71.50	70.79
Gunnison	80			— No comparable building type —							
Walker Field	60			— No comparable building type —							
RPI	81	Police station	Albany	97.9	1.015	1981	53.80	53.46	74.40	73.93	87.10	86.55
Touliatos	12			— No comparable building type —							
Phil. Auto	9			— No comparable data on retrofit —							
Princeton (Arch.)	9			— No comparable data on retrofit —							
Kieffer	18			— No comparable data on retrofit —							
Comal County	3			— No comparable data on retrofit —							

Sources:
1981 data from *Means Building Systems Cost Guide* 1982—7th Edition (S.F./C.F. Cost Section).
1982 & 1983 data from *Means Systems Cost* 1983—8th Edition (S.F./C.F. Cost Section).

These references were chosen instead of Means' *Square Foot Costs* to gain range from one-quarter to three-quarters of data base.

COMPARISON OF PASSIVE SOLAR COMMERCIAL BUILDING TO R. S. MEANS DATA BASE

EXPLANATION

As can be seen on Table B-1, comparable data could be found in R.S. Means for 11 of the 19 buildings for which there is construction cost data. The R.S. Means *Systems Cost Guide* was chosen because this data base is built from real building information and because costs are reported in a range from the lowest quarter of the data base through three-quarters of the data base.

With the Means data base, it is also possible to modify a given value by various factors to approximate a particular building more closely. For this analysis, given values were modified by four factors to gain the best comparison possible between the data base and the passive solar buildings. The modifications were:

- Select the building type most similar to the solar building
- Select a multiplier for the closest city to the solar building
- Select a multiplier to compensate for the size of the solar building
- Match the year of construction as closely as possible to the same year of Means data

These modifiers are combined and applied to the data given. The result is shown in the "Modified" (MOD) column in the table.

TABLE B-2
COMPARISON OF
PASSIVE SOLAR COMMERCIAL BUILDINGS
TO F.W. DODGE DATA BASE

	Name	Cost/ ft² $	Building Type	Size Range (000 ft²)	Year	Gross Building Cost $/ft²		
						Low Avg.	Average	High Avg.
PROJECT DESCRIPTION			**COMPARATIVE DATA**					
N E W	Two Rivers	149	———————————— No comparable building type ————————————					
	Abrams	36	Elementary school	30-40	1981	$41.20	$50.50	$56.00
	CUMC	47	———————————— No comparable building type ————————————					
	Blake Avenue	59	Vo-Tech School	20-80	1981	47.00	55.00	69.00
	Mt. Airy	88	Public library	15-60	1982	69.54	78.76	90.42
	St. Mary's	74	———————————— No comparable building type ————————————					
	Johnson Controls	57	Office	*	1982	53.62	66.39	72.11
	Princeton Park	46	Office	*	1982	53.62	66.39	72.11
	Security State	64	Branch bank	2.5-3.5	1981	53.50	75.00	90.00
	Essex-Dorsey	65	Senior citizen center	2-3	1982	37.79	43.34	51.31
	Shelly Ridge	85	Community hall	15-20	1983	43.14	48.01	55.52
	Gunnison	80	Air Terminal	20-30	1981	62.00	70.00	76.00
	Walker Field	60	Air Terminal	20-30	1982	66.86	74.07	83.85
	RPI	81	Police Building	18-24	1981	69.00	75.00	79.00
	Touliatos	12	———————————— No comparable building type ————————————					
R E T R O F I T	Phil. Auto	9	———————————— No comparable data on retrofits ————————————					
	Princeton (Arch.)	9	———————————— No comparable data on retrofits ————————————					
	Kieffer	18	———————————— No comparable data on retrofits ————————————					
	Comal County	3	———————————— No comparable data on retrofits ————————————					

*Not Given

Sources:
1981 Data is from *1982 Dodge Construction Systems Costs.*
1982 & 1983 data is from *1983 Dodge Construction Systems Costs.*

COMPARISON OF PASSIVE SOLAR
COMMERCIAL BUILDINGS
TO F. W. DODGE DATA BASE

EXPLANATION

The F. W. Dodge data base, Table B-2, works differently than the Means. In the case of the Dodge, one can select building type and year, but there is no modification process. Instead, Dodge reports the size range of the buildings in the data base and gives three average figures for that building type: low average, average, and high average.

The Dodge data base is valuable for this comparison because it reports several building types not in the Means data base. In many cases, both data bases report on the same building type; in no case are the ranges or medians similar. This analysis does not attempt to resolve these apparent differences.

TABLE B-3
COMPARATIVE DATA FROM
NONRESIDENTIAL BUILDINGS ENERGY CONSUMPTION SURVEY
(NBECS)
1979 CONSUMPTION AND EXPENDITURES

| | | NBECS DATA | | | | |
| | | DATA BY TYPE & REGION[1] | | DATA BY TYPE & SIZE[2] | | |
Name	Comparison Building Type	Region	Avg. Bill + Avg. ft^2 ($)	Size (000 ft^2)	Avg. Bill + Avg. ft^2 ($)	Range For Comparison
Kieffer	Retail/services	North Central	$0.61	<5	$0.95	$0.61-0.95
Johnson Controls	Office	West	0.63	10+	0.92	0.63-0.92
Security State	Office	North Central	1.02	10+	0.92	0.92-1.02
Mt. Airy	Office	South	0.89	10+	0.92	0.89-0.92
CUMC	Education	North Central	0.46	5-10	0.60	0.46-0.60
Comal County	Education	South	0.57	<5	1.33	0.57-1.33
Blake Avenue	Education	West	0.43	10+	0.40	0.40-0.43
Phil. Auto	Auto sales/service	Northeast	0.80	10+	0.60	0.60-0.80
RPI	Health[3]	Northeast	N/A	<5 or 10+	0.73 or 1.02	0.73-1.02

[1] Nonresidential Buildings Energy Consumption Survey—Part 2 (December 1983-Table 3).
[2] Nonresidential Buildings Energy Consumption Survey—Part 1 (March 1983-Tables 11, 12 & 13).
[3] Most closely approximates 24-hour occupancy.

COMPARATIVE DATA FROM NONRESIDENTIAL BUILDINGS ENERGY CONSUMPTION SURVEY (NBECS) 1979 CONSUMPTION AND EXPENDITURES

EXPLANATION

The Nonresidential Buildings Energy Consumption Survey (NBECS) is a careful accounting of both building characteristics and energy use. It was conducted once in 1979 on a carefully selected sample of about 6,000 buildings. It is significant because it is the largest single data base existing across all nonresidential building types based on real building experience and not on computer modeling.

From documents available to date, it is possible to obtain utility costs by building type and region or by building type and size not by type, region, and size simultaneously. For this analysis, it was decided to report data both by region and by size as a range, rather than to select either. Costs by region are based on all fuels. Costs by building size are limited to natural gas and electricity. This unfortunate difference could not be resolved within the scope of this analysis.

It should also be noted that NBECS reports "Average ft^2 per building" and "Average expenditure per building (in dollars)." It is easy enough to divide the second by the first to arrive at average cost per ft^2 as was done for this analysis. It is not clear why NBECS did not choose to report this figure directly.

Finally, the NBECS data base reflects 1978-1979 utility rates. Analysis of base case estimates (see Table B-6) suggests that between 1979 and 1983 electric rates increased to 148%, and gas rates increased by roughly 30%. It would be much better for this comparison to increase NBECS data to match the year of operating data for each passive solar building. This is not possible, however, from the NBECS published data alone.

TABLE B-4
COMPARATIVE DATA FROM
BUILDING OWNERS & MANAGERS ASSOCIATION (BOMA)

PROJECT DESCRIPTION		BOMA OFFICE BLDG. DATA					Modified Data[2] $/ft²/yr
Name	Location	Comparison City	Size ft²	Location	No. Bldgs.	Avg. Util.[1] $/ft²/yr	
Mt. Airy	Mt. Airy, NC	Charlotte, NC	<50,000	Downtown	1	$1.35	$1.49
Johnson Controls	Salt Lake, UT	Salt Lake, UT	<50,000	Suburb	3	$1.30	$1.43
Security State	Wells, MN	Minneapolis, MN	<50,000	Suburb	12	$1.00	$1.10
Kieffer	Wausau, WI	Madison, WI	<50,000	Suburb	2	$0.62	$0.68

[1] Average electricity + average gas, excluding water, sewer, and other charges.
[2] All BOMA data is per *rentable* ft². For this analysis, 10% is added to all BOMA figures to approximate costs per gross ft².

COMPARATIVE DATA FROM BUILDING OWNERS AND MANAGERS ASSOCIATION (BOMA)

EXPLANATION

The BOMA *Exchange Report* annually publishes office building operating costs for selected cities in the United States. This data base was used for comparison with the four projects in the program which were most similar to office buildings. The four nearest cities with data were selected for comparison. BOMA disaggregates by building size and location. The best comparison was selected in both these cases. However, the smallest BOMA size category is "under 50,000 ft^2," which is significantly larger than the passive buildings in the program.

It is important to note that the BOMA data base can be quite small for a specific category. The number of buildings reporting data is shown on Table B-4. With so few buildings reporting, it is possible for an operating cost figure to be skewed badly by one or two "bad" (high utility cost) buildings.

Finally, BOMA reports operating costs per "rentable" ft^2, which is a smaller number than the "gross" square footage of a building (the basis for the passive buildings). For this analysis, 10% was added to the rentable ft^2 costs as reported in BOMA to approximate the gross ft^2 costs for comparison. Although reasonable, the 10% figure can be debated. It is an easy matter for a reader to alter the data to satisfy a different opinion.

TABLE B-5
COMPARATIVE DATA
FROM
AIA FOUNDATION: SCHOOLS DATA BASE (AIA/F)

Typical New Jersey Elementary School (NJ DOE Audit Sample 10/80)

- 39,000 ft²
- Utilities Cost $0.78/ft² annually
- Use is 124K Btu/ft² (Point of Source)
- Electricity is 7.4¢/kWh; Gas is $4.20/MCF
- 5,000 HDD average

Typical New Jersey Secondary School (NJ DOE Audit Sample 10/80)

- 118,500 ft²
- Utilities Cost $0.81/ft²
- Use is 125.83K Btu/ft² (Point of Source)
- Electricity is 7.4¢/kWh; Gas is $4.20/MCF
- 5,000 HDD average

Average Maryland Public School

- 108,500 ft²
- Utilities Cost $0.78/ft²
- Use is 76.5K Btu/ft²
- Electricity is 7.1¢/kWh; Gas is $6.40/MCF
- 4,700 HDD average

The figures above were modified by the following percentages to reflect more clearly significant climate differences:

CUMC, Columbia, MO—Current electric rate of 8.16¢/kWh; 5,100 HDD Avg.: No Change

Comal County, N. Braunfels, TX—Current electric rate of 6.48¢/kWh;
1,600 HDD Avg.: −67% = 0.25 Elementary
0.26 Secondary

Blake Avenue, Denver, CO—Current electric rate of 6.45¢/kWh;
6,000 HDD Avg.: +20% = 0.97 Secondary

COMPARATIVE DATA FROM AIA FOUNDATION: SCHOOLS DATA BASE (AIA/F)

EXPLANATION

The AIA Foundation has recently completed a survey of available data on energy use and cost in elementary and secondary schools. They found that data on school operating costs per ft^2 is much more limited than one might expect. In fact, most energy use is reported in Btu's per ft^2 which facilitates comparisons across the United States independent of local utility rates. Unfortunately, in this case, it would be valuable to have that utility rate information.

Maryland and New Jersey report utility cost data by ft^2 (as shown in Table B-5). That data was used for comparison with schools or school-like buildings in the Commercial Buildings Program. This data was modified in two cases to reflect significant differences in climate. Because heating is the principal energy use in schools, this modification was done based on heating degree days (HDD). Utility rates were judged to be close enough not to require further modification.

TABLE B-6
COMPARATIVE DATA FROM DOE
PROGRAM BASE CASE DEFINITIONS
(1980 DATA UPDATED TO 1983)

Name	Year	BASE CASE ELEC $/ft²	BASE CASE ELEC ¢/kWh	BASE CASE GAS/OIL $/ft²	BASE CASE GAS/OIL $/th	Total	Year	FUEL COST INFLATION ELEC ¢/kWh	FUEL COST INFLATION ELEC % +	FUEL COST INFLATION GAS/OIL $/th	FUEL COST INFLATION GAS/OIL % +	REVISED BASE CASE ELEC $/ft²	REVISED BASE CASE GAS $/ft²	REVISED BASE CASE TOTAL $/ft²
CUMC	1980	0.06	4.4¢	0.27	$2.50	0.33	1983	8.16[1]	+ 85%	NA	+30%[a]	0.11	0.35	0.46
Blake Avenue	1980	1.17	4.0¢	—	—	1.17	1983	6.45[5]	+ 61%	—	—	1.88	—	1.88
Mt. Airy	1980	0.69	4.12¢	—	—	0.69	1983	6.47[2]	+ 57%	—	—	1.08	—	1.08
Johnson Controls	1980	0.53	6.4¢	0.12	2.86	0.65	1983	708[3]	+ 11%	NA	+30%[a]	0.59	0.16	0.75
Security State	1980	1.01	7.3¢	0.12	3.06	1.13	1983	7.4[4]	+ 1%	5.63[b]	+84%[b]	1.01	0.22	1.23
Gunnison	1980	0.51	2.6¢	—	—	0.51	1983	6.45[5]	+148%	—	—	1.26	—	1.26
RPI	1980	1.07	5.0¢	—	—	1.07	1983	10.7[6]	+114%	—	—	2.29	—	2.29
Kieffer	1980	0.33	5.4¢	0.17	5.60	0.50	1983	6.81[7]	+ 26%	NA	+30%[a]	0.42	0.22	0.64
Comal County	1980	0.47	4.6¢	0.13	3.35		1983	6.48[8]	+ 41%	NA	+30%[a]	0.66	0.17	0.83
Phil. Auto	1983	0.42	10.0¢	0.11g	6.04g	-------------------- ACTUAL BUILDING PRE-RETROFIT --------------------								1.46
				0.93o	6.57o									

[1] Missouri Public Service Co.
[2] Carolina Power & Light
[3] Utah Power & Light
[4] Wells Public Utilities
[5] Public Service of Colorado
[6] Central Hudson Gas & Electric
[7] Wisconsin Power & Light
[8] Texas Utilities Co.

[a] Average U.S. Natural Gas Price Increase 1980-1983 = 30% (computed from *Annual Report of Energy Conservation Indicators*— U.S.E.I.A.—January 1984)
[b] Peoples Gas

Note: RPI base case was changed to reflect 24-hour use (see "Explanation").

Source: Merrill Lynch Utilities Research Group
(Report Dated August 1984)

COMPARATIVE DATA FROM DOE PROGRAM BASE CASE DEFINITIONS (1980 DATA UPDATED TO 1983)

EXPLANATION

As explained in Chapter I, each design team in the project was required to propose or define a base case to represent good, but not necessarily energy-efficient, design within the area and of a similar type as the passive building being designed. This base case selection process was further judged by a jury of program monitors to evaluate the fairness of the base case selected. In several cases, the base case was another building owned or operated by the passive-building owner. In most other cases, comparable buildings were found or carefully specified.

In nearly all cases, base case utility costs were reported at 1980 utility rates. These rates and the resulting estimate of base case annual utility costs are shown in Table B-6. In order to make a more fair comparison, these base case costs were modified to reflect approximate utility rates for 1983—the year for which we have the majority of actual building operating data. Current local utility rates were taken from a national survey prepared by Merrill Lynch. Natural gas rates were increased by the national average increase for the period from an EIA report.

In the case of RPI, the base case was modified more substantially to reflect more closely current use of the building. The original base case had assumed occupancy eight hours per day. In fact, the building is now used on a 24-hour basis. Lacking better information, lighting cost was doubled and both heating and cooling costs were increased 20% to reflect this change in use.

APPENDIX C

PROJECT TEAM MEMBERS

PROJECT NAME	CONTACT	SOLAR DESIGNER	ARCHITECT	INSTRUMENTATION TEAM
Johnson Controls Branch Office	John Schade California Energy Commission 922 Vanderbilt Way Sacramento, CA 95825	Donald Watson, FAIA 730 Main Street Branford, CT 06405	Douglas Drake Johnson Controls, Inc. P.O. Box 423 507 E. Michigan Street Milwaukee, WI 53201	Brent Neilson Johnson Controls, Inc. P.O. Box 31806 Salt Lake City, UT 84130
Two Rivers School	John Rezek Department of Transportation & Public Facilities Research Section 2301 Peger Road Fairbanks, AK 99701-6394 Fairbanks North Star Borough 520 5th Avenue PO Box 1267 Fairbanks, AK 99701	Richard Seifert Cooperative Extension Service University of Alaska Fairbanks, AK 99701	Janet Matheson 2035 Hilton Street Fairbanks, AK 99701 Charles Bettisworth 1501 Cushman Street Fairbanks, AK 99708	Richard Seifert Cooperative Extension Service University of Alaska Fairbanks, AK 99701
Essex-Dorsey Senior Center	Carl Kuppe Baltimore County Aging Programs and Services 611 Central Avenue Towson, MD 21204	Peter D. Paul The Paul Partnership 27 W. 20th Street New York, NY 10011	Bob Dolny/ Barbara Sandrisser The Paul Partnership 27 W. 20th Street New York, NY 10011	Nancy Coleman Essex-Dorsey Senior Center 600 Dorsey Avenue Essex, MD 21221 Bob Dolny The Paul Partnership 27 W. 20th Street New York, NY 10011
Abrams Primary School	Jack Hale, Supt. Bessemer Board of Education 412 17th Street, North Bessemer, AL 35020	David Peacher Adams Peacher Keeton Cosby 2201 Morris Avenue Birmingham, AL 35203	David Peacher (See Solar Designer)	Roland McWilliams, P.E. McWilliams Associates 1824 28th Avenue, South Bessemer, AL 35209
Mt. Airy Public Library	John Vest City of Mount Airy P.O. Box 70 Mt. Airy, NC 27030	Marc Schiff Edward Mazria & Associates P.O. Box 4883 Albuquerque, NM 87196	Gary Morgan DPR Associates 2036 E. 7th Street Charlotte, NC 28204	Bill Sanders J.N. Pease Associates P.O. Box 18725 Charlotte, NC 28218

PROJECT NAME	CONTACT	SOLAR DESIGNER	ARCHITECT	INSTRUMENTATION TEAM
Philadelphia Municipal Auto Shop	Richard Tustin City of Philadelphia Department of Public Property Room 1650 1070 Municipal Service Bldg. 15th & JFK Blvd. Philadelphia, PA 19107	Charles Burnette, Ph.D., AIA Charles Burnette & Associates 234 South 3rd Street Philadelphia, PA 19106	Charles Burnette, Ph.D., AIA (See Solar Designer)	Charles Burnette (See Solar Designer)
Blake Avenue College Center	William Bowden Colorado Mountain College P.O. Box 10001 182 W. 6th Glenwood Springs, CO 81601	Matt Crosby Thermal Technology Corporation Box 130 Snowmass, CO 81654	Peter Dobrovolny Sunup Drawer 340 Old Snowmass, CO 81654	Peter Dobrovolny (See Architect)
Comal County Mental Health Center	Randy Wyatt Comal County Mental Health/ Mental Retardation Center 511 North Street New Braunfels, TX 78130	Dan Deffenbaugh Southwest Research Inst. 6220 Culebra Road San Antonio, TX 78284	Joe Stubblefield Joe Stubblefield, Architects & Planners, Inc. 120 Anastacia San Antonio, TX 78212	Dan Deffenbaugh (See Solar Designer)
Community United Methodist Church	William H. Miller College of Engineering University of Missouri at Columbia Columbia, MO 65201	Nicholas Peckham Peckham & Wright Architects 1104 E. Broadway Columbia, MO 65201	Nicholas Peckham (See Solar Designer)	William H. Miller (See Contact)
Shelly Ridge Girl Scout Center	Judith Helder Executive Director Girl Scouts of Greater Philadelphia 7 Ben Franklin Parkway Philadelphia, PA 19103	David F. Hill Burt Hill Kosar Rittelmann Associates 400 Morgan Center Butler, PA 16001	Frank Grauman Bohlin Powell Larkin Cywinski 182 N. Franklin Street Wilkes-Barre, PA 18701	Nancy Wisner Occupancy Forms Shelly Ridge Program Center Manor Road, P.O. Box 55 Miquon, PA 19452

PROJECT NAME	CONTACT	SOLAR DESIGNER	ARCHITECT	INSTRUMENTATION TEAM
Gunnison County Airport	Dorothy M. Johnson Gunnison County 200 E. Virginia Avenue Gunnison, CO 81230	Jan F. Kreider P.E. & Associates 1455 Oak Circle Boulder, CO 80302	Leon H. Waller Associated Architects of Crested Butte 207 Elk Avenue Box 1209 Crested Butte, CO 81224	Jay Yans Associated Architects of Crested Butte 207 Elk Avenue Box 1209 Crested Butte, CO 81224
Kieffer Store	Gordon D. Kieffer 821 Turner Street Wausau, WI 54401	Bruce Kieffer 2701 Petty Road Muncie, IN 47304	Bruce Kieffer (See Solar Designer)	Bruce Kieffer (See Solar Designer)
Princeton School of Architecture	John Hlafter, Director Office of Physical Planning Princeton University MacMillan Building Princeton, NJ 08540	Harrison Fraker, Jr. Harrison Fraker, Arch. 575 Ewing Street Princeton, NJ 08540	Jim Haufman Harrison Fraker, Arch. 575 Ewing Street Princeton, NJ 08540	Lawrence J. Lindsey Princeton Energy Group 575 Ewing Street Princeton, NJ 08540
Princeton Professional Park	Mike Glogoff 2303 Whitehorse- Mercerville Road Mercerville, NJ 08619	Lawrence L. Lindsey Princeton Energy Group 575 Ewing Street Princeton, NJ 08540	Short & Ford R.D. 4, Box 864 Mapleton Road Princeton, NJ 08540	Lawrence L. Lindsey (See Solar Designer)
RPI Visitor Center	Richard E. Scammel Rensselaer Polytechnic Inst. 110 8th Street Troy, NY 12181	John Tichy or Walter M. Kroner Rensselaer Polytechnic Inst. Mechanical Engineer School Troy, NY 12181	Walter M. Kroner (See Solar Designer)	J.A. Tichy (See Solar Designer)
Security State Bank	Pat Hart Security State Bank of Wells 32 S. Broadway Wells, MN 56097	John Weidt John Weidt Associates, Inc. 110 West Second Street Chaska, MN 55318	Jon Thorstenson Gene E. Hickney & Associates, Inc. 6950 France Avenue, South Edina, MN 55435	John Weidt John Weidt Associates, Inc. 110 W. Second Street Chaska, MN 55318

PROJECT NAME	CONTACT	SOLAR DESIGN	ARCHITECT	INSTRUMENTATION TEAM
Touliatos Greenhouse	Plato Touliatos 2020 Brooks Road Memphis, TN 38116	Plato Touliatos (See Contact)	Plato Touliatos (See Contact)	Plato Touliatos (See Contact)
Walker Field Terminal	Mike Boggs, Airport Mgr. Public Airport Authority Walker Field Terminal 2828 H Road Suite 211 Grand Junction, CO 81501	Jan F. Kreider, P.E. & Associates 1455 Oak Circle Boulder, CO 80302	John Porter John Porter, Architects & Planners P.O. Box 806 Grand Junction, CO 81501	David Yoder Yoder Engineering Benchmark Plaza Suite 307 P.O. Box 5740 Avon, CO 81620
St. Mary's Gymnasium	David R. Gallagher (on behalf of the most Reverend Thomas Welsh) 210 N. Glebe Road Arlington, VA 22203	Belinda Reeder Archetype Suite 202 1841 Columbia Rd., NW Washington, DC 20009 William Glennie Design Analyst 225 S. Harrison Street Princeton, NJ 08540	David Gallagher Architects Group Practice 300 N. Washington St., #330 Alexandria, VA 22314	Robert P. Schubert Assistant Professor Architect & Environmental Design Virginia Polytechnic Inst. & State University 201 Cogwill Hall Blacksburg, VA 24061

INDEX

Date Due

...ned	Due	Returned